ACT RIGHT
(Everything You Need to Know that they Didn't Teach You in Acting Class!)

"Mara and Erin have done a great service by providing an invaluable resource for young performers or others new to the business. *Act Right* is chock full of the kind of information not available through such traditional means as acting books or classes. As an experienced producer myself, I am grateful that they have filled an information void that previously existed."
— Steve Marshall, Producer/Writer, *WKRP in Cincinnati*, *Growing Pains*

"As the founder of the Theatre Department at University of Alaska, Fairbanks, I highly recommend *Act Right* by Mara Purl and Erin Gray. It's exceptionally well written, and the most practical book on the technical aspects of an actor's work. It's invaluable for anyone going into professional acting work in TV or film."
— Lee Salisbury, Chair of Drama, University of Alaska, Fairbanks

"I am blown away by the clarity and completeness of Erin Gray & Mara Purl's book. If you want to be a professional actor...and you want to work...*Act Right* is required reading."
— Joan Van Ark, Actress (*Knots Landing*), Director, Producer

"The 'Shooting' chapter was so complete and well written, that I have nothing to add — except my endorsement of *Act Right*: a must read."
— Dan Hamilton, Emmy Award-winning Director, *As the World Turns*, *Guiding Light*

"As the First Assistant Director on *Star Trek–Deep Space Nine*, frankly I wish every actor who came to work on our show read this book first. It's a wonderful book, full of step-by-step instructions for the novice. I'm very impressed. *Act Right* is an incredibly good idea, and very, very well done."
— B.C. Cameron, *Deep Space Nine*, *Spin City*

"Congratulations on *Act Right*, the great book on acting. As an actor, writer, producer and PR person, I was impressed by the presentation, content and overall style. I'm recommending it to the cast of the show I'm co-producing. Cheers to Erin Gray and Mara Purl."
— Gordon Durich, Public Relations, Los Angeles

"*Act Right* is a wonderful guide for anyone wanting to break into the industry and I applaud Erin and Mara for giving today's generation and those to come a source of aid and inspiration while following their dreams. Bravo!"
— Judy Moose, Public Relations, Las Vegas

"As an actor who did a recurring role in 'Gunsmoke' year after year, I learned a lot the hard way. If only I could have read *Act Right* by Mara Purl and Erin Gray, I think I would have been much more successful, much faster!"
— Ted Jordan, Actor, Los Angeles

"What I like the most about *Act Right* is the anecdotal and real-life knowledge it provides. In acting school I was taught how to hit a mark but not how to relate to a crew."
— Ken Arnott, Actor, Chicago

ACT RIGHT

A Manual for the On-Camera Actor

Erin Gray & Mara Purl

Haven Books

Act Right
PUBLISHING & SEMINAR HISTORY:
The material in this book first appeared in the professional seminar
"Hitting Your Mark" ©1989 by Erin Gray & Mara Purl
and in the original manuscript "Hitting Your Mark"
©1994 by Erin Gray & Mara Purl
Library of Congress TXu 641-803
©1998 "Act Right" First Edition by Erin Gray & Mara Purl
Library of Congress TXu 851-872
©2001 Revised Edition by Erin Gray & Mara Purl
Portions of this material also appear on the
Publisher's Web Site: http://www.havenbooks.net
©1998, ©2000 and ©2001 by Haven Books.

All rights reserved.
Copyright ©1989, 1994, 1998, 2001 by Erin Gray & Mara Purl.
No part of this book may be reproduced or transmitted in any form or by any means,
electronic or mechanical, including photocopying, recording, or by any information
storage and retrieval system, without permission in writing from the publisher.
For information address:
Haven Books
10153 ½ Riverside Drive, Suite 629
North Hollywood, CA 91602

Cover Art by Ron Covert
©2000 by Mara Purl & Erin Gray
Cartoon Art by Mike Warner
©1997 by Mara Purl & Erin Gray
Copy Editors: Vicki Werkley & Jean Laidig

Published in the United States of America.
ISBN 1-58436-000-3
Library of Congress Catalog Card Number 98-70321
Manufactured in the United States of America
First Printing: 1998
Revised Edition First Printing: 2001

<u>Quotations From The Following Works
Are Used By Permission:</u>

"Acting In Film" by Michael Caine
©1990 Applause Theatre Book Publishers

"Close To Home – Sex, Lies, & The Wedding Video"
©1991 M.Purl & E.Gray, PurlGray Enterprises

"Friday The 13th – The Ninth Life of Jason Vorhees"
©1991 Sean Cunningham, Cunningham Productions

"Independent Feature Film Production" by Gregory Goodell
©1982 St. Martin's Press, Inc.

"Milford-Haven – TV" by Mara Purl
©1995 Mara Purl, Milford-Haven Enterprises

"The Actor and the Camera" by Malcolm Taylor
©1994 A&C Black Publishers, & Heinemann Publishers

DEDICATION

This book is dedicated to actors everywhere who are about to embark upon a noble profession. We hope this makes your path easier and more successful, so that you can go about the business of creating worthwhile art.

This book is also dedicated to crew members everywhere, whose training, wit, wisdom, Zen-like patience, mastery and long hours make not only the actor's work, but the entire project, possible.

This book is additionally dedicated to all who appreciate film, television and video (streaming or otherwise) whether as professional critics, avid fans, or occasional viewers. It is our hope that our book will afford you a glimpse into a complex and difficult world, where many earnest professionals labor so that others may relax and enjoy.

Finally, this book is dedicated to collaboration. It is our hope that by reading it, professionals in our business, both above and below the line, will come to appreciate all that their colleagues do toward creating a finished piece of work and that all our readers will realize that together, we can do so much more than we can individually.

ACKNOWLEDGMENTS

Since publication three years ago, we've been working on the revised edition of Act Right. The original book was 7 years in the making – including 10,000 (recycled) pieces of paper, 107 computer disks, 22 rewrites, 6 computer systems, 4 word-processing programs, and untold numbers of speeches and seminars.

The entire process has been an adventure every step of the way. The goal of completing it has been a light shining on a sometimes challenging path. Since beginning this project, we have each gone through a divorce, and each gotten re-married. We have become mothers, step-mothers, god-mothers, and aunts. We have become best friends and partners. We have had important birthdays. We have moved homes and offices. We have taught ourselves computer literacy. We have formed new companies and learned accounting programs.

Most importantly, we have become teachers. There comes a time in life when a person realizes that he or she has learned a few things and that it is time to share what has been learned. That time came for us when we started this, and now sharing what we know has become a thrill and a passion. We teach classes. We give this book as an all-day seminar. We mentor as a way of life. We are growing up, and are starting to become the people we have always hoped we would become.

We have bared our souls in these pages, exposing our shortcomings, tattling on our own foolish mistakes, and occasionally sharing moments when we got it right. We have also asked many of our friends and colleagues to do the same, and we owe them a tremendous debt of gratitude. We thank each of these consummate professionals, without whom our book would be incomplete.

We thank our diligent proofreaders, not only for catching our mistakes, but for giving us excellent suggestions — Amelia Norfleet, Megan Van Dusen, and Nicole Gold.

We thank our professional editors Vicki Werkley (bless her eyes) and Jean Laidig (bless her alacrity) for their generosity, thoroughness, diligence and expertise.

We thank our extraordinary husbands, who both give us mental and physical room to work, as well as support while we spend a great deal of time away from them. We couldn't have done our book without them. We thank our daughters: Amelia Norfleet, whose love for the book has encouraged us, and Samantha Gray Hissong, who somehow always managed to interrupt us at just the right times.

And we thank you, our readers, for taking the time to read our book and for giving us such a steady stream of compliments and feedback. We have loved hearing from you and look forward to hearing more! We welcome your comments and share them with others through our web sites. We encourage you to keep learning. We intend to do the same ourselves.

COLLABORATE:

Latin root: coll (with) labor (work)
1. *To work together especially in a joint intellectual effort*
2. *To cooperate reasonably, as with an enemy occupying one's country*

— American Heritage Dictionary

The film differs radically from the other representative arts...which are the unfettered expression of an individual mind. The normal method of film production, on the other hand, requires the cooperation of many craftsmen and technicians working together as a team.

— Ernest Lindgren
"The Art Of The Film"

It has been computed that 246 different trades, crafts and professions are brought into making a single American film.

— Screen Actors Guild

That action is best which procures the greatest happiness for the greatest numbers.

— Hutchinson

As a casting director, I am constantly amazed that actors see the casting process as a war rather than a collaboration. We are all on the same team.

— Ricki Maslar

ERIN'S PREFACE

When I got my first job in Hollywood, the good news was that it was a starring role in a four-hour mini-series with an ensemble of major stars. The bad news was that I was plunged into such a high-profile situation that I had no chance to make a mistake in private.

Not only had I studied acting religiously with some of the best teachers in New York, I'd also been a successful model in New York for several years. I'd been fortunate to land several hundred national television commercials and had become the spokeswoman for some of the largest companies in the country, such as Bloomingdale's, Max Factor and Breck. As far as I was concerned, I was a consummate professional. I was comfortable with the camera, acquainted with lighting, had great working relationships with directors and crews, and was more than ready to tackle what I felt was the next logical step in the career to which I was completely dedicated.

Here was something I'd been praying for. I arrived at the set on my first day of work, and it wasn't until I was standing in a huge parking lot, surrounded by the trucks, equipment, and crew members — all of whom were busily going about their jobs — that I realized I had no idea what to do!

I literally didn't know who to talk to, who to check in with, where to report for work, or what was expected of me in any way. My confidence gradually faded to anxiety until a make-up person walking by said, "Don't you think you better get to make-up?" Thank goodness she said something!

It was that first, terrifying day of work that made me decide to write this book. May it spare my future colleagues a day of anguish, and help them to get to the depth of their talent, having mastered the all-important details of this complex and fascinating business.

Erin Gray

MARA'S PREFACE

The first time I auditioned for a commercial, I was asked to stand in front of the camera the moment I arrived. I'd already memorized the ad copy, done detailed preparation and was ready to give an award-winning performance. At this point the director said, "Slate." I thought he was addressing a crew member and waited for him to say "Action," which he never did. "Slate! Slate!" he repeated, yelling with such vehemence that it shattered my concentration. My mind raced through the options. He wanted me to bring a "gray" interpretation to the copy? We would be shooting this commercial on location on a slate roof? I froze, and he came unglued. Finally I said I had no idea what he was talking about. Even then, he didn't explain the simple fact that in commercials, it's the actor who does his own "slate" — the brief announcement identifying the take on film or tape before the take begins.

None of my life-long experience acting in the theatre had prepared me for this, nor had several years of performing in a Japanese television series. However, by the time I started on "Days Of Our Lives" I had learned some valuable lessons — to listen, learn and memorize every technical detail I could. Working on the soap sparked an interest in creating a show of my own and eventually "Milford-Haven" took shape as a radio soap opera that reached across airwaves from the U.S. to the U.K. Acting, writing and producing have thoroughly convinced me that a comfortable conversance with the technical aspects of a show frees us as performers. Like any other producer, I'm inclined to rehire performers who know what they're doing, not only artistically, but technically as well. Perhaps most importantly, I feel passionately that all the actor's careful and painful preparation through years of study should not be undermined by lack of technical awareness.

Arriving on a set is like landing in Paris and not speaking French. What we've created with Act Right is both a dictionary and a guide book. We want you to feel like citizens, not helpless tourists. I believe strongly that talent often gets lost in the complexities of this business. May our book help you to become a better actor by being able — in every sense of the word — to... act right.

Mara Purl

INTRODUCTION TO THE REVISED EDITION

Welcome to our first revision of Act Right. Our industry is changing rapidly, and we want to keep you abreast of the times.

Technology has changed our world since we first published Act Right. In the short span of three years, the Internet has become a factor in our business. We remember a world — not long ago — when there were no such words as "info-tainment," "fax on demand" and "download from our website." So we want to point out how these devises have changed our particular industry. Perhaps most importantly, we ourselves are learning and growing, so we want to pass along our new perspectives and insights to you.

Our book has enjoyed an enormous response which each week grows larger. To the many readers and performers we've met at book signings and seminars all over the country, we extend heartfelt thanks and feel tremendous gratitude that our book and seminar have been helpful. If we've learned anything in the past three years, it's that there was a great need for this book and that is inspiring us to keep it up to date.

Please note, we've added a new chapter to this edition. Although Act Right is a comprehensive technical manual, in the new chapter we respond to many of our reader's and student's questions by sharing more of our personal philosophy about preparing for, staying in, and creating success through this business.

Everybody wants success. But underneath it all, we're all also looking for success in life. Acting *per se* won't bring you success in life, but the things you learn from and bring to your acting work can help you define and achieve the particular success you hope for.

Your efforts in this business will be both individual and collective. One of the most important things we had to define in writing this book in the first place was a theme, and it wasn't until we included the word "collaborator" that we knew we were on the right track. The business of creating theatre, film, television and video is nothing if not a collaboration.

This is not to say we are advocating "art by committee," or claiming that the only way to get a career going is to dilute your own sensibilities, bury your individuality, or compromise your soul.

A painter can work in the solitude of his loft; a writer can commune alone with her computer; a potter can find himself in the spin of his wheel. But when it comes time to work as an actor, you cannot do so alone.

When you're studying your craft, a certain degree of focus and even selfishness is called for. Indeed, unless you can achieve that focus and carry it through the audition process, chances are you won't get the job at all.

What we want to emphasize is: once you get the job, you've been hired to join a team. No one works in a vacuum. Over and over again in our experiences, and through the interviews we conducted, what came up was the fact that to have real success in this business, you must learn to be a team player. And sadly, the other thing that was frequently mentioned, is that most actors don't know how to be one.

You must walk a line between your individual vision and your place on the team. And we will never try to tell you this is easy. You'll have to cultivate discernment and judgment. On one hand you'll have to listen closely to your instincts, and on the other hand, you'll have to hone your diplomatic skills.

Because this is a collaborative art, and each artist makes his or her own unique contribution, there is no formula for how a project will go. We don't want to overwhelm you with rules – or pretend that there are hard and fast ways of doing things. But we feel that an informed actor can better navigate the sometimes twisting pathways of a professional engagement. This is a guide through the labyrinth.

This book will help you land that all-important first job; and then it will guide you step by step through exactly what is required of you in each phase of a complex and demanding work day. The experiences related throughout this book are largely our own and those of co-workers, and sometimes even hearsay — one of the best sources of anecdotes. All of the combined experiences of casts and crews are by now a colorful history which has added a rich glossary of new terms to the English language. We keep finding these special words — and have passed them along to you in our Glossary.

Your proficiency with technical terms and professionalism in the complex hierarchy of a set will determine the extent to which you are hireable for your next job. Unfortunately, sometimes these seemingly minor details carry more weight than your acting ability. This is one situation where ignorance is not bliss. Ignorance can destroy your concentration, undermine your reputation, and interfere with your most fervent dream of success.

You've already worked so hard for so many years, you don't want to ruin your opportunities by overlooking the technical details, which are frighteningly mysterious when you don't know them — and simple when you do.

A word about format and structure. In each chapter, we've quoted professionals who work in the particular department we're discussing. You can therefore assume when you're reading "Auditioning" that we're quoting casting directors; when you're reading "Matching" we're quoting editors, and so forth.

We've designed our book to be used in multiple ways, because you'll always have a new situation to deal with in this business. If you have the time or inclination, by all means get cozy with a cup of your favorite brew and read the book from beginning to end.

But if your first job starts tomorrow and you're already having difficulty with wardrobe, flip to the wardrobe chapter. If you're already in the middle of shooting and don't have a grasp on "matching," flip to that chapter.

And if you're really in a hurry, you always have the option of skipping the anecdotes – they're all
> ***bold, italic, and indented.***

But we encourage you to read through the text itself, which will give you the nitty-gritty.

Here's your chance to turn every job into a complete success, and have a good time doing so.

TABLE OF CONTENTS

a.	Dedication	i
b.	Acknowledgments	ii
c.	Collaboration	iv
d.	Erin's Preface	vi
e.	Mara's Preface	viii
f.	Introduction	xi
1.	ACTING RIGHT	1
2.	PREPARATION	31
3.	PICTURES, RÉSUMÉS, REELS & WEB SITES	45
4.	AUDITIONING	67
5.	SCRIPTS	97
6.	PRE-PRODUCTION TO PRODUCTION	117
7.	WARDROBE	125
8.	ARRIVING ON SET	147
9.	CALL SHEET	157
10.	MAKE-UP & HAIR	169
11.	PROPS	189
12.	REHEARSAL	197
13.	SHOOTING	213
14.	MATCHING	255
15.	SOUND	267
16.	STUNT WORK	287
17.	DAILIES	301
18.	THE BUSINESS OF THE BUSINESS	307
19.	THE INTERNET AND YOU	317
20.	GLOSSARY	327
21.	BIBLIOGRAPHY	349
22.	ERIN'S BIO	358
23.	MARA'S BIO	362
24.	STUDENT RADIO DRAMA	366
25.	ACT RIGHT BOOKS & SEMINARS	368

ACTING RIGHT

Covered in This Chapter:

- The Artist
- The Business Person
- Ethics
- Practice Awareness: Be, See, Know
- Change & Changes
- Setting Goals & Establishing Mission Statement
- Talent & Fame
- Visualization

Knowing is the beginning of action. Acting is the completing of knowing.
  — Wang Yang Ming, Ming Dynasty

Men are free to act, but must act to be free.
  — Jean-Paul Sartre

What lies behind us and what lies before us are tiny matters compared to what lies within us.
  — Ralph Waldo Emerson

ACTING RIGHT

This book is designed to help you behave correctly from day one of your career as a professional actor. Our book focuses on technical and professional information.

The title of our book — Act Right — has other implications aside from doing what is technically correct from a filmmaking point of view. We use the term advisedly and, in fact, often talked about our own commitments to "act right" long before we developed our book and seminar. When we talk about "acting right," we also want to share an awareness that right behavior in all aspects of your life cannot help but affect your career as well.

To "act right" is fundamentally to do what is morally correct, to make the ethical choice and to show it in action. This underlies all we do, all we say in this book, and is the foundation of what we are sharing.

> *Acting is a venture into soul — your own, and that of your character. When we get it right, we become a transparency for Soul itself.*
> —Mara

We're going to wax philosophical here, so if this isn't your cup of chai, please feel free to skip this chapter and move on to the practical details of our book. However, we include this material because we would be less than honest if we didn't. The work of being an actor exists on both conscious and unconscious levels, and must be tackled from the points of view of both head and heart.

We'll be sharing a lot of information with you about the fact that this is a *business*, and to succeed, you'll need to acquire good business habits. We'll also talk about how, as an artist, you need to stay in alignment with your inner values and principles. One way to approach this is to consider your acting career as a spiritual journey as well.

There is no formula – no lock-step track – for getting into and succeeding in this business, and we don't want to give you the impression that there is. Goal-setting is excellent – we advocate it and will share more on that thought later. But not everything can be measured in straight lines. Instead of thinking linearly, try also thinking circularly. That's not to say we're going to advise you to go in circles! What we mean is, as a performer – and as a person – you want to be well-rounded. That means cultivating all aspects of yourself. Our friend K. Callan agrees with us.

> [Actors] know the business is a circuitous route. You enter the circle any place and don't usually get to choose where. Some young actors waltz in, get attention, an agent and a job, and aren't seriously unemployed for ten or twenty years. When things inevitably slow down, they have to learn the business skills that other less fortunate actors began to learn on day one. There are no steps to be skipped, as it turns out. We all just take them at different times.
>
> – K. Callan
> Actress, Author

As an actor, you're asking your *self* to become its most vulnerable: open to all possibilities, ready to respond to all stimuli in the quicksilver of a moment on camera. Our "selves" are crusted over with conditioned responses, which must be carefully peeled away in the safe arena of good acting classes. But now we're asking those same selves to go forth into a sometimes-brutal world to seek employment. There must, therefore, be a balance. Ideally, our practice is the art of science and the science of art.

One way to express this balance is in terms of the right and left brain. The left brain, which tends to see things in a linear fashion, is vital for getting your filing system organized and getting you to the set on time. Meanwhile, the right brain is intuitive and tends to be free and fluid, to go with the flow.

We encourage you to take a certain amount of time each day in the cultivation of your own wholeness, addressing who you are spiritually, emotionally, intellectually and physically. We all must nurture and care for our physical body daily. We're asking you to do the same for the other "bodies" you possess.

To succeed in this business you'll have to learn to cultivate both sides of yourself – the artist and the business person. You might think of this as cherishing your inner child while at the same time cultivating yourself as an adult. And you might think of it as a balancing act between your subjective and your objective sense of life.

The Artist

> "I believe in the power of art to change lives. I believe in the power of art to save lives. I've seen it first hand. The power of art lies not in the development of a skill, nor in its ability to reach us emotionally, eliciting laughter or tears, shock or diffidence; the power of art is its revelation that human potential is limitless."
> – Jane Alexander

Where does the bug for acting come from? Some say it's all in the genes; some say it's all in one's upbringing; some say it comes from some chance occurrence. For us, all of the above are true. We've both been acting since we could walk and talk. But that in itself is not what created careers in this business.

We thought you might enjoy hearing some of our childhood experiences. Perhaps they'll be similar to your own, or to those of your children.

> When I was a child I thought the hearth in front of the fireplace was a stage – don't ask me why. I assumed that since we had a stage in our house, it was supposed to be used every night, and I saw to it. Every day after school, I wrote a skit; and every night after dinner I announced to my parents and sister that it was "show time." They dutifully watched me perform, unless I'd written parts for them too, in which case they had to join me "on stage." Later,

my dad bought us some fabulous marionettes and then built us a gorgeous puppet theatre. From then on, every weekend I did a full musical. Nothing was more intoxicating and encouraging than to hear the audience laughing at my jokes and being enthralled by my stories. I had the bug early, and I had it bad.

—Mara

At age five I was cast in a play in which I had only two lines. Nevertheless, I took this performance very seriously and was looking forward to having my mom see my big moment on stage. Peering out from behind the curtain, I realized she wasn't in the audience. I was devastated! As I made my entrance, I was trying to suppress by disappointment. But just as I was about to say my line, "Doctor, Doctor, come quick quick quick!" my mother appeared at the back of the hall. As I said my second line, "My baby is sick sick sick!" tears came cascading down my face. I heard a gasp from the audience, riveted by so much emotion exuding from a child's performance. I probably got more accolades for that one performance than for any in my whole life. Everyone said I had so much emotion in my line! If my mother'd been on time, I might never have become an actress.

— Erin

This story points to one of the most important lessons for every actor: Use your own experiences to fuel your work. To be an artist is to cultivate the subjective sense of yourself and your life, for to portray anything through your art you must have a unique point of view. You won't ever arrive at a unique point of view unless you think about it, honor it, feel your own feelings, notice and record your own sense of life events.

As an artist you must go deep: deep into yourself, deep into life. You have to face difficult life issues; you have to make a conscious effort, give yourself tasks and exercises to help you dig deep enough to come up with something meaningful. Everyone who's ever been in a good acting class has had to face something buried and possibly unpleasant about themselves. It is from these deep moments of humiliation, humility and self-awareness that honest and riveting art is born.

> *One of the classic exercises taught by all the teachers from the Group Theatre, including Stella Adler, Sandy Meisner, Bobby Lewis, Lee Strasburg, and others, is what's called the "private moment" exercise, where you enter a private space and do in front of the class something you would normally never do in front of another human being. You can imagine what some people chose to do. Once in Tad Danielevsky's class at NBC I did an exercise bathing myself. There's no way to do something like that without setting aside your usual "shame" considerations. After that, I never quite felt I had the same level of privacy from my classmates. The beauty of it was I became much more open as an actress.*
>
> *– Mara*

We strongly believe that to be an artist, you must learn to honor and nurture yourself. In America, we don't live in an artist's society, we live in a business climate. If you say you're in business, you're immediately respected; if you say you're an artist, people wonder when you're going to get a "real" job.

If we lived in Florence or Kyoto, it would not be important that we return quickly to the office after a 45-minute lunch; it would be important that the flowers on the table be in the right vase, and that the pasta or soba be flavored just so, and that we take the time to enjoy the meal fully. Instead, here it matters that we return our e-mail on the same day, get the report done before close of business, and churn through a certain volume of paperwork weekly.

We can buy a day planner for our business, we can use a computer program to run our business, and we can fly business class to our meeting on the opposite coast. Can we fly anywhere on "Artist's Class"? No. Can you buy an artist's day planner? (Not yet, but we're working on it.)

With our modern efficiencies and technologies, life has improved in many ways, but in another sense, something gets lost. Today there seems to be only one speed: frantic. We gain time by using computers, airplanes and the Internet. What do we do with that newfound time? Most of us probably use it in still more high-speed pursuits. The time we're losing in this era is the time for reflection.

How can a revelation occur to you if you don't give it the time to surface? Pythagorus struggled to understand a certain mathematical theorem but at last gave up and went home to take a bath. It was during his moment of quiet reflection he uttered his famous expression "Eureka!" meaning "I found it!" Recognizing the value of the twilight area of consciousness, Einstein attempted to keep himself on the cusp of waking and sleeping by sitting in a chair in a deep meditative state without falling asleep. He accomplished this by holding some metal balls in his hands – if he fell asleep, he'd drop them. .

> *I remember a time when I was a teenager trying to work on a trigonometry problem I was bound and determined to solve. At 2 am I was still going over and over the problem, and my brain was like mush. I took a moment, walked into the kitchen and got some cookies and milk. When I returned to my room I sat down and suddenly I had the answer. I didn't know how, but I knew I had tuned into some sort of intuitive sense of a Higher Awareness. It felt other-worldly, and it felt right, so I wrote it down. I proceeded to solve the problem backward – and it worked. The reward came the next day when it turned out I was the only student who'd solved the problem.*
>
> *– Erin*

> *When I write an episode for my radio drama Milford-Haven, I consider the arc of each character and of each scene. Obsessing over getting it right, I sometimes miss the deeper point of a scene. When I sense I'm too bound up in logic and detail, I go for a walk – preferably by the ocean or in the mountains. I focus on nature, on the harmony of all things around me. Almost invariably, sometime*

during the walk, something falls into place — an idea I hadn't thought of — and the story takes on the depth and power I was hoping for.

— Mara

We must find the ways to re-synch ourselves with the forces of nature and the internal timing of revelation. We enjoy reading Deepak Chopra, who talks about the fact that spending time in nature gives us access to infinite creativity, freedom, and bliss.

So, although being an artist is a subjective thing requiring self-exploration, it is also a process of connecting with a higher consciousness. When we get it right, we feel we've glimpsed something larger than ourselves. When we see something of universal truth, we can then experience, share and manifest it.

Without imposing our own philosophical or religious views, we would just like to share our belief that as artists, we have an opportunity to become transparencies for, or transmitters of, higher truths. Indeed, art in its purest form is a truth-telling method that transmits clearly and universally through all ages and all cultures.

Because of the unique way in which the practice of acting makes demands upon both imagination and self-examination, acting can be a place to wake up, a place to become your better self, to unify yourself.

Remember that the artist is hungry — hungry for the feast of soul: a visit to a museum, a stop in a café to watch people, a deep conversation with a friend, a walk in the park. Our society is not structured to provide these things in any automatic way, so we must arrange for them, schedule them, take advantage of such moments when we see a chance to make them happen. All this will help develop and nourish the artist's soul and thus help to rebalance the mind-body-spirit continuum.

We must give ourselves permission to acknowledge the importance of nurturing ourselves. In our culture we're often made to feel guilty if we're "indulging" ourselves as artists. We're perceived as being irresponsible and childish. In fact, we're being free-spirited and childlike because as artists, we must "play." In fact, the French word for "to act" is the same as the word "to play."

Inside us there will always be the 6-year-old who wants to go splash in puddles and can happily hum songs to block out the nasties of the world; there will always be the rebellious teen who trounces off to a café with his buddies. Your job as an artist is not to kill off these aspects of personality, but to recognize them and integrate them.

The Business Person

The next reality you must deal with is that you have to interface with a business without losing who you are as an artist. You must learn to be professional. This is where you cultivate your objective sense of yourself, an objective point of view that will help you see yourself as others in the business see you. And this impartial view is not only helpful, but vital, if you are to succeed.

If a casting director sees you as ten pounds overweight, you will probably have two responses. The subjective response might be "I carry those pounds well and know how to dress, and besides, it makes me look like a regular person, and I'm not trying to be a fashion model." Your objective point of view might be "That suit would look a hundred percent better if only I'd lose those ten pounds." Or perhaps a producer looks at you and thinks, "He's been working out at the gym too much, and looks too muscular to play the part of the lawyer in my film." Your subjective response might be "I worked hard for those muscles and I'm proud of them! If you don't realize how great I look, it's your loss!" Your objective response might be "This character is an over-the-hill cop, and I'm going to have to lose some muscle tone if I want to play this part, no matter how much my vanity might suffer."

> There was a young actor who played a recurring role on "Silver Spoons." He played the nerd with stringy, long, unshaped hair. He

wasn't attractive in a traditional sense, but I always wanted to see what he'd look like with a great hair cut. I offered him some advice one day, but he straightened me out. "No," he said, "I wouldn't get hired as a leading man. This is my look." He was practical. He was right.

– Erin

The more you cultivate your own objective sense of yourself, the less thrown you'll be by criticism. When casting directors tell you your nose is too big or your hair is too thin, do you want to stand there blushing and walk away hurt and angry? Or do you want this information to be something you already know and have already turned to your own advantage? The better you know yourself, both inwardly and outwardly, the more centered you'll be when someone in the business says something blunt. They may appear to be heartless, but in reality it's "nothing personal." It is their job to select the right person for the part at hand, and if you know yourself and what your strengths and weaknesses are, you are helping yourself, and helping the professional who's trying to hire you.

Another great skill you'll begin to develop as your objective sense of yourself becomes clearer, is that you are, in fact, not right for every single role. Sometimes when we start out as actors we have the grandiose feeling we can handle any part, male or female, ugly or pretty, fat or thin, smart or stupid. From a subjective point of view we're right – and it's good to stretch and explore as an artist. But when we're considering ourselves as a business commodity, we can cultivate the wisdom to know which parts we should go for and which we should not.

Ruben Cannon was casting various series for Stephen Cannell and I was asked to go in on a "general" audition, which went very well. Anxious to get me into one of their shows, they asked me in to audition for the part of an ugly girl who returns home for a high school reunion. This presented a problem because I couldn't convincingly play "ugly" – but I tried. I wore a baggy dress, left my hair straggling, and wore no make-up. When I arrived the director

looked up, said "Too pretty" and I was dismissed without being allowed to read. I went in because my agent wanted me to. But in retrospect, I shouldn't have gone in. My audition had nothing to do with my acting ability, it had only to do with my look.
— Mara

I wanted to do a favor for a friend who asked me to participate in a short sitcom pilot. I can go into a playful, girlish — but immaturely sexual — character, which is fun, but doesn't work with how I physically look. In this case the situation was worsened by the fact that the jokes were in poor taste and were silly. Even though I had fun doing it, when I saw it on film I was embarrassed. I should never have done it because I'm just not right for that kind of role. On another occasion, I auditioned well and got hired for a comedy piece. But I was cast as a character actor and again, that's not the right role for me. I look like a leading lady so trying to be the character actor didn't work and I was fired.
— Erin

Part of Cary Grant's great talent was that he viewed himself objectively, and when watching dailies of his films always referred to himself up there on the screen as "him." He was clear about the difference between himself the artist, and himself the commodity that sold tickets and satisfied fans.

Here we want to share with you something you may not want to hear, but we feel we'd be less than honest if we didn't say it. Learn to make a living at something other than acting.

Some people choose as their "second job" something they can barely stand — we do not advocate this! It's terrible to consign yourself to spend most of your day doing something you hate. Ideally, we advise that you discover some kind of creative work as your second job. This may not be your heart's desire, but if it is creative, you'll still be spending much of your time cultivating your creative energy.

It's legendary that actors have to work at some menial task in order to pursue their craft. In fact, the joke is that in Los Angeles when you go to a restaurant you don't call for "Waiter," you say "Actor!" We suggest you pay attention to the atmosphere in which you spend much of your time. We know of an actress who's miserable because she spends her evening wearing a cat-suit serving drinks to drunks. Although she says "I have to work in a bar" in order to pursue her acting career, we know of better choices she could make.

As you begin to do well as an actor, you'll find, as we all have, that this is a terribly uneven business. It's not as though you "break into the business" and work from then on. Instead, you may do a series one year, and never get a job at all for the following year. How will you handle this? By taking a 9-to-5 as an accountant? Would you want someone who hates accounting to be doing your books for you? We don't think so. However, if you have some ability in accounting, you might be able to work freelance at an extremely useful profession and still have time for your auditions.

We admire Harrison Ford's attitude. He became a contract player at Universal and worked regularly. But after a while the parts offered nothing new or challenging, and he was tired of exploiting the same territory, and afraid of becoming overexposed in nondescript roles. To solve his financial problems and keep himself going as an artist, he learned carpentry. When he didn't care to audition for yet another episodic role, he built a cabinet instead. He was defining who he was and his agents and casting directors began to think of Harrison as someone who would only do meaty, interesting roles. The rest, as they say, is history. We call this a "win-win" scenario.

Another thing to realize is there are other ways to use your acting talent, and other places to use it than New York or L.A. We have several friends who now use all they learned as actors to do other – and equally interesting – jobs. A dynamic couple we've known for many years were very successful actors; now they've each won Emmys working on Soaps, she as a writer, he as a director. One friend used his great looks, charisma and stage presence to became a successful auctioneer. Another former actress now is paid top dollar conducting professional seminars for a large corporation. Another actress became a highly thought-of drama critic; another chairs arts councils and foundations. Many former rock stars now work at radio stations where their in-depth knowledge of the music business makes them indispensable. We don't consider these individuals to be failures, but rather tremendously wise about their talents and how to use them to serve others and make wonderful successes of their lives.

Something else to consider is that different aspects of our talents and personalities grow at different rates and respond to different stimuli. Think of your life as a garden: different plants grow at different rates, need different amounts of water. Sometimes a tree gets too large and needs to be removed because it overshadows everything else. Sometimes you have to leave something alone and just let it grow. Acting may mean everything to you now. There may come a time when it loses some of its luster. That's all right. It may be an important signal that it's time to begin cultivating another talent like writing or giving seminars or directing or producing or painting. You're not as limited as you may think you are.

Sometimes it's important to grow where you *are* before you consider transplanting yourself. For example, if there's a local theatre group in your town, audition for the plays; if there isn't a local group, you might consider starting one. You may not be great in Los Angeles, but you might be a star in Memphis. This *is* success. Living in L.A. does not necessarily spell success. If you have a flourishing garden, does it matter where it grows? It matters how it grows, not where.

One woman we know did a careful assessment of her life: she enjoys living in Memphis where she owns her own home and where she has family members. By day, she works as a computer consultant and trouble-shooter in a legal firm where she earns good money and establishes her own hours. By night, she dons the stilettos, the wig, or the bag-lady make-up and has a great time performing the character roles in local productions, be they for theatre or for film. We just heard she's directing one play, starring in another, and was offered character roles in four feature films. She has a full, rich life. And in Memphis, she is a star. Many of her friends who left Memphis for L.A. are still pursuing dreams that have not been fulfilled.

We're often made to believe that once we find our true path, we never have to find it again. But the fact is, paths continue to expand, contract, shift, branch and change. As you begin your career, you must listen to your intuition and carefully consider your goals. The thing is, you have to keep doing this throughout your life.

> *My parents are immensely talented thespians and for all intents and purposes, my sister and I grew up with theatre as our family religion. Mom was a professional ballerina by age fourteen. Dad got a Masters degree in theatre from Yale Drama School. Because of two cataclysmic events – the Depression and World War II – neither of them were able to pursue their careers as expected and, instead, have led a very full international business life. But neither of them ever stopped being artists. Through the years they've done over a hundred productions, been honored by the National Theatre of Japan, and in retirement joined Equity and continued to write, direct and perform. Their latest claim to fame is a series of performances in "Love Letters." Every performance has been a sell-out.*
>
> *– Mara*

Balance can be a difficult thing to strike in this business. Everyone we know goes through a certain amount of soul-searching when career makes such heavy demands that our personal lives suffer. On the other hand, as artists we have an obligation to use our talents.

> *When I starred in "Buck Rogers," at first I thought all my dreams had come true. This is what I'd worked so hard to achieve. But I forgot to take into account that it didn't allow me to fulfill my role as a wife and mother, and this caused a lot of anguish for me. When the role ended, I realized it wouldn't work for me to perform in plays, because I wouldn't be there to put my son to bed in the*

evenings. When I got the job on "Silver Spoons" it was the perfect blend. I was able to be there for every Little League game and still do the work I loved. I was very fortunate to be able to find that balance.

– Erin

There may come a time when some of the goals you'd hoped to achieve have not been attained. This may seem to be a bad thing – but perhaps it's not. Another possibility is that you do achieve a goal you've wanted very badly – and then it may turn out it's not what you want after all. Jessica Lange wanted a big movie contract, and got it. When she did, she disliked much of the material offered and felt trapped. She vowed never to commit herself again to work she didn't enjoy. The point is – reassess, rethink, and respond to change. This is where the ability to "go with the flow" can be life-saving.

There are many aspects to cultivating a garden. Plant good seed: this is the classes, the tutorial sessions, the reading, the studying, the asking questions, the reading biographies and the bits and pieces of advice you cull from everywhere. Pull the weeds: this is getting rid of the unhelpful criticisms, the unrealized goals, the erroneous ideas. Sometimes you may need a bigger pot, fresher soil, less crowded conditions. Then recognize there may be times when it's important to transplant.

Ethics

What is the job of the artist? Conveying the truth.

> Speak the truth, and the character plays itself.
> - Barbara Stanwyck

Whether we are actors or storytellers, painters or photographers, filmmakers or writers, we are in the business of *truth* telling. The irony is that, many times in this business, we must do this truth-telling in an untruthful environment.

You're coming into a business full of sharks and charlatans. You have to deal with these people. And you have to live with yourself. You have to decide for yourself what your boundaries are. We can only point out the pitfalls.

We want to present you with a "temptation scenario" — a hypothetical series of questions for you to answer. Let's say you were offered a 3-picture deal by a major studio; you'd be starring in each of these projects; you'd be earning $1,000,000 for each. You could be assured your career would be launched, and then some. There are, however, three conditions you must meet in order to sign the deal: a) you must sleep with someone you neither know nor care for; b) you must defame someone you know by claiming they use drugs when you know they don't; and c) you must change your name and lie about who you are and where you're from.

Okay now let's say it's ten years later. The film series is over. The friend you used to have whom you defamed hasn't spoken to you in years. And your family have never forgiven you for disowning them. How do you feel about yourself? Can you live with it?

Of course this example is exaggerated...or is it? We bring it up to help you begin to ask yourself important questions. These may sound like "nice" problems to have. But we're talking about your center, your equilibrium. Even as you read this, you are creating the person you are and the life you're leading. "Integrity is a gift you give yourself."

Going through life and making right choices is important if you're going to like yourself. Through the course of your career, people may tell stories about you or try, in various ways, to misquote you or try to defame your character. These are some of the dangers of this business, particularly if you become a celebrity. But if you stay with your own truth, you will always feel secure within yourself. No one can take that from you. You can't change the past. But you can make the choice, from now on, to live a life of integrity. If this is all you have, you will still have all you need.

Sexual behavior is one aspect of the business that can be very difficult to deal with. As an actor, you are often asked to portray an expression of sexuality, which may or not be your own, or if it is, it may not be something you would normally share publicly. Yet here you are on a set – perhaps virtually naked, in front of co-star, director and the entire crew. You successfully perform your scene – but then what? How do you re-establish "normal" boundaries? How do you keep your signals clear to your co-star or crew member that you're "not available" and yet keep yourself uninhibited enough to do your part?

> *I was hired to do a recurring role on a popular drama series. I was to play the love interest for one of the leads and there was some light flirting between the actor and me as we got into our role. That's to be expected. But he then began to get into telling me lurid stories, and these persisted day after day. I became increasingly uncomfortable and began to realize he was making the make-up artist, the sound man and several crew members uncomfortable with what is now recognized as abusive behavior. When he invited me to his trailer, I tried to meet with him elsewhere and eventually I was avoiding him in the catering area, where I found others doing the same. It wasn't until I got home and my husband asked me how I was that I fell apart. Looking back, I wish I had said something on the set in front of the entire crew. What I didn't see at the time was that the crew really couldn't say anything and I should have. My next choice was to report him to the Screen Actors' Guild, and SAG takes sexual harassment very seriously. I later found out the leading lady had left the show. She would no longer put up with her leading man's constant verbal abuse, nor with the unprofessional climate which allowed the behavior to continue.*
> *– Erin*

You've heard the old expression, "if you don't stand for something, you'll fall for anything." This business is a perfect proving ground for your sense of character.

You've heard of the "casting couch," and you may think it's a myth, or just an exaggeration. In our experience there are good and bad people at every level of the business. Many of the casting people or directors or producers you meet are busy, professional and their jobs depend upon maintaining respectful relationships with colleagues. However, we've run into people in many different aspects of the profession who seem to be in the business for reasons of their own – personal power, ego, sexual role-playing...you name it.

> *One day a young woman who'd attended our seminar wrote me an e-mail about a troubling situation. While having dinner with her mother, she'd run into a well-known producer who'd approached her in a restaurant. Joining her and her mother at their table, he'd proceeded to give her a full critique about her hair, make-up, weight, clothing, career path and professional chances. He'd then offered to meet her later to tell her more. She declined, but then panicked that she'd thrown away a valuable opportunity. I reassured her, she'd made the right choice. Ironically, I'd had my own version of this scenario with that very same producer fifteen years earlier. I'd auditioned and been offered a job, providing I met him at his office after hours. When I declined, I lost the part. But here's the twist. The woman who was this producer's secretary at the time decided that day to quit. She then became an agent and opened her own agency. She called to tell me she'd been impressed with my stand for principle, and I became one of her first clients.*
> *– Mara*

And in case you feel women are the only vulnerable parties to this behavior, be aware it can be just as dodgy for men.

> *The casting couch works both ways because of the complete sexuality of the entertainment business. Remember – the most powerful word in Hollywood is "no."*
> *– Jim Lewis*

The best way to deal with any and everyone you meet in the business is to have your own boundaries in place. Some actors decline to do any nudity; some actors feel nudity is called for in certain roles; some have no inhibitions about nudity under any circumstances. This is purely a matter of personal choice. Be aware that your attitudes may change as you develop. The nude shots you do today may later come back to haunt you when your teenage son or daughter finds them on the Internet.

You don't have control over other people; you do have control over your own actions. Be conscious of your behavior. People will make assumptions about your attitudes based on the way you act. If you appear uninhibited, it can later be too late to claim you were taken advantage of in some way.

> *I was hired to go a feature film with a mega-star, knowing the previous leading lady had been fired. I needed to meet with the star to get final approval to do the role. This job meant a lot to me, both in terms of reputation and income; at the time my family and I really needed the money. When I met the star, he made it clear he wanted to have an affair with me. The script called for a certain amount of flirtation. However, I had to be very careful to watch my personal behavior. I made sure I was never alone with him in his camper; if he offered to come by my hotel room later, I clearly declined. I had to be sexually attractive to him to get the job; yet I had to maintain my own personal boundary. He kept the pressure up throughout the entire filming process, which began to take its toll. I became very depressed and distracted. The good thing that came out of this was, I made a pledge to myself never to allow anything to make me feel that devalued again.*
> — *Erin*

To be very crass — we heard it said once that in Hollywood if you don't have "fuckability" you don't have "hire-ability." We all have sexual energy. We can use it for good, or for ill. We can abuse it with too many partners, too much emphasis, and by manipulating others. However we can also channel that powerful energy into positive and creative life experiences.

In many Eastern philosophies this is addressed with clarity and without judgment. The thought is, there is only one part of our body where energy can expand and grow, and that's the sexual energy. The individual must then decide what to do with that energy – use it to indulge the senses, or use it to raise the consciousness.

When you enter this business, you are entering the land of temptation. It's the land of glitter, of money, of overindulgence in every sense – too much attention from the press, too much jumping in and out of relationships, too much materialism. This land of plenty is then in immediate juxtaposition to constant rejection, which tends to render the actor vulnerable. So here's the scenario: you're surrounded by excess to which you have, for the moment, no access. Parched and thirsty, you cross the desert heading for the oasis. What would be your tendency when someone invites you to jump into their deliciously inviting pool? Enter this land with awareness and keep yourself awake.

In your previous life – before Hollywood – you may have believed life to be fair, and that some basic ethic ensures that the deserving are those who get ahead. But Hollywood is not a meritocracy. It's more an autocracy with capricious monarchs who come and go, bringing favorites into glory, and beheading those who have fallen from favor. Though some of us take our status as public figures seriously, there are also celebrities who are treated like royalty but who accept none of the responsibility that actually comes with the job.

The external system in Hollywood is quite dysfunctional: often the most talented are those who never get the opportunities their talents deserve. So how can you even the score? By aligning yourself with a higher sense of Principle, whereby in your daily life you honor your talent, no matter the external outcome.

> *I was being considered for a leading role at a major studio. I'd already been accepted by the director and the studio was prepared to go with the recommendation of the producer. He called and*

> asked me to lunch. He was a bright, personable and energetic man, and we had a great conversation about the script and the shoot. I assumed this lunch was in a way yet another audition so of course I did my best to be responsive and enthusiastic, all of which was easy because I loved the project. Toward the end of the lunch he said, "You know, I can see to it you get this part, and I can help you get access to a lot of other good roles in the future. The only thing I need is for you to become my mistress." I was stunned. Desperately trying to think of something diplomatic to say, I replied that if I did that sort of thing, I'd certainly choose him. But the bottom line was I turned him down. We left the restaurant on cordial terms. The following day I received two dozen red roses. I never heard back from the studio about that, or any other part.
> – Mara

What we want to share with you is: It's important not to be duped, not to be confused, not to be mesmerized by what may temporarily seem so tempting. To some extent this exists in every business. But in the film and television business, it's so accentuated as to reach levels of absurdity. This business has so much fantasy mixed in with reality, it's sometimes hard to see where you are.

Change and Changes

> When Perry King and I did a play together several years ago, he became a dear friend. No matter how famous he became with his film and television work, his ability to stay centered always struck me. With humor, and self-deprecation, he shared the following:
> The Five Phases of an Actor's Life:
> 1. Who is Perry King?
> 2. Get me Perry King!
> 3. Get me a Perry King type.
> 4. Get me a young Perry King.
> 5. Who is Perry King?
>
> – Mara

In this business, legend has it that one minute you can be waiting tables, and the next minute you can be starring in a film. It's true, this can and does happen. But what it points to is a constant sense of fluctuation. It's best to be prepared for the opposite scenario as well – you can be famous one season, and happy to get any kind of job the next.

Careers in this business can be likened to the weather. There are seasons in life. Most of us get hired in the spring of our lives; men generally get hired right through the autumn years. Women are seldom given that opportunity. Careers also cycle like seasons: there are times when you may feel frozen out, but often these periods are followed by a spring thaw. If you used the "winter" well, by taking classes, performing in small theatres, honing your talents, you may find new opportunities unfolding like buds on a tree when spring returns.

In Los Angeles, it's more like the Southern California sky: clouds without rain. A lot of people make promises in L.A. that are never kept. This is generally not out of malice. It's more from a sense of politeness: no one wants to say no. So, you keep at it: take your classes, audition for everything reasonable, perform in as many productions as possible. Then, like the flash floods L.A. is famous for, you get a deluge. We all know the expression that "luck" is when preparation meets opportunity.

When it rains in this business, it pours: one offer leads to another, you find yourself edging toward the "hot" category, and you have simultaneous job opportunities, some of which you must turn down.

Of course these "high" moments are what we live for to some extent. These are the hopes that keep us going. However, it is only fair to warn you, this business tends to put you on a roller coaster. You will need to have tools to keep your inner compass in working order.

> Having starred in two television series, I thought I was now on my way to being able to pick and choose the roles I wanted in feature films. I was unaware that in the hierarchy of the business,

"television" people are not considered to be "film" people. Also, as was the case with many other performers, I suffered from a year-long writers' strike. By the time the strike was finally over, I was no longer "hot." Roles came more intermittently, and I had to audition just like everyone else. By then, roles I was right for were tending to go to younger actors who were "Erin Gray" types.

– Erin

The best advice we can give you is: don't get too depressed when things *don't* work out the way you want them to; and don't get too excited when things work out the way you *do* want them to. Strange as it may seem, this latter is the most important. If you allow "the business" to send you over the moon, believe us when we say it's a long parachute back to Earth, and it can be a hard landing.

If you got the part you've been after, great! Congrats. Now think about a few things. Are you a more valuable person than you were before you got the part? What do you need to be studying and preparing before you start the role? How can you prepare yourself best for the next several steps? Who can you talk with, what can you read, how can you progress? This way of thinking will help keep you grounded.

If you didn't get the part, too bad – or is it? Are you a less valuable person than you were before you didn't get the part? What do you need to be studying and preparing for your next performance or audition? Is it possible you weren't ready for this role? Might it have been a blessing not to have gotten it at this particular moment? We're not saying these things are necessarily true, but we encourage you to keep your perspective. Otherwise you're in not only for a bumpy ride, but perhaps a foreshortened career as well.

Another kind of change you must deal with in this business is that people are constantly transforming themselves. We liken it to living in a business of shape shifters.

It may seem maddening or frightening to think you're living in a town and working in a business where no one is what they seem to be. So, the way to turn this to your favor, is for you, too, to become a shape-shifter. Today you're waiting tables and scrounging for open calls in the trades. Tomorrow you're a regular on *General Hospital*. The following day you're the lead in a big budget feature film. As we said, it can happen.

Here's another scenario. Today you're temping, and later going to rehearsal at the small theatre company you joined. Six months from now a casting director remembers your performance, his memory jogged by all the postcards you sent, and you're auditioning for a new TV series featuring at least two characters you could do exceptionally well. Two years from now you've got two episodic appearances under your belt, and you're finally up for a feature. In the meantime you've taken classes, studied, read, learned more about life and about yourself, and your work is growing. It turns out that to be a shape-shifter is your natural state. Remember, this is happening for other people in the business too — and not just actors. The nerd in the mailroom where you leave your photos today, may be the executive producer for whom you audition tomorrow.

As *you* shape-shift, know what is motivating your changes. Are you having rhinoplasty because you met an agent who said he'd only take you as a client if you changed your nose? Are you starving yourself to achieve that anorexic look you think is the ticket to TV stardom? Are you losing touch with your real friends, those who tell you honestly what they think of you and your work?

No matter how many forms your career takes, stay in touch with people and activities that remind you who you are. Your core values will always be important.

Building Your Life, Setting Your Goals

There's a disturbing trend we've noticed in modern society, something we call "the lottery mentality." What we mean by this is not so much the literal definition of those who play the lottery, but rather those who rely upon chance, effectively making it one of their values. Whether from a sense of discouragement, lack of education, or fear, there are those who believe no amount of hard work will get them the success they desire, so rather than work for their dreams, they leave them mostly to chance. There are lucky winners in the world, but we have to say their experiences differ from ours. So in our book, we'll be showing you a way to integrate your artistic instincts with logic and dogged persistence.

Perhaps all this is a fancy way of saying don't wait for something to "happen" to you. Go ahead and "happen" to life instead. It may seem from where you stand that you have infinite time. In fact, none of us do. Life is short. If you had one year to live, what would you do? If that's what you're doing anyway, you're on your true path. If not, this is a good time to examine your goals. Do you have a life purpose, a mission you feel you're here to fulfill? Ten years from now, will you feel good about how you spent the decade? Twenty years from now, will you be where you want to be? It's not too soon to consider these sobering thoughts.

Wealthy parents may have made your young life easy. On the other hand, a divorce may have interrupted a happy childhood, you may have grown up in poverty, or you may feel nothing has ever quite gone your way. Whether you began from favorable or unfavorable circumstances, decide what you truly want, then go for it. We always say – what do you have to lose by trying?

There are some wonderful tools for defining your goals and discovering not just your next role – but your role in life. One of the best we've read is Stephen Covey's *Seven Habits of Highly Effective People*. You're coming into a wonderful but tough business. Don't you want to be effective?

Covey's book and seminars train people to write their mission statements, and few tools are more powerful for personal growth and understanding. The entertainment business tends to be a magnet for the good, the bad and the ugly. As you begin working and enjoying some success, it's easy to get pulled off center unless you actually know what you are all about. We encourage you to have your core values clearly in mind as you embark on the path of the performer.

We love the expression "go with the flow," which has its roots in ancient Chinese wisdom and encourages us to view the universe not as an adversary but as a partner in all we do. This expression is not, however, to be confused with "anything goes." To navigate the high seas, you still need a compass. "With a mission statement, we can flow with changes," says Covey, and this assures you'll be able to respond to situations that arise and still reach your destination.

Another book we recommend is *The Path of Least Resistance* by Robert Fritz. He describes what he calls the "pivotal technique" whereby you constantly reassess two vital things: one, where you are now, what he calls "current reality"; two, where you want to be, your goal. He describes "structural tension" as an important key to life.

> *In working with Robert Fritz's concept of structural tension, the image that came to me was two posts stretching a rubber band. One post is current reality – where I am right now. The other is the goal I'm working toward. If one or the other "post" isn't there, the rubber band is slack. If both are in place, I have "structural tension," and my life tends to move in the direction of bringing the goal closer to current reality.*
> *– Mara*

Talent & Fame

Talent and fame are two concepts much discussed in this industry. The first —talent – is either debated, as in "Does he have any talent?" or touted, as in "Oh, she's so talented!" The second subject – fame – is often publicly avoided, as in "I hate it when paparazzi follow me!" while behind the scenes it is avidly pursued, as in, "She's not a big enough name."

You need to decide where you stand on these two concepts so you're neither confused nor fooled by either of them. Chances are at the outset of your career you have talent and not fame. Of course some do enter the world of film with fame from another arena and no particular acting talent. Fame for the sake of fame is treated as though it were a currency, something that, once attained, can be spent. When you become "bankable," producers are willing to spend big money to include you in a project.

All of us in this business are trying to take an internal quality and make it externally successful. At the outset of your career, ambition — an internal thing — is often used as the measure of success — an external thing. Both of us were asked by early agents, "Do you want to be a star?" Of course, the answer was "Yes!" The agents were trying to warn us. If we never became famous, did we still want to be actresses?

From an internal perspective, there's nothing wrong with ambition. You'll need it to fuel your career. But think about whether you're a sprinter or a marathon runner. Ambition can be likened to sugar — a great short-burst fuel. But for the long haul you'll need something more substantial. Goal-setting, core values and mission statements may be closer to the balanced diet you'll need to create a full life.

From an external perspective, it is sometimes a struggle to discern the underlying logic in this business, because we think in terms of what we deserve.

> *One of my favorite moments in the film "Unforgiven" is when Clint Eastwood looks at Gene Hackman, just before shooting him. Hackman's character says, 'I don't deserve this' and Eastwood's character says, "Deserves got nothing to do with it." You can't take "deserve" to an agent, you can't take "deserve" to a casting director or producer. What you can do, it take "deserve" to yourself.*
> *- Beau L'Amour, Producer*

This is a tough business. Don't look for confirmation of who you are from outside yourself. It will forever elude you.

One day we were on a morning hike we often take. Although we consider our trail to be sacred ground, there was one day when it became all too "Hollyweird." As we came up behind two producers, we overheard them commiserating about the burden of dealing with well-known actors who were calling them, begging for auditions. "Didn't she see she was wasting my time?" one of them asked about an award-winning actress of international renown. "And who does he think *he* is?" the other said about a Grammy-winning recording star. "Of course, I flattered him, because we do need him for that one event." They were more interested in bringing in an "unknown" because they could get him cheap, and he had "star quality" (however that's defined for the next ten minutes). They went on to say, "Of course we don't know if he can act, but we can take care of that."

We wanted to scream at them, "You idiots! See how you feel when this neophyte has wasted 10,000 feet of film and cost you double your budget!" They were only too eager to take major, proven talents and them on the trash heap. And here's the clincher. In the next moment, a very well-known actor walked by them going the other direction. "Hi, Steve!" they shouted and waved. "We just *loved* your last film. Gawd, you were Great! Can't wait to see you do the Oscars!" "Yeah," said Steve, pulling down his hat and walking by them as quickly as possible. He knew better than to take them seriously.

Visualization

Visualization is a tool used widely today in business, in sports, spiritual training and in psychology. But visualization was first an artist's tool that other disciplines have borrowed. And in the business of film and television, it is the foundation of everyone's work.

A writer must visualize her story in order to create the script; the director must visualize the completed film before he shoots a single frame; a casting director must visualize who's right for the part; a costumer, the correct color and line; a set designer, the period and architecture, and so it goes through each department.

Actors must do even more visualizing than their colleagues, because not only must they visualize themselves in the role; they must visualize a career in the first place in order to make it a reality. If you're reading this book, you're probably serious about having an acting career. If you're an artist, you have strong visualizing powers. We encourage you to visualize your own success and match this visualization with right behavior, taking the important steps we've outlined in this book.

But in using your imagination, you are unleashing a powerful force in your life and in the lives of others. Will you be a force for good or for ill? Will you visualize yourself beating others in a race for a coveted role? Or will you visualize yourself doing superb work that illuminates the role and serves the story?

You have a choice how you use your personal power. We ask you to practice the higher use of imagination, thus honoring yourself and your profession. This will make you a success in *life*— not just in "the business." This will mean you truly have learned how to *Act Right*.

PREPARATION

Covered In This Chapter:

- Schools & Classes

- Reading

- Credits

- Editing

- Workshops & Theatre Groups

- Advanced Class Work

Action must be founded on knowledge.
— Beaconsfield

The most important thing in any show is preparation.
— Abby Singer
Producer

PREPARATION

Acting is a unique profession. Although talent is essential, talent itself is not enough to ensure you'll become a working actor. Many talented actors are never heard of and never really have a career.

We won't presume to tell you too much about how to act, since there's such an abundance of experts who teach and write on this subject. One thing we feel strongly is that the important things you'll bring to your acting work you learn from life itself, so we hope you view life as a continuing education, filled with reading, observing, interacting and personal experiences.

We'll say this again and again — you must take responsibility for developing the skills and strategies necessary to become a pro. At times there seems to be no rhyme or reason to this profession. There is no rule book to follow, or set of rules which will ensure your success. There is, however, a lot of good information in the following pages that will help you make good choices. There are certain rules — and one cardinal rule is to be prepared, and we mean for *anything*. You never know when you'll be asked to dance a waltz, crack a joke, sing a cabaret torch song, wield a sword, or cartwheel over a couch. Some of these skills may be beyond you. But do your best to learn.

Students interested in film and TV have asked us whether or not they should "do theatre." We answer emphatically — yes! We acknowledge that theatre requires a completely different set of technical skills. And in this book, we are not dealing with theatre. We are focusing entirely on acting for the media of film, television and any other form which involves a camera lens.

There are those who believe film and television actors should never do theatre. We think this a sad commentary on the disconnection young actors have from their performing roots. As long as humans have existed, they have performed. For many of us, this is a basic drive, an inherent impulse. Through the centuries, people have experimented, learned and perfected performance techniques. Those of us who perform are adding to a long, colorful tradition. So it is well to know our heritage.

Theatre is the beginning, middle and ultimate experience for the actor — a living, breathing exchange between performer and audience. So — if and when you can — take every opportunity to perform in a play. This will in some ways always be foundational work, both grounding and challenging you as an actor.

The various forms of work you do in front of a camera will require fine tuning of technique — less volume, more going on behind the eyes, awareness of a whole new technical world — but it will always require a basic understanding of what you do "live." This is particularly applicable for auditioning, for example.

As we mentioned earlier, there are many pathways into a performing career. Each of us had quite a body of experience before beginning our television work, coming from two totally different backgrounds, one of us in theatre, one of us in modeling. We've always found is fascinating to compare notes from these two extremes.

> *When I was asked to go in for a general audition by the casting director of "Days of Our Lives," I expected to return to see her a few days or weeks later for an actual audition. But I'd been recommended by another casting director who'd seen me in a play. Apparently that recommendation carried a lot of weight. After reading my resume, she asked a lot of questions about my theatre work. I remember telling her one funny story about ad libbing when my co-actor forgot his lines. After a very pleasant interview she thanked me for coming in. By the time I got home my phone was ringing. She was calling me to offer me a part. I got the job not by auditioning, but largely because I had theatre experience. In soaps, "the show must go on." She knew I could be trusted to come up with some kind of performance no matter what happened on the set.*

The most important asset I brought to acting from my modeling career was my awareness of my entire body and of the space I occupy. When I was modeling I would shift inch by inch from one position to the next with a clear sense of where each appendage and each body angle was. At the same time I always knew where the camera was and what it was seeing. This gave me a level of comfort which translated well to the technical requirements of a set.
— Erin

Understand that in the modern world, there are many forms of performance. As an actor, not only must you be able to shift from part to part like a chameleon, you must also shift comfortably from format to format.

When you do theatre, you have a rehearsal period, you speak loudly enough to fill the house (be it large or small), you "cheat" downstage so you can be seen and heard. But if you take those same techniques into an intimate close-up on film you'll blow the sound man out of his chair and pop out of frame as soon as you turn your head. When you work in Sitcom you have to allow for audience reaction to jokes. But if you wait for a laugh when you're doing a soap opera you'll be there till Christmas.

The point is, you need to be flexible enough to move from one medium to another, and you need to be a diligent enough student to pick up the nuances of each particular format.

The fascinating thing about theatre is that it's a *living* art form. Thus, through performing the classics, one can participate in a palpable, vibrant form of this rich history. To perform a part in a play by Euripides, Shakespeare or Ibsen is to travel in time and relive, in some measure, what our theatrical ancestors experienced.

Another way to participate in this historical unfoldment is to study the development of acting itself. Most students of the theatre agree that Stanislavski was the first to develop and write about an actual technique. He is the father of "the method" and in various forms, this is still what all acting students learn today.

SCHOOLS & CLASSES

There are many schools and anyone can call himself or herself a teacher. So it's very important that you check out a teacher's reputation. In the books and articles you read, actors will often mention where they studied. Also, check the biography section in playbills, for actors often list their teachers or schools.

When researching schools, see how long they've been around and find out about the instructor's own background. Still, the best way is through recommendations from people you respect.

Not all classes will be right for you, nor all teachers. When searching, ask your prospective teacher if you can audit a class. There's nothing wrong in asking, and if it's allowed, it is the best way for you to see for yourself if this is the kind of person you can work with, or if his or her technique appeals to you. Many teachers will not allow auditing, as they feel it may be disturbing to the class. If you feel right about a certain class, the only way really to find out about it is to take the class. You should have a good idea if the class is really helping after about a month.

We recommend you study with more than one teacher, although not necessarily that you study with more than one at a time. After you've been with one teacher for a while, explore other options. Each teacher will offer you another perspective, method, approach, or insight. Also be aware that there are different levels of classes as you gain experience. If you're a beginner, don't attend a class with seasoned professionals.

There's a history of teaching in the American Theatre and as an actor it's your job to find out about it. Essentially, it started with what was called The Group Theatre — a group of thespians (including writers, directors, producers and actors) who traced their roots to Stanislavski. Many of them became the great American drama teachers and this in turn has led to a certain hierarchy of schools of thought. Lee Strasberg, Stella Adler, Sanford Meisner, Robert Lewis and Uta Hagen are among the members. Some of their schools still exist. Many have students who teach the "Strasberg" or the "Adler" or "Meisner" method.

> *It had been a goal of mine to study with Bobby Lewis. Fortunately, I was accepted in a master class he taught in L.A. Mr. Lewis's approach to the rehearsal process is simple, direct, brilliant. It was both art and science, sparks flying and light bulbs turning on. I'd been acting for years before I took his class, but after his class, I felt I had a solid, irrefutable foundation.*
> — Mara

Once you're in a class, be sure to make the most of it. For example, if you're not given a specific scene to work on, take the time to find plays, read them, and find a scene you'd like to work on. Choose material that inspires you.

All actors should be familiar with the classics — Shakespeare, Moliere, Chekhov, etc. But you should also find scenes to work on that fit the kind of character you might be cast as. If you're from Texas and have worked on a ranch all your life and still have an accent — until you get rid of it — use it to your advantage by finding characters that have those qualities.

In most classes, scenes will be given to you, or recommended. It's up to you to do your work. That means making sure you're prepared, finding the time to read, to memorize and to rehearse with your partner. This is not the time to be shy, or to be lazy. This is your work, the career you've chosen. Make the most of it.

We've often been in classes where students complained that they never got the chance to get up on the stage. And yet, in all those cases, it was really the fact that the students themselves were never ready. They hadn't rehearsed enough. They had personal problems. They were too busy to find the time... etc., etc., etc. Tad Danielewski – who directed professionally for twenty-five years before he became a well-known teacher and coach – always said, "There are no out-of-work actors. Only actors who don't do their work."

We could almost always spot the actors who were going to succeed. They were the ones who worked the hardest, were the best prepared, and were the most willing to face their fears and insecurities.

> *It was no surprise to me when a fellow model and acting classmate Susie Blakely successfully made the transition from modeling to acting. She not only had a scene up every week, she was studying in two different schools. When I did a scene with her, she'd meet me on street corners, between modeling jobs, to run lines. She was the first one in our class to land a major role in a mini-series. It was the coveted role in "Rich Man, Poor Man" and it started her career.*
> *— Erin*

As we write these words of wisdom, we find we're both getting knots in our stomachs remembering the years of class study. Probably this is because you are never more vulnerable than when you are in class. You are judged by your peers. You are asked to make a fool of yourself in the most intimate of ways. You are asked to perform private moments in front of others which no sane person would share with strangers. There are moments in class that surpass most human experience in catharsis. There are moments in class when you only wish the bowels of the earth would swallow you. All this – and you're not even making money. Are you still sure you want to be an actor?

READING

As this is the business you have chosen to be in, it behooves you to know everything you can about it. So, start reading. We feel very strongly that there are three major categories of appropriate reading for actors: the trades; biographies; and scripts and plays.

For the "trades" – *Variety, The Hollywood Reporter, Backstage* – are the majors. *Backstage* tends to focus on theatre. In *Variety* and the *Reporter* you'll find who's the head of Studio X this week, so in case you run into him or her at a party, you'll know who you're talking to.

Biographies about people who have made their living in this business can be invaluable. Many are heartbreaking tales of woe. Some are uncanny success stories. Many detail the path of excesses. But in most of these real-life stories, you'll also find some sort of focus, drive and wisdom which may be helpful to you.

Undoubtedly your acting teachers will have given you this information, but if you haven't yet read Stanislavski, we consider reading his four books to be vital foundation work. Likewise, we recommend both Michael Chekhov's and Robert Lewis's important books. We've included a longer reading list in the appendix, but we encourage you to ask your acting teachers and peruse the shelves.

There's never an end to what you can glean from reading good material. Read all the plays, screenplays, teleplays, playlets, scenes and dialogues you can get your hands on. Some are awful. Some are great. Some are flat on the page but come to life in class or in production. You'll learn from reading everything, be it good or bad.

The major source for finding plays is the Samuel French chain of bookstores, which has outlets in Los Angeles, New York and London. (All of them carry our book, by the way.) In New York there are also the Drama Bookshop and the Applause bookstore. Even if you live in Gary, Indiana you have access to these via phone. And before you get that far, there's always your local library, which will give you a good start.

Through the various Internet book stores you can also order anything you like, and you have the advantage of being able to see what other readers think about a particular book. Amazon.com, Borders.com, Bn.com (barnesandnoble.com) are all good sources for books. (Again, all of these sites carry our book, though we've found amazon.com is the only one which ships immediately; the others offer a six-week delay.)

The Internet is also a good source of information, even if you don't care to use it for buying books. If you don't have a computer, you can use your public library's computer. You can access interviews, videographies, filmographies, biographies and other kinds of information, which you can either save as computer files or print-outs. Some organizations have created pages chronicling the careers of well-known performers. One example is http://www.tv-now, which lists (with regular updates) many stars, their credits and which of their film/TV projects are currently running. (A list is given in our chapter Useful Web Sites.)

We've found great sources for information in every form — print, audio, and video — at the broadcasting museums. Two of the major ones are the Museum of Broadcast Communications in Chicago (which has a wonderful web site) and the Museum of TV & Radio, which has branches in both New York City and Los Angeles. Their archivists are well-informed and their collections comprehensive.

Another great source for materials is the Motion Picture Academy in Los Angeles, which has a formidable library of scripts. Scripts may not be taken from the premises, but you are permitted to copy scenes from the scripts they have on file. There are sometimes early versions that changed by the time they became final shooting scripts.

One of the many benefits of becoming well-read is that you can start cross-connecting the names and pieces with which you are familiar. For example, Andrew Bergman wrote a number of plays popular among dinner theatres throughout the country. He later directed "The Freshman" with Marlon Brando and Matthew Broderick. If you know something about Bergman's plays, you then have a level of understanding and perception about his work as a director, which would otherwise elude you.

It's also interesting to screen films and with the video rental business flourishing, your task has been made particularly easy. One way to do it is to choose themes. For example: have a Brando week, or a Marilyn week. Or choose a writer or a director you find interesting and follow their work chronologically over a period of their career. Examples are: Martin Scorsese or Sydney Pollack or Robert Altman. And don't overlook the masters who laid so much of the groundwork for the film industry, such as Frank Capra, Alfred Hitchcock, or Billy Wilder.

CREDITS

Are you in the habit of doing the dishes while the opening credits come on the TV screen, or walking out of the movie theatre when the ending credits roll? This is a good time to break that habit and begin thinking of the credits as a guide book to the people who work in this industry. Everyone else (in the business) does. Sadly, you may need to use your VCR pause function to actually read some of today's TV credits, as they go by much too quickly for humans or other life-forms to read them.

> *Before I start a project, I ask my manager for credits on everyone. I want to know where someone comes from — particularly the Director and Director of Photography.*
> *— Joan Van Ark*

It's funny. You can always tell when you're sitting in a movie theatre in Los Angeles, as opposed to most other American cities: the crowd doesn't start its mass exodus when the first name appears. Remember these are the people you'll be working with — and the people you aspire to work with. You may feel that you'll never remember all these names. We think you'll find that just by making the effort to read the names, some will begin to register. Directors, producers, casting people and any and everyone in a position to hire in this industry take this even more seriously — they make notes.

I recently had an interview with a Director who was looking for a Director of Photography for his next pilot. He explained that during the process of looking for a DP he made detailed notes about things he liked and didn't like in programs which were on the air. My name apparently came up several times under the "plus" column and this is what got me the job.

— Richard Hissong ("Friends;" "Mad About You")

EDITING

In general, when you watch programs and films, begin paying attention to the way things are edited. What does that mean exactly? It means that you should take an active stance rather than a passive one in viewing. Think through the options the director had in putting together the scene you're watching. Realize he or she made choices about master shots, close-ups, which of the actors is on camera at any given moment and so forth. We will discuss the finer points of varying shots subsequently. For now, be aware of these options, because your work will ultimately fit as an important part of a complex puzzle. The better the piece, the more indispensable to the overall project.

WORKSHOPS & THEATRE GROUPS

We firmly believe that just because you have started working — that is, being paid to act — this is no excuse to stop studying. In a perfect world, none of us would need to do sit-ups in order to have toned abs. However we make those trips to the gym to keep ourselves in shape. So it is with acting. Musicians call it "chops." To keep them, you have to play regularly. So look for classes, scene groups or theatre groups and "work out" with them. Many are listed in the trades. Your local SAG or AFTRA (or ACTRA in Canada) office will have listings. We also recommend word-of-mouth as a good source.

Continuing to participate in workshops and theatre groups helps you to keep and to continue honing your skills. It also ensures that you are a member of the acting community, contributing to the collective body of work, and making all sorts of contacts which will continue throughout your career.

ADVANCED CLASSES & WORKSHOPS

Even a well-launched career may require fine tuning. Sometimes a well-structured class taught by a good teacher can give a successful actor who has hit a "plateau" just the breakthrough he or she needs. Sally Fields, for example, had done two successful TV series when she went to study with Lee Strasberg. She tells a story of becoming furious one day in class, pushed to her emotional limit. She used her new-found emotional awareness and poured it into an audition for a mini-series called "Sybil." Her work was stunning and later gave her access to the kind of parts which earned her an Oscar. We think she'd agree she could never have done so without the advanced class work. Helen Hunt valued her teacher so much that during the acceptance speech for her first Oscar, she lifted the statuette and said "Thank you Larry Moss," a teacher who specializes in intensive, advanced sessions.

As an alternative to an advanced class, consider joining a workshop. Workshops are structured as places where actors can "work out" — a place to try scenes, find scene partners, do acting exercises where feedback is available. Just as it's important to maintain some degree of physical exercise throughout our lives, we believe it's critical to continue using your acting talent in a variety of ways throughout your career. We're never too old to learn. And talent which is being used has no chance to get rusty.

Some workshops are attached to a theatre company. Some function separately and then progress to the point of giving showcases.

> When I first moved to L.A., I found out that Tad Danielewski — who had extraordinary credits as one of the directors of the great early television programs like "Playhouse 90" — had started a workshop. It cost no money to join. But one had to have some credits and one had to audition. He believed in nurturing talent and he believed the TV

studios were foolish if they didn't support young actors. So he asked them for free space and got it. We met weekly at NBC where we did acting exercises and scenes. Tad ran these workshops in both Los Angeles and New York and any of us were free to attend any of the workshops whenever we could. This was a fantastic place to get thoughtful, insightful feedback and to keep the juices flowing.

— Mara

At one point I joined a theatre group. To get in, there were three requirements: some acting credits, a referral and an audition. This was a group of seasoned professionals who wanted to keep working. There was a rule that you couldn't direct yourself, but that was great. You could chose another member to direct you, and you had to subject yourself to comments from your peers. I found both the positive and the negative feedback to be helpful — after all, that's what the business is all about. Sometimes we got far enough along that we developed a full performance and actually put on a play.

— Erin

Both of us participated in showcase performances during the early stages of our acting careers. Some of these productions require the actor pay to participate. Though this may sound counter-productive, use your own judgment. Sometimes the money is well spent, if it gives you a good platform to show casting directors what you can do.

Remember these groups are terrific not only for continuing to hone your acting skills, but for developing new skills, like directing. We believe it's both soulful and smart for actors to expand into directing, producing, writing, as their careers continue to unfold.

PICTURES, RÉSUMÉS, REELS & WEB SITES

Covered In This Chapter:

- Pictures

- Résumés

- Academy Players Directory

- Video Reels

- Web Sites

- Record Keeping

- Information For Your Agent or Manager

Make sure that you and the photographer "click." Don't be frugal. Don't pick the cheapest photographer you met just to save a few bucks.

— Lesley Bohm
Professional Photographer

Change your picture every year and a half, or whenever there's a significant change in your look.

— Ursula Shelehov
— Photographer,
Former Manager of Warner Brothers Photo Lab

The most important thing is, don't lie on your résumé.

— Joy Todd
Casting Director

PICTURES

Even with the advent of video résumés, even with faxes, even with modems, even with interactive, on-line, real-time, downloadable, high-res, digitally enhanced, full color imaging – yes, you still need pictures.

The black-and-white "glossy" is still one of the actor's key tools of the trade. Without pictures, you can't get an agent, your agent can't submit you, the casting director can't find or remember you, the director can't make a decision about you...and so it goes. So one of your first tasks is going to be getting a good standard shot and getting it duplicated.

How do you go about finding a photographer? Check the trades – photographers will sometimes advertise in display or classified ads. Check union publications – SAG and AFTRA sometimes have listings. Peruse the shelves at the drama bookstores such as Samuel French to see what books focused on actors' photographs might be available. Most importantly, when you find a shot you admire, find out who the photographer was. Word-of-mouth is still the best way to find a photographer. The bottom line is that you need to find someone whose work you like. Check with other actors. Look at their photos.

Another way to find photos of other actors is to ask your agent if you may look through his or her clients' photo files. If that's not acceptable, ask your agent to show you which photos he or she likes – and about which he or she gets positive response from casting directors. Are the photos clear and interesting, and do they look like the actor they represent? Have they captured the essence of the subject's personality?

As to price, we feel it's a good idea to comparison-shop. Find out the price of a sitting, as well as any additional costs such as film, processing, contact sheets, prints, retouching, etc.

Ask who keeps the negatives. If the photographer keeps the negatives, ask him or her for how long and if he or she regularly purges the office files. Ask to be notified in case you want to purchase the negatives later, or ask if you can have the negatives duplicated. Our advice is to make sure either to retain the negatives, or make arrangements to buy them eventually. Buy them for an additional fee if necessary. We've learned the hard way that sometimes the very shot you later decided to duplicate has now been discarded for lack of filing space — or has perished in a fire that destroyed the photo archives.

Ask who develops the photos. The photographer? Or do you have to have that done? If he or she does the blow-ups, ask how many are included in the original price. If you want additional blow-ups, ask how much more per shot.

Some photographers offer different kinds of sessions — a "head shot" session, for example, versus a complete series of shots. These shorter sessions will be cheaper and will be all you need to get started.

Be prepared to spend several hundred dollars on this project — at least $300 for the base fee, and a few hundred more for retouching and duplication. If you need your images to be scanned, that can be another expense. In addition, you'll need to pay for wardrobe, hair and possibly make-up, unless you're an expert at these yourself.

One of our favorite photographers is Lesley Bohm and she suggests an intermediate step. After going through the contact sheet (filled with tiny pictures impossible to see except with a loop) she recommends having a few favorites printed in a 3x5 size. These are easier to see and choose from. Then afterward, you have some great postcard sized shots to refer to.

What should your picture look like? Very simply — you. Your picture will serve as an introduction, a chance to glance at you before people actually meet you. It also serves the important purpose of being a reminder to producers, directors, et al, after they've met you. We'll say this again: make sure you look like your picture! It's of no use to present yourself in Shakespearean costume and then walk in in jeans. It's of no use to submit a picture with long hair when your hair is now short. It's of no use to present a picture of you ten years ago, unless you're one of those rare people who looks exactly the same no matter which decade it is.

There is all manner of wizardry available through the magic of photographic and digital technology. Digital retouching is a fantastic tool – but it must be used wisely.

First, don't give yourself a nose job or a chin job or an ear job or a face lift with photographic retouching. As we said – the goal is to look *like* your photo. If you have a few wrinkles, remember this may be exactly what the casting director wants for the role. Similarly, your cute button nose may be the thing that gets you the part.

Second, resist the temptation to make your head shot "artistic" in some way, and save those impulses for some magnificently imaginative album cover.

Third, there IS a place for digital retouching, and it's in correcting errors in what is otherwise a terrific shot. There might be a fold in your blouse, a tiny shadow under your chin, a piece of jewelry that's too much, or an arm skin tone that's too bright compared with the skin tone of your face. Retouching is made for solving these kinds of problems and it can be well worth it to invest the relatively small amount of money required to redeem an expensive – and otherwise terrific – photo shoot.

> *In one of my recent photos, I had my hand in the shot. As it turned out the hand drew too much attention away from my face. I had the retoucher remove the entire hand, which had been against a black sweater. Cutting and pasting, he used the black sweater material to cover the area where the hand had been. Now the photo is one of my most usable shots.*
>
> *– Erin*

> *If I'm in the sun for sixty seconds — like, say, I have to walk across the parking lot — the end of my nose turns red. I don't like to use a lot of makeup, which can give a caked-on appearance. So in some of my photos, a retoucher removes the slight "shadow" which the red becomes in a black and white photo.*
> — Mara

Many cities have excellent photo labs. In Los Angeles, one of the best — and one of the best-kept secrets — is the Warner Brothers Photo Lab, which processes all in-studio stills, but also does a retail business with the public. You must call to make arrangements for a drive-on pass in order to get there. The long-time head of operations gave us a lot of good advice:

> *If you're older, you may be tempted to ask for an over-retouched photo. Don't have that done. Look like your photo. Make yourself pleasant looking, but not like you look 20 years younger than you are.*
> — Ursula Shelehov

About new pictures — if you have changed your look, either by cutting your hair or growing a mustache, of course you need new ones. We also recommend that you have fresh pictures at least every two years, even if you do look exactly the same. Why? Because casting people get tired of looking at the same old glossy.

You can keep up with the demand for fresh pictures by organizing new photo shoots periodically. You can also keep up, to some extent, by having a variety of shots taken at one sitting — and then not using all the shots at once. Hold one or two back until you get that call — "Do you have any new pictures?" "Of course," you'll say. "I can get them to you this afternoon." You'll look very prepared and professional.

Unless you have dramatically changed your look, it is generally not necessary to do new photos more than once every year or two.

> *We have actors here who are selecting two shots from a shoot, and then a few weeks later they come back in to get new pictures. Why? "Well my agent said the reason I haven't gone on calls is that I need new pictures." It's the oldest ploy in town. You don't need pictures any more frequently than once a year. The agent is just trying to get the actor out of their hair.*
> — Ursula Shelehov

What about the style of your picture? First of all, styles have changed somewhat in recent years. It used to be that the head shot was the only shot used in theatrical casting — that is, a shot from the neck up. The idea was to give people a very clear look at your face, and nothing else. For commercials, the rule was to create a composite — three smaller pictures on one 8x10 sheet: a head shot, a full body shot and a "character" shot. The trend now is to combine these — that is, to create one main shot, but instead of a head shot it's often a "three quarter" shot, that is, from top of head to about the knees. This gives prospective employers a chance to see less of your face, but more of the whole you.

What style should you choose for your picture? Our advice is to choose your most comfortable, natural look. Try to dress yourself in a "neutral" look — ready to go anywhere. But also try to portray the essence of yourself. From one picture a casting director should be able to see your potential in many different roles. If it's too frilly you may type-cast yourself as a "period" actor; if it's too athletic you may limit yourself to "athletic" roles. If you look too tailored you may only be considered for the "lawyer" roles.

As far as clothing is concerned, we find in looking through the stacks of the pictures we use the most, the clothes are basic and comfortable. We also find that either black or white work extremely well. When we prepare for photo shoots, we might wear a white shirt in one, a black sweater in another, or a white sweater in one, a black tank top in another. Ant this works well for both men and women.

There's a myth than one should never wear black and never where white in a photo. We don't agree. Lesley Bohm recommends both (see her complete list of tips, below.)

In our opinion, black frames the face best. When it comes to white, experiment and use your own judgment. White can give you the advantage of additional light which bounces onto your features, giving you a natural "fill" – i.e. no dark shadows, no lines. The disadvantage is that, if the white is truly bright, it can be so much brighter than your face that it tends to draw the eye away from you. Our advice is to take both black and white clothes to the shoot and use them both. Then if in your favorite shot you're wearing white, you always have the option of retouching and slightly darkening the white.

Many people say that when they look at a photo, they look first at the eyes. And this makes sense because in film and television "the eyes have it." There should be something going on in your expression. But this must come from within. There are two ways to approach this picture of you. One is to use the picture to mask your "real self" by putting on some kind of persona. The other is to use the camera to help you peel away layers of posturing and let it help you reveal who you really are.

When there's something coming through those eyes, casting directors – and everyone else – will see it clearly and more often than not, remember it. So when you do your photo shoot, think the thoughts you need to think so that something is going on behind the eyes. If it works for you, bring your loved one – in the flesh, or in your imagination – so that your eyes glisten and have depth. Here's a small but valuable piece of advice. Always have a playful and secret thought tucked into the back of your mind that you can think of when you need to. This works well for still photo shoots of all kinds. The viewer will sense that you are withholding something intriguing and will want to find out what that something is.

A word about lighting – and this affects your decision whether to shoot indoors or outdoors.

Available light is always better, unless you have a really great photographer who can do excellent lighting. A woman looks best with diffused, available light. Harsh light doesn't work well.
— Ursula Shelehov

Aside from your own wardrobe and hair choices, lighting is the single most important choice you'll make for your photos. There are good and bad things about both studio and location shoots.

If your photographer can give you soft, diffused lighting and a background that is not too stark — gray is better than bright white — then you'll probably have good results and perhaps better ones than you'd get if you're squinting into the sun on top of a scenic mountain top. However, if you have soft lighting at a certain time of day in your back yard and you feel comfortable there and fidgety in an unfamiliar studio, then try the great outdoors.

We've done hours upon hours of both indoor and outdoor shoots and gotten great results from both, but usually have thrown away many more shots than we've used. Remember that if you get one or two good photos from a single shoot, it's been a success.

When you have chosen the shot you're going to use, take it to a good photo lab that specializes in large quantity duplication. The number of duplicate photos you order will depend upon whether you need to supply your agent and/or a manager, along with supplying your own stock. At most duplicating labs, prices go down after the first one hundred, so we would suggest that as a minimum number to order. The standard size and style for professional photos is 8x10, black and white. The finish is up to you — glossy or matte — with or without a border. But here you have an opportunity to highlight your photo.

Make your photo a little different. Stay within the basic parameters, but choose either no border, or not a glossy finish.
— Ursula Shelehov

Be sure you're identified on each and every picture. Choose a clear type font you feel represents you. Then staple a copy of your résumé to each and every picture and take these on each and every interview. You may think that your agents have already submitted your picture – and maybe they have. Nevertheless – take responsibility.

Even if you keep returning to the same casting director on call-backs for the same part – take your photo. The first one could have been given to the director, who left his folder at home. It could be the casting director wants to keep the first one on file. (Good!) There could be any number of positive reasons why that first shot isn't available. Be prepared. Be professional.

We asked our favorite L.A. photographer what her suggestions would be for your photos. We liked what she came up with so much, we'll share the whole list with you.

Lesley Bohm's Top Five Tips for Actors Going to a Photo Session.

1 – Bring a variety of clothing that you feel and look good in. Textures are great as well as solids, but no busy patterns. Black and white are both good.
2 – Be focused. Make sure you get enough sleep the night before and that you are in the right state of mind. Do not go to your photo session if you're stressed out about something. I.e., you broke up with your boyfriend/ girlfriend/ fiancé, there was a loss in your family, etc.
3 – Bring along whatever will help you get the expression you're going for. I.e. favorite music/ boyfriend/ dog/ picture of Brad Pitt, etc.
4 – Don't be frugal. Don't pick the cheapest photographer you've ever met just to save a few bucks. Less is not always more. Also, if you can afford to get the best make-up and hair artist, do it. Excellent make-up and hair make the difference between decent pictures and phenomenal pictures.
5 – Make sure that you and the photographer "click" and feel comfortable with him/ her. This will make your photo session more enjoyable and that is the most important thing. Have fun!

PHOTOS – IN SUMMARY:

The Don'ts:
- Don't use a candid snapshot.
- Don't use a shot that shows you much younger.
- Don't use a production shot showing you in character.
- Don't have a picture that looks unnatural.

The Do's
- Do update your picture regularly.
- Do have a stack of photos & résumés ready at all times.
- Do take your photo (and résumé) to every single casting session.

RÉSUMÉS

Résumés serve two basic functions: to inform and to remind. When you're not present, résumés tell a producer, director or casting director about your experience. When you come in for an interview, it acts as a reminder of who you are and what you've done.

Your résumé should be clearly laid out, concisely stated, and as full of good information as possible. An acting résumé should not be longer than one page under any circumstances. When your page is full, the rule of thumb is to drop the old, and make room for the new. However, if something is particularly prestigious, keep it, even if it's old. Consult with your agent and/or manager on this. Think of your résumé as a constant work in progress, which will make it a true reflection of your career. It will be changing as you gather experience, and so each time you meet – or re-meet – with casting people, you'll have new information to share.

There are certain things your résumé must have – in addition to your credits – and they are as follows:

- your name, address, telephone number, answering service, pager number, e-mail address (only if you check your e-mail!)
- your agent's name, address and numbers.
- your union affiliations, if there are any as yet.
- your height, weight, eye color.
- your age range (see notes below)
- your special skills, which may include things you might not think of: languages, accents, athletic abilities.

The most important thing your résumé includes is: how to reach you. In this business, it's essential that there be a way for someone to contact you at all times. If you move around a lot during the day, get a pager, or a cell phone, or a combination of the two. If you tend to move from apartment to apartment, get a mail box so your mail doesn't have to chase you around town.

Many people disagree with us, but we recommend not including your age. Our feeling (and our experience!) is that you'll be cast according to how you look, and your looks may or may not exactly match other people's preconceived ideas of what "20" or "30" or "40" looks like. If, however, you have a very clear idea that you look a certain age, use that on the résumé, or put an age range such as 25-30 — not too wide a range which simply looks boastful.

> *Someone came in to read for the part of a seventeen-year-old. I asked her how old she was and she said, "seventeen." "Oh come on," I said. "How old are you really?" "Eighteen," she said. Uh-huh. Then a few minutes later, I asked her again. This time she admitted to being twenty-two. By the end of that interview, she finally came clean — she was twenty-nine. "You know what?" I said. "You could have gotten away with seventeen." I think the actor needs to stick with his or her story. I don't really care how old someone is. What I care about is: are they right for the role? If they are, I'll fight for them when I talk to the director. But I need to know the actor and I are going to tell the same story. If you're going to be honest with someone, be honest with me.*
> *— Amy Lieberman, Casting Director*

Something we feel strongly about: don't lie on your résumé. There's no doubt about it — if you lie, you will be caught. Do you think there's a theatre no one's ever heard of, and that you can list yourself as having done the lead when you didn't? Don't believe it. The Director you audition for today may have been doing props backstage in that theatre, and know perfectly well who did the lead. There is nothing wrong with not having experience. Just go out and get some. Always, always be honest about your work.

THE BEGINNING RÉSUMÉ

When you're starting out and don't have professional credits, you can still have a professional résumé. Make a list of all the roles you have played in high school, workshops, and community theatres. List the ones that were most significant under a heading such as "representative roles." This is the right way to "fatten" your résumé honestly until you have more experience. List your teachers, your classes, and all your legitimate acting activities.

Another word about pictures and résumés: after your first few jobs and after you've established yourself with an agent, you may feel you no longer need to carry your own picture and résumé. You may feel this is your agent's job. However, we disagree. We advise you to leave your attitude at home and carry your own materials instead. If you bring your own picture and résumé, this indicates a level of commitment and preparedness, which is not lost on most casting directors. As we will say many times, take responsibility for your own career.

ACADEMY PLAYERS DIRECTORY

This won't apply to you if you are not yet a member of any of the performing unions, so you may either skip this section or read it for future reference.

The Motion Picture Academy, which has a long and colorful history, began publishing its Players Directory in 1965 and it's been virtually indispensable from day one. When you go into any producer's, director's or casting director's office, what do you see within arm's length of the phone? The Academy Players Directory.

This directory is the bible of casting, so, of course, you need to be listed in it as soon as possible. The cost is $75 annually and it's worth every penny.

The directory has categories. Women may choose from among: Leading Woman, Ingenue, Character/ Comedienne, Child Female and Stunt Woman. Men may choose from among Leading Man, Younger Leading Man, Character/ Comedian, Child Male and Stunt Man. (For all categories except children, you must be eighteen years of age or older to be listed.) You may list yourself in more than one category for a small additional fee.

The directory now has a tremendous added bonus for NO additional fee: the entire directory is now on line. So, for your $75, one cropped head shot and your full one-page resume is instantly available to all producer, director, casting director and agent subscribers. And as a further added bonus, a link to your own web page can be added at the end of your resume.

At your first opportunity, we urge you to enroll in this vital professional listing. And at the beginning of every calendar year, write yourself a memo to renew your listing, as only payments for one year are accepted.

One more goodie. If you have Internet access, you can update your resume online ANY time. Instructions are included on the Players Directory web site and there's no need to wait for someone else to do the update for you.

Unless you're a subscriber, you won't have full access, but you can peruse the site and we encourage you to do so. Add this to your list of key web sites: www.acadpd.org.

VIDEO REELS

The bad news is, video reels used to be optional for actors. That has all changed. They are now compulsory.

The good news is, you can put together a video reel more easily than you might think.

We realize that, if you're just getting started, it may indeed be that you literally have nothing on tape and if this is your situation, our advice is to start building a library of tape as quickly as possible. Get yourself taped doing a scene in a workshop; have someone tape a theatrical production you're doing; tape whatever you can. Carefully save and label these tapes, as these will be your permanent archives. A video editor will one day be grateful that you know what you have.

If you're looking for professional cinematographers to help with this process, start networking with people. Many professional crew people between jobs like to keep a hand in by working on personal reels during their time off.

And if you want a more structured — and more immediate — way of jump starting your reel, there are companies offering various kinds of services. Some studios will videotape you on a built-in set while you perform a scene. Or try contacting a local university or college which has a film department. You might find eager students looking for a chance to try their hand at shooting, directing, and/or editing.

You may be far enough along that you do have a few things on tape, but still feel none of it usable. This isn't necessarily the case. We encourage you to think creatively here. If you have what you think are dreadful old tapes of this and that, sit down and view them with the eyes of an editor. See if you can find thirty seconds here, or fifteen seconds there, which show a color, a mood, a moment. Then imagine quick cuts from one to the next. Have a studio videotape your head shot as an opener for your tape and close it with another head shot and with contact information. You may find you have a three-minute tape after all, and that three minutes — if it's well-structured and not boring! — might serve you very well indeed.

As your career continues, make it a point regularly to acquire professional quality tape of your performances. First, try to get it in your contract that you want a professional-quality (3/4" or 1", not 1/2" VHS) copy of the show in which you appear. From this one professional master, you can make your VHS copies to give to others.

If you work on television and you find muscling a tape out of the production office virtually impossible, there's an alternative. In major cities there are video services that will pull your performances off the air for a fee. Tell them what kind of tape you want used (again, always choose professional quality, not VHS) and give them the date and time of the show. They have banks of machines they use for clients. They'll give you a professional tape, labeled, and ready to be used the next time you edit your reel. If you live in a smaller city, suggest this service to a local video production house. Hire them to do it for you and get them started.

WEB SITES

We see a future just around the corner when producers who want to see your previous work will be directed to your web site and download from a selection of scenes you've uploaded.

We wrote that paragraph about ten minutes ago, and guess what? The future is here. Strictly speaking, it may not yet be an absolute requirement to have your own web site. But the Internet is changing so quickly that the rules may have changed by the time you finish reading this sentence. Sooner – not later – many aspects of our business will shift to web-based technology, so start heading in that direction now, even if only preliminarily.

We each have web sites now (eringray.com and marapurl.com) and are finding them to be invaluable on many levels. We can't tell you the number of times a prospective client interested in booking us for personal appearances requests that we send (via overnight courier, at our own expense) our résumés and head shots. Instead, we suggest they go to our web sites now – no need to wait till tomorrow – and download whatever they need.

If you can afford to register your own domain name, do so, even if you're not yet ready to create your site. If you have the resources to design and support your own site, the advantage is obvious: for full info on you including resumes, photos, or current performance dates, producers and casting directors can find updated information in just a click or two, even if you're not yet listed in the Players Directory.

> My agent called recently, saying a producer in another part of the country needed my resume and latest head shots and that I'd have to send them overnight. I was able to say – just have him download

whatever he's interested in from my web site, www.eringray.com. He'll have it sooner than tomorrow. He'll have it today.
— Erin

A book organization on the East coast had asked about my availability to be a featured speaker, but I wasn't able to call them back immediately because I was flying all day and didn't get their message. In the meanwhile they checked the Internet, found my site, www.marapurl.com, found my events calendar and tentatively booked my talk. Without my web site, they might have booked someone else.
— Mara

If you don't have your own domain, almost every ISP (Internet Service Provider) offers a Home Page as a part of their basic service. Take advantage of this and upload your own basics: head shot, resume, contact information. Even the "bragging rights" are a big advantage in this business. (As you stand by the pool at your next Hollywood Party and the producer says, "Is your number listed?" you answer, "You don't have to remember a phone number. Just remember my name — and check my web site.")

There are also some intriguing new sites you can link to and/or explore. We've listed some of them at the end of the book. But here's an example. At www.reelmind.com, actors (and composers and film makers) can join for free. Once you're a member, you're given your own page — another place either to upload your info, or create a link to your Home Page. The advantage of this site is that it supports a large enough bandwidth, that you actually upload your reel to the site, making it available for one and all to see.

One of the key attributes of the Internet is the instant accessibility. Another key attribute is linking. Some people are afraid of "linking out" because they feel users will lose track of their site. Actually, that's not an issue, as every browser has a "back" button and most will give you a list of sites recently visited.

If you think of your site not only as a place to showcase yourself and your work, but also as a resource for helping people find fascinating or useful connections, your site will be visited again and again and that kind of "traffic" can be a marketable commodity.

> When I do book signings around the country, people ask me all kinds of questions — where else they can find my books, where I find my ideas, how I got involved with some of the issues I write about. I direct them to my site at www.marapurl.com. From there they can click to the publishing company, or to the site for my fictitious town Milford-Haven. They can also click over to our domestic violence web site, or to some of the sites I use for research. Our world is so full of information, that it can be overwhelming. What helps, is providing people with a useful path through the maze of factoids.
>
> — Mara

In designing either your home page or your site, we do caution you not to over do the special effects. First, too many graphics and bells and whistles can make your page so slow to load (for those still using modems, as most people are) that no one will want to bother with your site. Second, even for those with DSL lines and lots of RAM, if your message is obscured by an overblown graphics and text, it may annoy your would-be employers. Be imaginative, but keep it simple and tasteful.

We also recommend keeping the site in keeping with your own persona. If you have a great sense of humor, by all means add something humorous to your site. If you're elegant and deep, let your site reflect those qualities. If you're active and athletic, let viewers see that too. If you don't "match" your site, this can be as much of a problem as showing up with a photo which looks like someone else. If your site is funny, those who meet you will expect you to be humorous. If you can't think of one funny thing to say, you will have set yourself up to disappoint the person you're meeting.

To see what we mean, take a look at some other artists' sites. Amanda McBroom (singer, songwriter, playwright, actress) is a stitch in person, and her site (www.amcbroom.com) reflects her unique sense of wit. Also take a look at Linda Purl's site – www.lindapurl.net. She's a thoughtful, elegant person and her site reflects these qualities. The composer Mark Wolfram showcases his orchestral recording sessions in Europe, but since he also happens to be a Lakers fanatic, fans can find a fantastic basketball resource at his site www.markwolfram.com. Actress Alyssa Milano features interesting location shots. The Doobie Brothers are a group of musicians with eclectic interests, many of which are linked to their fantastic site at www.doobiebros.com and the web design is a superb visual reflection of the band. Surf the net and find your favorite actors – and anyone else who catches your fancy. You'll find all kinds of interesting information.

If you know nothing at all about computers, we recommend you start learning. There are some terrific books around – such as the "For Dummies" series – to help get you started. After all, you don't want someone else to be in charge of how you communicate with the world.

RECORD-KEEPING

As we've said, part of our personal philosophy is that you, as a performer, should take a great deal of responsibility for your career. One of the ways to exercise this is to do detailed record-keeping. We'll mention this as another theme throughout our book. And we go into more detail on this subject in the chapter "Your Data Base."

The first list we suggest you create and update regularly is a running log of all the meetings you have. This should include, for example, all casting meetings.

Second, keep a list of all the details of each of your jobs. This means your salary, your scripts, your production crew lists and who the casting people were. There are many uses for this list – we'll share some in a moment.

Third, keep track of everyone you meet in the business. Whether you're a high-tech Palm Pilot carrier, or an old-fashioned collector of business cards, find a way to keep track of the people you meet, how they're connected to you and how to find that name again. Take notes on the meeting ("met at grocery store, has the same kind of dog, produces sit-coms") and cross-connect them in your data base in some meaningful way so you can find them again.

We have some people listed in six categories: Producers, friends, Christmas cards, charities, events and board members. Now when we do events, be they screenings or book signings, we invite everyone from the relevant list. We can find these names by zip code, or by category. Believe us when we say, some day you're going to want these lists. And people do appreciate being remembered and included.

We now also keep an e-mail list. We co-hosted an hour on KIIS-FM recently and because we sent a quick e-announcement that morning, many of our contacts tuned in. Think how useful this can be when you're performing in a showcase or appearing in an episode!

INFORMATION FOR YOUR AGENT OR MANAGER

Take the information you've already recorded for yourself, and keep a running list for your agent.

When (not if) you change agents, this list is one of the first things the new agent will ask for. Did you have a good experience with a certain producer? Or did you have a run-in? If this information is available up front, your agent won't have egg on his or her face when making a call on your behalf. Instead, your agent will be the one with the upper hand, which will work in your favor. Perhaps he can mention how much you enjoyed working with that producer. Or, if you had a negative experience, this can alert your agent to be careful in negotiations on your behalf. As a part of this list, your agent will want to know your quotes — i.e. what you earned on each episode or movie.

We also advocate creating a list which includes your own vital statistics, and this should be updated regularly by you — not by someone else. It should include your measurements and sizes. Be truthful about them, and be more thorough than you might think you need to be. Include hat size, glove size, shoe size and so forth. You never know when you'll be doing a historical drama or something that requires unusual items of clothing. Who will use this list? Every costumer/head of wardrobe with whom you ever work. For more on this we refer you to the Wardrobe chapter.

AUDITIONING

Covered in This Chapter:

- Casting Directors' Responsibilities

- General Preparation

- General Auditions

- Philosophy

- Rules of Auditioning

A wise man adapts himself to circumstances, as water shapes itself to the vessel that contains it.
— Chinese proverb

Getting an acting job from an audition has as much to do with being the right person in the right place at the right time, as it does with talent.
— Trish Deitch Rohrer
Premiere Magazine, February 1990

Don't waste your time agonizing over parts you clearly aren't right for.
— Malcolm Taylor
Director, "East Enders," "Coronation Street"

My producers and directors do not want to participate in an actor's preparation for the audition, nor do I. They only care that you are "in your zone" when the audition time comes. Do your homework, leave it at the door, and trust your instincts.
— Ricki Maslar
Casting Director

AUDITIONING

Auditioning is like taking off in an airplane. A plane isn't built to trundle down a piece of asphalt on wheels. It's built to fly. But unless it can make it down the runway, it can never get up into the air. Actors aren't built to audition, they're built to act. But unless you can zoom down the audition runway with the right energy and attitude, you'll never get the chance to fly as an actor.
— Mara

At first we were not even going to include anything about auditioning in this book, because there are volumes written on this subject alone. However, the more we reviewed our own and others' experiences, the clearer it became that the actual work of being an actor begins with the audition. This is the first time you are going to present yourself in your capacity as a professional actor.

What we're going to give you in this chapter is as much cross-referenced advice from various Directors and Casting Directors as we feel will truly be helpful to you. However, we also have insights — and strong feelings — we want to share with you from the performer's point of view.

We find the auditioning process is quite different from the acting process. And unfortunately, being good at one doesn't necessarily mean being good at the other. Both of us know numerous actors whom we consider absolutely brilliant and extremely versatile and yet who cannot conduct themselves successfully in an audition. Some of these gifted people have been seen on stage by diligent casting directors who've had the wisdom to hire them. But many gifted people sink themselves sooner or later, by not being able to "wow them" in the casting room.

Auditioning is one skill. Acting is another. First GET THE PART. Then you can redefine it.
— Joy Todd

Some casting directors have been performers, studied acting, and/or developed a great awareness of the acting process, and when they give advice, it is from this learned and compassionate point of view. Many other casting directors, however, have come into their profession through a different avenue. They do not know the process an actor goes through to audition, nor do they understand that it's quite a different process from that which one goes through in actually preparing for a role.

The building of a character, as you know already from your own studies, is a delicate, complex procedure, involving the layering of experience, research, and imagination. For all this, you need the time and commitment you can only give when you've got the part. The abbreviated version of this – what you do for auditioning – is different for myriad reasons.

Some casting directors may seem fairly heartless about this and will basically say, "If you don't know how to audition – learn." They feel it's a skill like any other of the skills expected of an actor. Of course they're right. It is expected and you'll have to master it to the best of your ability.

Try to think of this process from their point of view, and be aware of how many responsibilities they have....

CASTING DIRECTORS' RESPONSIBILITIES

- Read script; break it down character by character
- Make preliminary casting suggestions, checking them with Director
- Send character descriptions to breakdown services
- Go through photos and phone calls from agents' submissions
- Choose audition scenes from the script, checking them with Director
- Schedule actors, one every 10 minutes
- Make notes on each actor
- Schedule actors' call-backs
- Notify actors of call-backs

- Prepare printed schedule for Director; arrange pictures and résumés in order to present to Director during call-backs
- Schedule second call-backs for Producers and/or writers
- Schedule actors for Studio Executives
- Schedule actors for Network Executives
- Negotiate actors' contracts and fees
- As needed, hire "under fives" for TV and daily hire "extras" for TV or film

GENERAL PREPARATION

As an actor you should have your own special bag of tricks from which to draw just the right treasure at just the right time. Particularly when you are starting out, you may be asked to do prepared audition pieces. You should have several ready at all times. And they should be varied, showing off your own versatility and range.

One piece should be comedic. Another should be from modern drama. And one piece should certainly be from the classics, even if you're not planning to march down the street and audition for "As You Like It." Which brings us to a word about Shakespeare and the Shoot-Em-Up, Bang-Bang Action Film. Never the twain shall meet? Then why is it that the star of "Mad Max" and "Lethal Weapon" tackled "Hamlet" and one of the directors of "Star Trek" is a Shakespearean scholar? From the perspective of several centuries, this playwright has, for some, become cloaked in an aura of "classicism" wherein his words seem archaic, his themes larger than reality and his plays irrelevant. You should take note, however, that not only does Shakespeare continue to be performed around the country and around the globe, but his plays are always being redone for the silver screen with great success.

What we want to emphasize is that you should become a well-rounded performer, developing a familiarity with different styles. This will give a flexibility and range you can't otherwise achieve. No doubt your acting classes will have prepared you for this. (If not, this is such a vast topic unto itself, that we recommend some good classes, and a lengthy perusal of the drama book shelves at the very least.)

GENERAL AUDITIONS

Many times your first contact with a casting director will be on what's known as a "General." This is where a casting director gets to meet new talent, or talent that is new to him or her. And although there may be no specific role that's right for you at this moment, you have an opportunity to show something of who you are and what you're able to do.

A word about casting directors: their stock-in-trade is new talent and every casting director spends a tremendous amount of time searching out and becoming aware of new talent. (Some casting directors actually cultivate talent by conducting workshops.) Casting directors go about finding this new talent in several ways. They go to plays, showcases, comedy clubs and anywhere else they can, to see what new talent is bubbling and percolating around town. Another way they accomplish this very important aspect of their work is to schedule general auditions on a regular basis. Many casting directors make it a point to see three people per day on general auditions and they do this week in, week out, all year long. This is an extraordinary commitment they've made to finding you – and it behooves you to be just as diligent and committed in meeting every casting director you can.

General auditions are as varied as the casting directors who take them and we've heard varying kinds of advice on how an actor should conduct himself or herself. Then too, like every other human being, casting directors have good days when their schedules are relatively open and all is right with the world and bad days when they can just barely tolerate their jobs and want to get to the business at hand.

"Sometimes I want to talk about the person's credits and background," said one casting director. "But sometimes the most helpful ones are where we may talk about everything from babies to astrology!" So here's one piece of advice we'll probably repeat ad infinitum throughout this book: be prepared to be flexible!

PHILOSOPHY

First we want to share with you a bit of philosophy about the audition process. It is very demanding... and can be maddening. In few other lines of work is a person expected to get educated, show up prepared and dressed appropriately, be professional and proficient, then return home not only without a paycheck, but with little or no acknowledgment that he or she was ever there!

And so, a philosophy becomes a prerequisite. We find most everyone we talked to — on whichever side of the casting desk they find themselves — agreed that there must be a sense of pride and joy in the process itself, that the actor must come to terms with the job at hand, thinking of that job as the audition and of the audition as an important part of their job.

> I always tell people that as an actor, going on the audition is the job. That's the gig. You've done your job that day. And the monetary reward may not come that week. But a year from now, two...you never can tell in this business how it's all going to come together. As long as when you do go out, you have done your work for that day. It has nothing to do with rejection. That's the gig. Going on auditions is what actors do. The other rewards will come in time. I always refer to a story I heard about Betty Thomas, when she got the job on "Hill Street Blues." She didn't have an agent at the time. A casting director had seen her a year and a half earlier and remembered her as being a good actress. She had the physical look that they wanted and remembered her. He found out where she was, brought her in, and hired her. So when did she really get the job? A year and a half before she finally came in, because she did her job when she first auditioned.
> — Mel Johnson

> *Alan Thicke auditioned for "Moonlighting." We had to read David and Maddie in front of executives and he wasn't right for that project. Three months later, I was casting "Growing Pains" and I remembered that Alan was really good even though he didn't get the part. I stuck my neck out and suggested him to the network executives, who said, "The talk show host?" I had to talk them into seeing Alan, but he got "Growing Pains," which was a successful series for seven years. He still mentions my name every time someone asks how he got the part.*
> — Robin Nassif

Another important aspect of being in this business is to follow your instinct. We feel very strongly that you must allow instinct to have as much importance as logic. And this can have specific application to the audition process in many ways. If you have an instinct to do something, call someone, take a certain action, our general advice is — do it.

> *"Coulda woulda shoulda oughta" — that's what I call it. Follow your hunch. When I'm doing my seminars, one of the things I lean on so heavily is positive thinking. Henry Ford said, "Think you can? Think you can't? Either way, you're right." For example, if you're wondering and agonizing about whether or not to call a casting director and feel that you should, then make the call. The worst thing they can say is: I can't see you.*
> — Joy Todd

This leads to a related point about this business: and that is the critically important factor of "timing." All the adages we've heard so often — "being in the right place at the right time," "it's who you know," and so forth — certainly apply. These can perhaps be understood as a kind of energy flowing between and amongst those who are participating in this larger picture — a kind of collective consciousness. If this is true, then following your instinct is perhaps one of the most important ways to participate — to tap into the whole. Some people call this "synchronicity." If you have an intuition, a "gut feeling" to do something — follow your instinct.

Let's say you go to a casting director's office on a strong hunch. We think you'll experience some of this synergy. Maybe he or she unexpectedly comes out of the office at that moment, sees you, and you're right for the part. Is this chance? Many people think it is rather an element of this "synchronicity" of life which may be more evident in the arts than in any other field.

There are no coincidences. Follow your hunch.
— Joy Todd

In some ways you'll have to work harder at an audition than you may ever have to work on the job. You're lacking virtually every element of support when you audition, and yet you must bring a full sense of vision and reality to the part — and therefore to the piece.

And speaking of reality — there's a particular lack of it in the casting situation. When you're working on stage or in a film, you create a reality. Everyone there is helping you to do so: props, sets, wardrobe, fellow actors, director, etc. All those elements are missing in the casting room, so the thin hold you have on that special reality you're trying to create must be created by you alone.

Auditioning is by far the most difficult aspect of your craft to do well. When you audition, you're expected to perform with nothing. You will seldom, if ever, have an actor to work with. Most often you'll be reading with the casting director, who must somehow manage to read the appropriate words and simultaneously focus on your performance. You may get very little energy or meaning from their reading. Or it may go the other way and you'll get far more energy thrown at you than you're comfortable with. Furthermore, the casting director may "play" four parts to your one, so you'll have to pretend you're working with a room full of people. You will have no props, no atmosphere and seldom a sense of space in which to move. Sometimes you'll be stuck in a chair when you know you should be pacing. Sometimes you'll be standing when you should be lying down.

As if it isn't bad enough that you'll have to work in a "vacuum" — it can sometimes be worse. You'll actually have elements working against you. On a professional set there's a rule of silence out of respect to actors who are trying to remember lines and stay in the mood. No such luck in a casting session! You could encounter everything from someone telling jokes just outside the door, to construction noises, to competing actors doing their own rehearsal.

The stories of nightmare auditions are legion in this business. Some are tremendously funny, some are tragic and all of them are informative. We'll share some of these subsequently.

Some casting directors may seem to be ogres. However, most of them are wonderful people whose reputations and jobs are riding on the discernment they exhibit in choosing just the right cast out of many hundreds of applicants. They may not have the emotional or physical strength to always be nice or aware of everyone's delicate feelings while they're doing their very stressful jobs.

> *They're not emotionally empty, but they're emotionally drained. When you've got dozens of people, one right after another, presenting themselves, with their energy and their nerves, with their need for approval, desire to get the job and where you try to give back something to them to try to help them be their best and be open to their performance, you run out of emotional energy.*
> — Barnet Kellman

Remember that casting people are professionals, and that their jobs depend upon your existence. Without talented people who are committed to the acting profession, there would be no casting directors. As such, they are taking notes, remembering names and faces, and noticing a great deal about you.

We'd like to pass along an interesting suggestion that a Director mentioned to us, which might give you a very concentrated exposure to the auditioning process:

> Auditioning is probably the world's most unsatisfying process for everyone. I recommend that actors volunteer to be the reader for a casting director and spend a day of your life on the other side. What you'll learn will change your life. You'll see all the mistakes, awkwardness, that get in actors' way, but also you'll see who you're auditioning for.
>
> — Barnet Kellman

RULES

> There are rules — but there are no rules.
>
> — Joy Todd

As Ms. Todd's very pertinent comment suggests, this is a business of paradoxes. It's a business of inspiration, improvisation, seizing the moment and following your gut instinct. There are, however, some guidelines. Here are some general and some specific comments from the casting directors, directors and actors we canvassed. Some of the comments we heard more than once. All the information we found to be valuable and we have categorized it as good general rules.

1. What Questions Should You or Your Agent Ask Before the Audition?

Not only should you ask every question you can think of about the part, you should also ask who's going to be at the audition. Entering the room forewarned and forearmed gives you a sense of confidence you couldn't otherwise have. If you already know that "Tom" is the director and "Sue" is the producer, you won't have to be busy memorizing names when you're already nervous about remembering lines.

2. Understand the Type of Role

Take a careful look at whether you're auditioning for comedy, tragedy, sitcom, episodic, feature, industrial… they each have their requirements. Know as much as possible about what you're auditioning for – not only the role itself, but the type of role. If, for example, you're going in to see the network people who cast comedy, be aware that they basically expect you to have all the skills of a stand-up comedian. They expect you to break the ice, take center stage, put everyone at ease with your honed improvisational skills, and then on top of that, do a respectable audition.

If, however, you're auditioning for a dramatic piece, a stand-up approach may work against you. Again, the important thing to do is assess the situation you're stepping into. The energy, focus, style, approach, and general attitude with which you enter the room are going to be projecting information long before you open your mouth.

3. Comedy

Auditioning for comedy is, to some extent, a realm of its own, requiring particular skills.

> When people come into that tense room full of network people, producers and casting directors, if they have an improv background, they do much better because they know how to break the ice. Don't forget the producers and everybody else are nervous too! They want this person to be the last person they have to see. Stand-up comedians often come in and are neurotic and a riot. So funny! They put everybody at ease right away. They know how to break the tension.
> — Robin Nassif

Not everyone agrees with this, so again, you'll have to know your material, and assess your situation.

> Stand-up comics have honed that "attitude" thing, which is what executives are looking for at this point. A stand-up comes in with an outlook and world view, which they've spent years refining. It's a very

specific thing. It's really not related to acting, which is about allowing many characters to show through you. To me it's always worked against people because I have trouble imagining them as anything else. Stand-ups don't automatically translate into actors.
— Barnet Kellman

Actors with a good solid background in drama have a great deal going for them. However, in comedy you must cultivate a light touch. What this amounts to is allowing the audience to have room to laugh. There can still be a serious moment that happens in the scene. And yet, as is so often the case in life, we see the humor in it and suddenly the whole moment is lifted off the ground. This is something almost ineffable, and therefore, virtually impossible to explain or describe. But in another way, it's completely tangible. Finding it, knowing it, experiencing it and presenting it, will open the door to comedy.

In auditioning for comedy, although you won't be giving your ultimate comedic performance, one thing you'll have to do is find the jokes, find the punch lines and get these under your belt. It won't work if you're looking down at the script and stumbling through the punch line. Even if you've memorized nothing else in the script, have these down. If you don't know what the punch line is, find yourself a class or a coach who can help you with comedy.

In an audition situation you may or may not get a reaction laugh — but whether you do or not, you should know to take the proper pauses. This, too, is a critical part of handling comedy.

4. Grooming

One rule should be obvious, but we'll say it anyway — pay attention to your grooming. If you're presenting yourself to other people, be clean and be groomed to whatever standard you expect of yourself. If you're groomed from head to shoulder, but your dirty feet are hanging out of rundown sandals, you may leave an impression you didn't intend. You make a statement with your whole self, so be mindful of the entire package.

5. Pick Up Your Material

Generally when you're going to audition, the script or sides you'll be working from are available anywhere from a few hours to a few days before your meeting. Even if it's inconvenient, find a way to get those materials in hand. It's expected of you, and your confidence and performance will be dramatically impacted by your level of preparation. Some casting directors feel so strongly about this that they say there is "no excuse" for not getting the materials before the meeting. Don't have a strike against you before you even get in the door.

6. Sides or Script

Sometimes you'll be given a full script from which to prepare. Sometimes you'll only be given "sides" – the particular scene or scenes you'll be reading. For the audition, bring whichever you feel comfortable with. The important thing is to make the lines <u>yours</u> – mark the script, do your "left page" (if you don't know what that means, read Robert Lewis's "Advice To The Players"), do whatever you need to do to "own" the part.

7. Memorization and Accuracy

And now for the eternal question: do I memorize my lines for audition or not? Generally the answer is yes. If you have so much as an hour to prepare, get the lines down as well as you can. If you can't get the whole scene down, choose the beginning, ending and key moments, particularly in comedy. Choose the moments that require the best timing, and have those clearly in mind.

Then do yourself a favor. Practice a technique we've heard referred to as "thumbing the page." Place your thumb on the page and as you deliver your lines, slide it down the page so that if you absolutely must look down for a moment, you don't have to search for the right line.

> When we do a network reading we want people to hold their scripts, rather than suffer through forgetting their lines. We don't have time for them to grope. We're looking for the basis of what they're going to

be doing. We are not looking for a memorized performance.
— Robin Nassif

As Ms. Nassif's comment indicates, there's some room for flexibility. However, no matter how you bend the rule, remember always to respect the text. Whether or not you memorize the lines, it is best not to intentionally change the text. Rewrites are not your job when you're auditioning, and some people feel very strongly about this.

I have a pet peeve. Coming from a theatre background, I want to hear the actor say the words written. I do not want them to "improve" it. When I would cast plays in New York, I could tell people from California who had spent time on episodic sets or in acting classes where you "make it your own" or "adapt it for yourself." Comics often cannot do the line as written by somebody else, but must make it come out of their own persona, but that doesn't make it easy for those who like a well-wrought text.
— Barnet Kellman

8. Dressing for the Part

There are two schools of thought about this. There's something to be said for paying no attention to what you wear, because any casting director worth their salt will see through wardrobe to the performance anyway.

Dressing for the part is not necessary. But if it works for YOU, do it. Do what makes YOU comfortable. It's your five minutes. It's your career. I did specify "no make-up" for a recent casting call, because that's what we needed for this part. Most people adhered to this request, but Betty Buckley, for example, came in full make-up, dressed to the nines, because that's what works for her.
— Jeannie Wilson

On the other hand, elements of clothing are sometimes the very thing you need to help you get "into" the part. Generally the more extreme the character, the truer this tends to be. We both have stories to share on this topic....

> I was asked to read for the part of a prostitute for a Stephen Cannell TV series. This is so far away from my own look that I had to spend a few hours preparing — teased hair, big nails, short, tight black skirt, major shoes, etc. I had to drive myself to the audition, and on the way, two guys in their black leathers on a bike did their utmost to pick me up. The more I shook my head in protest the more fascinated they were. I finally outdistanced them, but then had to park the car. Of course, Cannell's building is on Hollywood Boulevard, and I had to walk down that street. Let's just say I got the part about 12 times before I ever made it to the elevator. I arrived upstairs, completely frazzled, and went in to meet the director. He looked up at me over his glasses, considered me for a moment, then said, "No, no, too classy." I wanted to say — could you just come downstairs with me for a minute? Even though I didn't get the part, I was asked back two weeks later for a role which was perfect for me. They had noticed a great deal more than I realized they had that day.
>
> — Mara

> I was known as the all-American girl, and the casting director refused to see me for the part of a high-fashion model who hung out with rock stars and did too many drugs. I had my agent beg and finally was told that if I got there at exactly noon, she would see me. Well, at 11:00 I had, wouldn't you know, an additional audition for an "all-American girl." The night before, I worked with a stylist who put together exactly the elements I'd need for my "hard" look and I had all these in a paper sack. In the taxi rushing to my noon appointment, I was putting on gold lamé and big earrings, baring my midriff and pulling on tight pants. The taxi driver's face was nothing compared to all the truck drivers who got a glimpse of me running the last few blocks after the cab got stuck in traffic. I marched into the office and was told I was five minutes late and would not be seen. I took matters into my own hands and asked the secretary if the director had arrived yet. No, she said. So I sat

there in the foyer, knowing that the director would have to walk right past me. I sat with my sunglasses on, legs akimbo, with about as much attitude as I could muster and paid no attention to the gentleman who strode through in his safari jacket. Seconds later the secretary's phone rang. "They'd like to see you," she said. I didn't get the part. But I got a screen test. And the director — Irvin Kershner — and I met years later backstage at an awards ceremony and shared a good laugh.

— Erin

One further comment about dressing — don't wear clothes or accessories which get in your way. They can interfere with your work and distract not only yourself but the casting director as well.

There was the actress who came in with bangle bracelets — all she could do was push them up and down her arm. Then there was the actress whose hair was in the way — she was constantly flinging it, tossing it, getting it out of her way. These things totally distracted these actresses from working.

— Joy Todd

9. Props

For the most part, props are not a part of auditioning. You have so much else to deal with. This is not the time to add to your responsibilities. And remember, whatever prop you might think of using, you will already have one hand occupied with your script. On the rare occasions where you may choose to use something, we feel it's important to keep it simple — a tissue, a pair of glasses, something you're completely familiar with and are comfortable using.

Keep it simple. If you get the part, they'll give you the props. Pantomime. Don't bring a phone into my office — believe it or not there are those who have. Don't bring your cup and saucer. It tells me you don't know how to do it. I don't need the props. You're telling me that you need the props.

— Joy Todd

Having said all this, there are exceptions, when including props might be the perfect thing. We repeat, however, that this is rare, and most probably — as in the following story — is more appropriate for theatre than for television or film.

> I get an anxiety attack when I see someone start with the props in an audition. I feel I'm seeing their homework and I'm anticipating that all the focus is going to be on the object. Therefore, it's going to be the story about the lighter or the cigarette. The scene is not going to be what it's really about. Yet, there is no hard and fast rule regarding props. For example, when I was casting a play called "Breakfast with Les and Bess" actress Holland Taylor walked in and rearranged all the furniture in the rehearsal space, unloaded her bag, cluttered the desk with objects, arranged the whole thing. By this time my mind has checked out. There's no way I'm going to cast this person. I look at the résumé and sure enough, I see she's a Stella Adler student so I'm now convinced I'm going to see classroom work. She then made it work (much to my relief.) If you make it work, great. Usually it will get in an actor's way.
>
> — Barnet Kellman

10. Be On Time!

The casting director's day is scheduled in tight, brief increments of time which must be adhered to. If you absolutely cannot avoid being late, have the courtesy to call, or have your agent call. If they're expecting you any moment, they're not free to eat a sandwich, take a phone call, or see someone else. If they've sat and wasted half an hour, believe us, they'll remember you and not the way you wish. If on the other hand, they realize you're delayed, this allows the casting director to fit in someone or something else.

> Being late is a giant No No. My advice is to be there a half hour early, rather than being there five minutes late. Many times the producers have a one-hour lunch and that's it. There was a comedian we had seen in a nightclub whom we loved. We asked him to come in and read. He went to the wrong floor and, unsure what to do, he waited 15 minutes.

By then he was so late, that blew the meeting. We rescheduled him and he came in, but the room was less enthusiastic than it had been for the original meeting.

— Robin Nassif

11. Small Talk in the Foyer

The situation in the foyer as you wait for your audition can be a tricky one. On the one hand, you don't want to appear cold or rude to others who're reading, or to professionals who're there to meet with you. On the other hand, this is your moment and you must take the focus you need to prepare for your audition.

12. Small Talk in the Casting Room

Use your time with the casting director wisely. Don't take it personally if he or she is short with you. This is not the time to chat. If you want to chat, ask for a "general" meeting when the casting director isn't on the hectic pre-production schedule. Once you enter the casting room to audition for a specific part, remember that the clock is ticking, and every second counts — for you.

13. Picture and Résumé

Hand it to the casting director, so he or she can hand it to the director. Don't by-pass the casting director and attempt to hand it directly to the director.

14. Take Your Moment

Yes, you should be courteous, yes you should respect the situation, take stock of the room, know what you're coming into. But remember — this is your moment. You are there because these people want to see what you're going to add to their project. If you have nothing specific and interesting to bring, why should they hire you? Your point of view is important, and just as important is your ability to know and believe in yourself. So, collect yourself and take your moment.

A key component of this is making your own choices about the material and sticking with them. Even if your choices are different from those the director may ultimately want, if you've made choices at all, this in itself is indicative that you have something to offer. This is far better than spending your time second-guessing what you think the director, casting directors, producers, writers, and everyone else might or might not want. Chances are, they may not know themselves what they want at this early stage of the project.

> *The Director doesn't know what he wants at this point. He's looking for the next collaborator in this project. It doesn't mean a finished performance, but it does mean a point of view. You know it when you see it.*
>
> *— Barnet Kellman*

Here we should mention another bit of philosophy. We've said there's a difference between auditioning and performing — and there is. And there's never a time when you shouldn't do your best. Your sense of commitment, your willingness to give it your all, your sense of joy in what you're doing, all show in the audition. What we feel is, there are those who treat their lives as though they were rehearsing, waiting for their "real" lives to begin. Then there are those who live as though today really matters.

> *When I go in, I don't audition, I perform.*
>
> *— Yaphet Kotto*

15. What Questions Should You Ask at the Audition?

Generally, you shouldn't ask a series of detailed questions about the part. Sound strange? Not when you realize that time is of the essence. You should make every effort to find out everything you can about this part *before* you get to your casting meeting. Do not think that by asking questions you'll show off your insightful and inquisitive nature. You'll show off those qualities better by being prepared. If for some reason you're dashing in at the last minute at the request of the casting director — or your agent — then you have a legitimate excuse. But such situations are rare.

> *Come in and get to work. If you take time to ask about the script, you should already know. If I ask you, "Do you have any questions?" make them real questions, don't use it as an opportunity to make small talk. I like it when an actor says, "No, I have no questions. I'd like to try it."*
> *— Jeannie Wilson*

One of the questions you may be longing to ask may be a legitimate one, having to do with directorial guidance. Again, it's a good idea to be prepared, having made choices of your own. But it's also extremely valuable that you indicate your flexibility and willingness to take direction.

> *Many casting directors will say do you have any questions? I always say, do not ask the actor if they have any questions. It puts the actor in the position where they feel they're supposed to have a question. Now you're obliged to answer. "Well, I actually was thinking orange." Now the actor has to go against their own instinct, and do what they think you want.*
> *— Barnet Kellman*

One more pitfall we want to point out has to do with the degree to which you share the preparatory work you've done for this audition. Our advice is not to get drawn into discussing your own homework. It's for you, not for the producers or the writers. It's been extremely useful to you, because it has helped you develop your choices. But the details may, for example, run counter to something the writer or director may feel strongly about. And as we've said, time is of the essence. Do your work, don't talk it.

This situation can change quite radically if and when you're on your third callback. By then you've progressed to the point of detailed conversations with director, writers, producers, who are now beginning to see you as a potential collaborator. But wait until you're in that situation before volunteering your private thoughts. Until then, keep them a mystery.

16. Stopping and Starting Over

If you feel your audition is going in the wrong direction, don't wait till you've gotten all the way through the scene before stopping yourself. Odd as this may sound, you actually can do yourself quite a favor. Our friend Jim Lewis, who has years of experience both in front of and behind the camera puts it this way:

> If your audition isn't going right — and you know when it isn't — just stop and explain to the casting director that you have a problem. "The gypsies took me away. I don't know where they took me. But I'm back. And I'd like to start again."
>
> — Jim Lewis

If you're brave enough to use Jim's line, at the very least you'll get a good laugh. Casting directors confirm that starting over is a good idea.

> Don't wait till END of scene, then ask to do it again. We don't have the time or patience and we feel that's manipulative. The minute you see the scene going bad, that's the time to ask to start again. We can't see every scene twice. And we won't concentrate the second time. Make the most of it — it's your audition, it's your time.
>
> — Robin Nassif

Here's an important note — this is an example of where the auditioning process is <u>not</u> the same as the shooting process. We'll deal with this issue further, later in the book.

> My favorite thing is when an actress says, "If Im going in the wrong direction, would you please stop me, and let me start again." This gives you a better chance at getting the part. Sometimes, if you've gone in the wrong direction they won't have time to let you read the whole thing again. So if you give them permission to stop you — you get that chance.
>
> — Jeannie Wilson

17. Eye Contact/ Physical Contact

Generally speaking, it is the casting director's job to stand back and watch you work — not to work with you. Some casting directors are excellent performers and coaches and on rare occasions might even work with you. But you should be aware that attempting to involve them in your work without their consent can make them uncomfortable, as well as interfere with their capacity to assess your work.

> *Actors — especially when they do emotional monologues — look at me, and there they are, digging out their soul. I feel so uncomfortable because they're looking right at me.*
> — Mel Johnson

When it comes to physical contact with the casting director, it's virtually never appropriate. It is intrusive and cannot serve any useful purpose.

> *Don't touch the casting director. Don't come too close to me, because I can't see you. When it comes to eye contact and playing to the casting director — ask them. I don't mind it. But some do. Ask — who should I play to?*
> — Joy Todd

This advice goes for hand-shaking as well. Don't walk into the room and in your usual forthright manner, offer your hand to the casting director, the director, or anyone else present. If they offer their hands, of course participate in the hand-shakes. Our experience is that most professionals in a casting situation prefer not to have to shake your hand. Don't take offence. There are good reasons. One is time. One is health. The people in this room may have to meet thirty or forty people today and they don't want to exchange germs with each and every one of them.

18. Dealing with the Space

One of the principal limitations you'll have to deal with is the space itself. Generally, you'll be in a small room and will have to convey a larger, or in some way, completely different kind of room or location. While it's good to show you have sufficient imagination, you will also have to adjust to the physical reality in which you find yourself.

> As my singing teacher used to say, "Play the room." I was auditioning once where the script had me shouting at the bad guy thirty feet away in a warehouse. In reality, I was in a room six by ten. In my mind, I had transported myself to that warehouse. It was only after I had finished the scene that I realized I had flattened the producer and director against the wall of the tiny casting room by shouting at them at the top of my lungs. "She has no problem with aggression," was the comment I received. It wasn't necessarily what I was trying to convey.
> – Erin

19. Reading with a Non-Actor

One of the classic elements that makes working so different from auditioning has to do with power. In a scene, a great strength can be giving your power to your fellow actor. Why? Because in the next beat, you get it back. It becomes the tennis fall in a spirited game. It works.

In an audition, however, you rarely have a true partner. Most often, you have a casting director who is busy *observing* you, not *playing* with you. You therefore must keep more of your own power than you would in the actual scene. If you're busy acting with a figment of your imagination – that is, you're making up what you think your true acting partner would do – then your reactions are gauged against someone who isn't there. The casting directors can't see that person and therefore can't actually feel or understand what you're doing. So, don't pretend that other person is there. Stay in current reality and accept the fact that they are *not* there. This may bring your scene up "too high" or make you feel you're "over the top" because you're having to drive the scene more than you would with a partner. Our advice is, go ahead and drive the scene. In our opinion, it's better to have too much energy in an audition than to have too little. Most casting people are too busy to have much imagination on the job.

20. Handling Extraordinary (Impossible) Physical Moments

We find there are three basically impossible situations you must often make work in a casting room: love scenes, childbirth, and murder....

Love scenes invariably have a kind of nightmare category all their own, as you will often find yourself having to play a passionate scene opposite someone of the wrong gender, sitting behind their glasses, behind their desk. Meanwhile you're attempting to retain some dignity while kissing your own hand.

Another category for the tragi-comedic audition moment is childbirth. It's extraordinary how many women have been asked to enter a casting room and give birth. It's hard to know how to handle this situation and it's probably best to ask for some basic guidelines – how loud, how physical, how realistic do you want me to get here?

> *I had to audition for a childbirth scene, and I got the role because I was the only one who actually lay down on the ground and screamed.*
> – Amelia Norfleet

The same applies to committing murder with some degree of realism in an unrealistic setting. Obviously, most casting directors will have you "indicate" this in some way, but find out some parameters.

21. The Bad Day

One thing we must address is the "bad day" syndrome. Everyone has them. It's just that it doesn't seem to happen in every profession that one bad day can actually ruin your whole year quite so often as it seems to in this business. We want to say very emphatically: one bad day cannot ruin your career. And we have many professionals who agree with us.

> *We study actors. We watch you and study you. If I see an actor who's done a good job for me in the past and he comes in and has an off day, he may walk off and think, "Oh, God, he never wants to see me again." No. He had an off day. We understand that. One interview where you're not right on is not going to destroy your entire career. So don't*

go beating yourself up. The thing is to keep plugging at it. If you stay at it a long time, sooner or later I'm seeing you again…guaranteed. Because I'm going to be around. If you're going to be around, we're going to see each other again.
— Mel Johnson

The wonderful thing about these comments — continued below — is that they remind you that you're not in this business to be an overnight success. You're in it to develop a talent in which you believe. He goes on to say:

We remembered one guy who did an awful audition, but there was a likable quality that we saw. We knew he was a novice, so in six months we tried him again. And there was an improvement. We'd seen he had been in classes and things were changing. He had gotten rid of the problems he had with physical mannerisms. And we thought, hey, he's really working. We acknowledge that. We recognize it. I always give an actor the benefit of the doubt. One lady had a year on a soap and she'd gotten immensely better for that. I remembered that I liked her look then, but the ability was a little off. And now she has the ability with the look and she works out fine.
— Mel Johnson

Developing your talent as an actor is an infinite process. It never stops. We hope you'll continue to hone your work and grow throughout your career. And believe us — auditioning never stops either, even after you've arrived, after you've become a star. To greater or lesser degrees, there are always auditions in life. But most particularly when you are starting out, understand that every single audition is going to teach you a great deal. Enjoy the process as much as you can. If you can't enjoy it, at least recognize its importance and value to you.

22. After the Audition — Feedback
We know, we know, you're dying to know, How Did I DO?? Here's our best advice to you: know your own truth.

We don't say this to be flippant, or to encourage you to develop the skin of a walrus. Some casting directors find it completely annoying to be asked to give you comments. Some enjoy it immensely and if honestly asked, will honestly give feedback.

Why we advocate knowing your own "truth," as we call it, is that logically, if you did well, you'll be the first — or the second, after your agent — to know. If you didn't, you probably already know that. If you had a terrible day, you may not want to further compound your problem by calling, or having your agent call, to annoy the casting director, who will probably just try to be polite in answering the question. You must know your own truth, as you will rarely get it from others in this business.

There are many reasons for this. You have the professional casting director who is too polite — and too busy — to give you some sort of critique. Even the most experienced casting director may simply not know what went wrong. Their training is usually not in acting, remember, so they don't necessarily know what your process is. Sometimes you may run into the inexperienced casting directors who know less than you do about what an actor does to prepare and express his or her talent. Do your best preparation. Do your best work. Then go home, and get on with your life.

Different casting directors have completely different feelings about feedback.

> *I love giving feedback to agents. If an agent wants me to be honest, I'll try to be honest about what the actor did right or wrong.*
> *— Robin Nassif*

> *Never call your agent or manager about feedback. If they liked you, they will let you know. If not, they'll just lie anyway. A casting person is not in a position to critique your work. They are only making a decision about a specific part. If you get feedback and it's bad, it's devastating. It's almost guaranteed that you will not get the truth. Never put the casting person on the spot. "How did I do? Will I get a call-back?" Don't do that. They don't want to hurt your feelings. Or*

they don't have the time. You only put yourself in a no-win situation. And don't assume you're not good.

— Jeannie Wilson

23. To Audition Or Not

First of all, we should say that we recommend, almost always, that you should audition whenever given the opportunity to do so. Having said that, there are a few exceptions, or exceptional situations, most of which cannot arise until you're further along in your career.

One is, if after you've been working for a while, you are finding that you're just no good at auditioning, consider the following comments from two casting directors:

An actor shouldn't necessarily be able to do any and everything.

— Robin Nassif

If you know you're wrong for something — go in anyway. Don't read. Instead, tell them in your two or three minutes, how wrong you are for the part. Tell them how much you wanted to meet them, how much you admire them as a casting director, but that you don't want to waste their time. What they'll remember is your performance, so don't read if you're wrong for it.

— Joy Todd

After an actor has gained considerable recognition for his or her work, often agents or managers will advise a star they shouldn't have to audition. Or perhaps actors finally get to a point where they think they're above the auditioning process. Remember that some things can only happen "in person."

I think it's a mistake when people don't want to read. Even if someone is further along in their career and their work is well known, that magic and chemistry cannot take place over the phone, no matter who you

are. There's no substitute for being in the room.
— Frank Abatemarco
Producer, "Star Trek Next Generation", "Dellaventura"

Our feeling is that if you want the part, you should be willing to audition to get it. Acting is what we do, and auditioning is all part of the process.

A film called "Awakenings" was being cast by a big casting director. It starred, among others, Robert DeNiro. An actress was needed to play DeNiro's mother, and DeNiro had requested Shelley Winters. The producers insisted that Winters come in and read for the part. She did — come in, that is. She sat down across the table from the casting director, resting a satchel on her ample lap. There was a moment of silence. She reached into the satchel, pulled out her Oscar, and placed it on the desk. She waited another moment, then reached into the satchel again, pulling out another Oscar, which she placed on the desk beside the first. There was a long pause this time. "Some people think I can act," Winters said. "Do you still want me to read for this part?" "No, Miss Winters," the casting director said.
— reprinted from Premiere Magazine Feb. 1990
by Trish Deitch Rohrer

Shelley Winters is a fine — and certainly a proven — actress and we don't feel qualified to judge her behavior in any way. We will only point out, however, that she did not do the role in "Awakenings," even though Robert DeNiro had requested her for the part.

24. After the Audition — Keeping Sane

This may be the most important rule of all. We've discovered it ourselves, but have also heard it from others. When you have an audition, plan something to do afterwards. Go to a workout class. Have lunch with a friend or colleague. Tackle a project on your desk that you've been meaning to get to. Whatever the activity is, do it. Get busy, and be too busy to ruminate and regurgitate over the audition in those first few hours. The soul processes slowly when given a chance to do so. Give yourself that chance.

SCRIPTS

Covered In This Chapter:

- Reading the Script

- Script Page Examples

- Binders & Covers

- Early Drafts

- Revised Pages

- Terminology

- Shooting Schedule

- Your Bible

- Text Analysis

Suit the action to the word, the word to the action.
— *William Shakespeare*

I wish actors would read the whole script. Even big stars will arrive on the set and say, "What are the jokes?" Many are a very quick read, and a very quick studies, but this means no awareness of context.
— *Abby Singer*

SCRIPTS

The first call you'll receive is, of course, from your agent, telling you that you got the job. **Congratulations!!** In case your agent forgot to remind you of this — you have just made it through one of the most complex and challenging mazes life has to offer. And you've emerged with the greatest of all possible victories — a paying job! Regardless of the doubts parents, teachers, colleagues, siblings, co-workers might have expressed, you persevered. So take a moment to pat yourself on the back.

Now the real work begins. Once you've been cast, the first thing you'll receive is your script. Probably you'll be asked to pick it up from the studio. Under some circumstances, it might be delivered to your agent or to you. Don't wait for that script to show up automatically. Find out what you are to do about getting it.

READING THE SCRIPT

You've already spent years learning how to prepare your character, so we won't dwell on this subject here. We'll focus instead on how to break down your script from a practical point of view.

> *At one of the first "Hollywood" parties I attended, I met a well-known writer and producer with whom I was making polite conversation. Since he was older and wiser, I was bold enough to ask if he had any words of wisdom for a budding young actress. He thought for a moment and said, "Yes. Always read the script." I was rather amazed by that comment, and said well, of course, I would read the script. "No, you don't understand," he replied. "You'd be amazed at how many actors only read their scenes."*
>
> *— Erin*

In case this point still seems too obvious to you, we thought we should tell you that when we asked a major television writer/producer "What do you wish actors would understand about scripts?" His answer was:

> I wish that actors would read the entire script. So many actors skip through the pages looking for "My part... my part... bla bla bla... my part my part."

He went on to make a further point about reading:

> I also wish actors would not just read the dialogue. I try not to insult the actor by putting in "he smiles," for example. I will say "he reacts," leaving room for the actor to make his own choice. But the actor should read the descriptive material as well, because it contains everything they need to know that's not in their lines.
> — Don Bellassario

The thing to remember is that your script is much more than just the words your character will say. It also contains the key to everything you need to know: plot development, character interplay, sequence of events, and so forth.

Three of the most important technical aspects of the work you're about to do are:
- the number of scenes you're in
- the time which elapses from one scene to the next
- the number of outfits you'll wear.

As you break your script down, you may come across incomprehensible abbreviations and unfamiliar formats. Take a moment to familiarize yourself with the following standard script formats.

SCRIPT PAGE EXAMPLES

Following are one-page examples taken from three different kinds of scripts:

- a feature film script
- a sitcom script
- a soap-opera script

While you may not be able to tell a great deal from singular pages, they will at least give you an indication of the styles used for scripting these differing dramatic forms.

SCRIPT EXAMPLE: Feature Film

"Friday The 13th:
The Ninth Life Of Jason Vorhees"

Screenplay by Dean Lorey

```
Shooting Script    7/7/92
Blue Revision      7/16/92
Pink Revision      7/22/92
Yellow Revision    7/31/92
Green Revision     8/5/92
Salmon Revision    8/11/92
Tan Revision       8/21/92
Orchid Revisions   8/24/92
```

The Coroner turns and walks to the door, passing by a mirror.

ON THE MIRROR

to see the reflection. It's not the coroner walking. It's

JASON VORHEES, HOCKEY MASK IN PLACE!

17 INT. HALLWAY OUTSIDE MORGUE - NIGHT

The Coroner/Jason strides out of the doors and walks past the FBI man.

>   FBI MAN 1
> So what's the verdict — is Jason gonna be getting
> up and walking around some time soon?

The Coroner/Jason stops and slowly turns back to the two smiling FBI men - there will be doom here very soon.

Over this, we hear:

>   CAMPBELL (VO)
> Tonight, on American Casefile...

                                                        CUT TO:

18 INT. STOCKROOM - DINER - DAY

FULLFRAME ON A TV SET

WHOOSHING SFX as the words "American Casefile" are stamped in red across the screen. Behind them, a graphic of Jason's hockey mask ZOOMS UP.

>   CAMPBELL (VO)
> Jason Voorhees - dead... or deadly?

                                                        CUT TO:

OMIT 19

20 VIDEO

Photos of the two FBI men from the morgue, dead and bloody, as well as photos of the dead assistant coroner.

SCRIPT EXAMPLE: Sitcom

"Close To Home"

Episode Title:
"Sex, Lies, & The Wedding Video"

Executive Producer
Kevan Schwartz

Producer
J.P. Luckenbach

Directed by
Hank Berrings

Teleply by
Celeste Sparling

Story by
Purl Gray

Show: #0505
Tape: 7/11/99

© 1991 PurlGray Enterprises

```
ACT ONE
SCENE FIVE
INT.  THE GARAGE - DAY
(AMANDA AND ASHLEY HAVE JUST RETURNED FROM A SHORT DRIVE TO A
NEARBY PARK)
                    AMANDA
          There's nothing like a hike first thing in the
          morning.
                    ASHLEY
          On the other hand, there's nothing like a good...
                    AMANDA
          (INTERRUPTING) Don't say it.
                    ASHLEY
          Good idea.
BEAT
                    AMANDA
          Well, now that we're single, we get to enjoy the
          great outdoors, to feel the wind through our
          hair...
                    ASHLEY
          To feel the wind through our thighs.
AMANDA LOOKS AT HER
          This means our thighs aren't touching.  This is good.
                    AMANDA
          No, this is great.  (Laugh)
                    ASHLEY
          (Laugh) It's always so great hiking with you.
                    AMANDA
          I love the fact that the first half of the hike we
          always talk about me.
                    ASHLEY
          Yeah, the uphill part.  And the second half we always
          talk about me.  The downhill part.
```

SCRIPT EXAMPLE: Soap Opera

"MILFORD-HAVEN"

EPISODE #1001　　　　　　　　　　PRODUCTION #184001

TAPE DATE: FRI., JAN. 29, 1999　　　TIME: 2:15 - 4:30 PM

AIR DATE: SAT., FEB 20, 1999　　　　TIME: 11:00 PM - 12:00 AM

NETWORK:　　　CBS-TV, HOLLYWOOD
　　　　　　　STUDIO #1
　　　　　　　CBS TELEVISION CITY
　　　　　　　LOS ANGELES, VA

EXECUTIVE PRODUCERS: FRANK ABATEMARCO
　　　　　　　　　　　MARA PURL
　　　　　　　　　　　MURRAY SHOSTAK

SUPERVISING EXECUTIVE PRODUCER: SHERRY HILBER

SUPERVISING PRODUCER:　　　KARI NEVIL

WRITTEN BY: MARA PURL　　　　　TAPE DAY
　　　　　　SHERI ANDERSON
　　　　　　　　　　　　　　6:00 - 8:00 A　　DRY BLOCK
　　　　　　　　　　　　　　8:00 - 8:30　　　Tech. Meeting
　　　　　　　　　　　　　　8:30 - 11:15　　 CAMERA BLOCKING
　　　　　　　　　　　　　　　　　　　　　　RUN THRU
　　　　　　　　　　　　　　11:15 - 12:30 P　lunch
　　　　　　　　　　　　　　12:30 - 1:45　　 DRESS REHEARSAL
　　　　　　　　　　　　　　1:45 - 2:15　　　Notes

DIRECTORS: DAN HAMILTON
　　　　　　ROGER CARDINAL

P.A.'S:　AMELIA NORFLEET
　　　　　LESLEY TYE

MUSIC COORDINATOR: MARILYN HARRIS

　　　　　A MH ENTERPRISES/ TREASURE ISLAND PRODUCTIONS
　　　　　　　　　　CBS TV PRESENTATION

MHTV - EPISODE #1101

TEASER

FADE IN

INT. CHRIS CHRISTIAN'S BEDROOM, MORNING

EARLY MORNING SUNLIGHT FILTERS THROUGH BLINDS AND LANDS ON THE SHEETS WHICH MORE OR LESS COVER CHRIS AS SHE LIES IN THE ARMS OF JOSEPH CALVIN. **WE HEAR** THE PHONE RING.

JOSEPH
Let it ring.

CHRIS REACHES FOR THE PHONE AND JOSEPH PLAYFUL WRESTLES WITH HER AS WE **HEAR**:

CHRIS (V.O., FILTERED)
You've almost reached Chris Christian with Satellite News, and if I'm not here I'm covering a story. After the beep you know what to do.

JOSEPH
I certainly do.

JOSEPH MAKES ANOTHER MOVE ON CHRIS WHO PLAYFULLY TRIES TO GET AWAY. WE **HEAR** THE BEEP AS THE IN-COMING MESSAGE BEGINS.

MR. MAN (FILTERED - VOICE OVER)
Ms. Christian, you know who this is. If you want to get the story you have only 24 hours to do so.

WE **SEE** THAT CHRIS HAS COME TO ALERT STATUS. JOSEPH TRIES TO WRESTLE HER AGAIN BUT THE MOMENT HAS BEEN LOST.

JOSEPH
Do you always get such mysterious messages?

CHRIS
Always.

BINDERS & COVERS

A word here about script covers or binders. You won't be given either. The script will come as sheets of paper held together with brads. Some actors hate binders and feel they're pretentious. Others find them useful for holding a pencil, notes, call sheet, production shooting schedule, lists of names and anything else one might need for work. It is, of course, your choice. We've always found some sort of script cover to be indispensable, particularly for work in on-going projects.

EARLY DRAFTS

Depending upon how early in the overall project you're hired, you may receive an early draft, which is hot off the writer's computer (or the studio's photocopy machine). On the Title Page you'll see the title and if this is early in the project, this is most likely a "Working Title" which will probably change by the time it's released or is broadcast. For example the script, "Sisterhood," was later televised as "Addicted To His Love." Sometimes the title page includes not only the writer's name, but the date the script was written and the WGA number. This is the Writer's Guild of America Registration number indicating that the script is protected by the Guild for copyright.

In later revisions, the title page will contain more information. There might later be the names of two screen writers. Also director's and producers' names will appear, as well as a production company.

If this is an early script, the wording will still be the way the writer let it flow from his or her thoughts and may include a great deal of descriptive material. You may find this very helpful. By the time the script becomes a "Shooting Script" it has gone through a transformation, which is the responsibility of the First Assistant Director. The First A.D. takes the writer's final rewrite and breaks it down shot by shot and then numbers these as scenes. This is what begins to translate the script into a working road map for all the crew members who must bring the project to life. If you've seen that earlier draft, you may be surprised to find some of its description missing. If you never saw it in the first place, you'll supply your own.

Film and TV scenes are numbered. There are some specifics that apply to numbering feature films and also specific differences between shooting on film and shooting on video. If you're doing a Sitcom, it could be shot on film, in which case the shots are lettered A, B, C, etc. If you're doing a Sitcom on video tape, the shots are numbered Act I, Scene V, etc., as is the case with our example page from "Alta View."

As to numbering, while this may seem obvious, we should perhaps point out that the word "scene" is not used in the same way as it is in the theatre. In a play, a scene is a unified series of actions that clearly have a beginning, middle, and end. In a screenplay the word "scene" usually means "shot" or "set-up". A "set-up" is just what it sounds like: getting the camera set up to shoot a particular thing, be it a panorama, an over-the-shoulder close-up, or a master shot of people at a dinner table.

In a feature film script, for example, scenes 3 and 4 represent continuous action; what the woman is doing in scene 3, she continues to do in scene 4. In a play these would be considered sections of one scene. For the purposes of shooting a film, it becomes necessary to have separate set-ups for the separate shots. This is why, in reading a feature film script, it can seem very choppy. The more you read, the better you understand the underlying flow of action.

Occasionally, you'll see a scene number and opposite it only the word OMIT. This means a scene has been left out. It could be for any number of technical reasons, or could simply be a matter of renumbering.

As the script continues to evolve, numbering can get quite complicated. Here's a key to how it works. Let's say a new opening scene has been added right at the beginning of the picture. The original shooting script will have begun with Shot 1. So how is this new opening shot numbered? The new opening Shot is number A1.

After A1, the new script might say B1 thru 1B omitted. From this we would be able to tell that at one point there was a series of "B" shots which preceded the original opening, and that the original opening itself once contained a 1A and a 1B. These might now be gone and the action would resume with 1C. Too complex? Don't worry about the numbering beyond knowing where to insert your new pages in the correct spots.

REVISED PAGES

Even with all the advance preparation that takes place before a project begins to shoot, things change as the film or episode begins. No sooner have you received your "Final Shooting Script" than you begin to receive "Revised Pages." As you begin to get inundated with pages of all colors, you'll need to be organized in your handling of these very important sheets — and at the same time maintain the thread of your own work with your script.

When you first receive your script, its pages will be white. However, once the show goes into production, you'll find yourself being given pages of different colors. What are these? These are revisions, and each new color represents yet another revision to the script. As each department begins to analyze the script and solve the various problems from a departmental point of view, the script must change accordingly. These changes, in turn, cause responsive changes from other departments, and so it goes. On the cover sheet for a script that's gone through these changes, you'll see a list of revisions with a list of colors with revision dates opposite each color. You may think these are arbitrary — but they are not. They always appear in the following order: Blue, pink, yellow, green, salmon, tan, orchid.

When you receive your first set of blue pages, what do you do with them? Take your old script apart, and insert each new page in its proper spot immediately. Be sure to place your new title page as the very first page in the script, because this will tell you at a glance which is the latest version you've received. If the Second A.D. asks you "Did you receive your blue pages?" you can glance at your title page and tell him or her exactly what you received most recently.

When new pages come in, <u>don't</u> assume these changes have nothing to do with you, even if your dialogue doesn't change. As the script changes come in, you'll also receive additional pages full of interesting information. You'll receive a complete list of characters for the whole film, for example, and a comprehensive "Set List."

As to the old deleted pages – we leave it up to you whether or not to keep them. Our feeling is keeping them is probably wise – at least until the end of production. Sometimes a mistake can appear on a new page, and if you can refer to older pages, you can correct it more easily. You may or may not want to keep them in your actual working script, which you carry with you.

Eventually you'll have pages to discard – perhaps not until the end of production. A word for the ecologically minded – throughout your career you won't believe how much paper will be generated to keep you working as an actor. Recycle these pages one way or another. If you have a place to take them for recycling, great. We've found we've never lacked for scrap paper by every phone and next to every bed. Turn the sheets over and cut them into fourths. You'll save a fortune at the stationers.

Another thought is to archive your scripts for posterity. We know of one actor who answered his fan letters on the backs of script pages, which added value and something special for his fans. Sometime in the future you might even auction your scripts for a small fortune.

Note that on a revision page there will be an asterisk (*) opposite specific changes. These mark individual lines, whole scenes, or whole pages that have been changed as of the revision matching the color of the sheet on which these changes appear. Asterisks appear in the right hand margin. Again, be sure to read these new pages even if you're not in the scene. Something on the new page may affect the script in a way that influences your character. And an overall awareness of production is always to your benefit.

TERMINOLOGY

FADE IN is a technical term meaning the image you're about to see will gradually appear from a black screen. Each shot is then listed throughout the entire script. Very important information is given for each shot. Each and every shot must be described specifically for the sake of every crew member from Director to Prop Master, from Sound to D.P. (If these titles are not familiar, please check the Glossary.) This is so that he or she knows exactly what's to be shot, where and under what circumstances.

EXT. or INT. Means the scene will be either an Exterior or an Interior shot. If an Exterior shot it will be either a Day or Night shot. And the specific location will also be described as briefly as possible. Information regarding the shots is generally CAPITALIZED, such as location and in some cases, key action. Names of characters are also capitalized in certain cases.

There is a uniform rule regarding indentations. Shot information is always flush with the left margin. Dialogue begins at the first indentation. Character names are always at the second indentation. Parenthetical remarks (such as "WALKING TOWARDS HIM") can appear at either the first or second indentation, depending on which script format is being used.

SHOOTING SCHEDULE

Part of the First A.D.'s task in breaking down the script is to prepare a shooting schedule. This will determine the order in which all the scenes will be shot. Although this preliminary shooting schedule is subject to change, you may request a copy of it. This will be helpful to you in knowing the order in which your scenes will be shot. You may, for example, find the director needs to film your character in jail before having filmed your character being arrested, or must film you being divorced before having filmed you as married. The worst situation — and it comes up all the time — is that you often must film your torrid love scene before you film the scene in which you meet your lover for the first time. You'll need to have done your preparatory work carefully in order for the development of your character to make sense.

YOUR "BIBLE"

We'll put in another plug at this point for having your own script binder. For one thing, because it's a good place to keep your own personal script notes. Remember that if you have notes that you want to keep, you'll need to transfer them to your new pages. You'll arrive at your own style for dealing with this, but we find adding your own lined paper to the script can sometimes prevent you from losing notes you meant to keep and can save you the time of rewriting notes that are important to you.

Consider your script to be your own personal "bible" — your road map, your driving directions, your journal. It's a place to write down your own choices. If the script doesn't say "frying eggs in the kitchen" and you therefore don't know what you're to be doing, choose or decide exactly what you see yourself doing at that point. Mark this down and later it may be an opportunity for discussion with the Director. If not, at least, it'll serve to remind you of your own process.

> I read the script about twelve times and I take notes and notes and notes. I read where it's quiet, without interruptions.
> — Joan Van Ark

As you begin to mark your script and learn your lines, take the time to analyze the technical aspects of the piece. Is this scene four days later? Has a month gone by? Is it just an hour later? Prepare yourself by having all this information carefully stated. Believe it or not, even with all the care taken to prepare this expensive project, with all the revisions that typically take place, mistakes can happen. You may find the script has you wearing a bikini at a dinner party, or has you wearing a business suit for a business meeting and the same suit for a meeting with the same characters two days later. If these are intentionally written into the script, then make note of that too, because there may be important comedic or dramatic reasons for such choices. Know which it is.

> I leave my whole script in my trailer. I pull out today's pages only and put them in brads and keep them always with me. I keep focused on them. And, of course, I mark my lines in yellow.
> – Joan Van Ark

Use your script as your sketch pad, the rough draft of your own work. Eventually you'll toss your script aside because all your script work will be done and you'll be ready to perform. For now, it's your homework and your homework will pay off.

TEXT ANALYSIS

There is an art to reading a script, and we recommend you treat the process as something serious – or should we say, sacred.

First, read the entire script through without interruption. Try not to read while taking phone calls, feeding the dog, watering the plants, or watching a ball game. Save your script reading time for a plane ride, a long soak in the tub, or best of all, curl up in your favorite chair and switch off the phone.

The point is, go into the "zone" when you read your script for the first time – the script zone. As you read, visualize where the characters will be standing, what they'll be wearing, what time of day it is. From this first reading you'll get all kinds of first impressions and first impressions only come once. These can be so valuable! Also, your uninterrupted read-through will give a sense of the flow and pace of the story.

Once you've read the script through, henceforward you'll probably only be reading it in segments. As you read your own scenes, start making notes about things you see or things you question.

As you continue to familiarize yourself with your script, you'll want to do what is called text analysis. During this process you'll plumb the depths of the script – assuming it has any depth – and probably surprise yourself as to how many things you'll discover.

Consider your script to be a treasure map, a cleverly disguised series of clues which will lead you into the center of the story and into the heart of your character. Write down any and everything you see written about your character and from there, start building a history for him or her. Where was the character born? To what kind of parents? Was the character raised in a nurturing environment, or left to his or her own devices? Does the character have loving relationships, or is he or she unrequited? Don't forget, we said the script would be full of *clues*. That doesn't mean everything is spelled out. It does mean you can infer volumes from what is written.

> *Without the past, you don't have a present. The text is the architect's blueprint, without which he can't build the building. The text is the roots of the tree, without which the tree dies, or never grows in the first place. Unless you know where that character is coming from in his or her history, you really don't have anything to share in the present.*
> – Bruno Ragnacci, Actor

We share something with our students. Know where your character is coming from and know where they're going. If this information is not provided in the script, make up your own version.

Next, take a look at the way the dialogue is structured. When your character speaks to others, is it adversarially, let's say the way an investigative reporter might speak? Or is it patiently, the way a kindly teacher might be? Is there a marked change in the way your character speaks, depending upon who he or she is talking to? Does your character say a lot of words without actually saying much? Or does your character hold back the Hoover Dam with his or her words, saying so much less than what they're actually thinking? A good writer will have worked hard to bring nuances into the dialogue and it's up to you to discern them.

Of course one of most fascinating things to look for in a script is not the text, but the sub-text. Good writers build this into their work, so that actors are swimming in layers of meaning.

Sub-text is like an underground river which flows and burbles in a way that can't be seen from the surface of the ground. You can only tell the underground river is there, because in an otherwise arid zone, a clump of trees grows nearby. They must have a source of water you can't see, right?

The characters in the script will show behavior — sudden anger or deep longing, let's say — and it's up to you to discover what source of experience or history is feeding that behavior, just as the underground river is feeding the roots of the trees. Sub-text is the secret unwritten story which fuels the script and makes it far more interesting than it would be otherwise.

Whatever classes or books you work with, cultivate your own "sacred" process of plumbing the depths of your script.

PRE-PRODUCTION

Covered In This Chapter:

- Initial Calls

- Production List

- Working Overseas

- Production Relationships

Every member of the cast and crew is responsible for a special part of the picture. Consequently, each of them views the project from a somewhat narrow perspective.
— Gregory Goodell
Independent Producer & Director

PRE-PRODUCTION

At this point one of several things will happen and the order and the timing may vary widely, or even wildly. Your job may begin a month after you're cast — or you may be told you're flying to Vancouver tonight.

This is a good time to point out that all this time you've been living in a parallel universe — one with which you're about to collide. The other universe which runs parallel to ours, is the one inhabited by crew members. Their lives are every bit as complex and valuable as ours. It's just that they speak a different language.

Many crew members have a more technical background that actors have and this gives them a different perspective. While you're busy tuning in to your character's motivations, they're concerned about focus. They may not understand you need a moment to get centered. You may not realize that if you don't hit your mark, you're ruining the focus and lighting they've worked so hard to achieve. There may — no, there *will* — come a time you just don't understand one another. You may feel they're being insensitive and they may feel you're being stupid. We'd like to do whatever we can to heal this great divide. It's time for pre-production: not too soon for you to become aware of how the other half lives.

INITIAL CALLS

You should definitely expect calls from two people: Wardrobe and the Second A.D. We've written a separate chapter on Wardrobe to deal with this. In addition to these, you may receive a call from the Production Coordinator, particularly if you're going to be working out of town or out of the country. In such a case the Production Coordinator will call you with travel information and other important details.

If time permits, the Director may call to welcome you to the show. However, particularly in television, where time is of the essence, this happens only about 50% of the time. If you feel talking with the Director is critical, leave a personal message with the production office and say specifically that you would like a couple of minutes for questions. You can have your agent call, but it's best not to, because that implies that there's a problem.

If you do have this opportunity to talk with the Director, then it's wise to have some key questions ready, because chances are the next time you'll see the Director will be on the set. Key question number one would be: Is there a number where I may reach you? Or would you prefer that I contact the First A.D. if I have any questions about props or wardrobe?

Immediately before you're to begin work, you'll receive a call from the person known as the Second Assistant Director. The "Second" will be your life-line to everything you need to know. Occasionally on the set your liaison may end up being the "Trainee." If so, you'll be told and introduced. The Second A.D. will tell you what time you're to report for your first day of work and where shooting will take place. He or she will also tell you what scenes will be shot that day and will try to give you an idea of the order, so you'll know which to prepare.

Although it is the job of the Second to call you, it is also a courtesy to you and responding to it is your first opportunity to win friends and influence people.

> It is wonderful if, when requested to do so, actors call the 2nd A.D. to verify their call time for the next day. We A.D.'s always sleep better knowing the actor knows his call and will for sure show up, hopefully, _on time._
> — B.C. Cameron

PRODUCTION LIST

Here's a bit of personal philosophy. Before you get off the phone, ask either the Production Coordinator or the Second A.D. for a Production List, which will give you the names, titles and contact numbers of all crew members you'll be working with. Once you get it, attach it to your script and refer to it regularly. You run the risk of slightly annoying the A.D. at this point, in that you've added one more thing to his or her extremely hectic schedule. But the advantage to you is that you'll know exactly how to address your make-up person by name, for example. If you explain this, you'll generally be respected for making the extra effort. Everyone likes to be called by his or her first name. Most crew members will know your first name within the first couple of hours. Do others the same courtesy and start building relationships.

Second, ask for a shooting schedule — particularly if you're in a lot of scenes. This is an outline of all the scenes and when they are expected to be shot. Note: this is only a guideline. The movie-making business is complex and fraught with problems and sudden changes.

This is also a good time to let this person know how you like to work and what your idiosyncrasies are. For example, we like to have at least an hour and a half for make-up and hair for the first day of work because there's usually so much to discuss. Since you probably won't have worked with these people before and most likely haven't had a pre-production meeting, there will be a number of things you might need to share with the hair or make-up person. Once you're used to each other, that time span can be shortened. Be aware that if there are a number of principal actors that day, they may not want to accommodate you. You must always be flexible, but it doesn't hurt to ask.

If you have heavy emotional scenes, ask to be notified immediately about any changes in the shooting sequence for that day. You may want to be notified anyway, but most assuredly awareness of sequence changes can help when there are tough demands being made on you emotionally, or if you have an immense amount of dialogue.

WORKING OVERSEAS

If you're going to be traveling to do this job — and most particularly if you're going to be working overseas — be very organized. Have a file or notebook of some kind containing all the phone numbers you've been given. You don't know what circumstances you'll be dealing with, nor which numbers you might suddenly need at some strange hour.

> I flew overseas to Australia to shoot a film for the USA/Sci-Fi Channel called "Official Denial." A few days before departure, I developed a rash on my neck and went to my dermatologist for a prescription to get rid of it. At first, it seemed to be going away. However, as I flew the twelve hours to Sydney, the rash started to get worse and began to crawl up my neck to my face. I started to panic, knowing I only had a few days before I was expected in front of the camera and realizing that with the time change, I would be arriving on a Sunday. Thank goodness I had my Production List with me — I went down that list until I reached someone who could get me to a local doctor in time to help me before shooting began.
> — Erin

Working overseas can run the gamut from working in another English-speaking country where language and basic cultural differences are minimal — such as Canada or Australia — to working in a European country where differences are pronounced but many things are similar to the U.S. — people sit on chairs, eat three meals, take taxis — to working in a Third World Nation where no assumptions can be made — cars stop and wait for sacred cows, high holy periods require fasting for two days. Many overseas working experiences are a delight, particularly if a) you've done some homework and b) you're smart enough to ask questions about things you don't know.

> When I was very young I did a series for NHK TV in Tokyo. In Japan, it's considered rude to "no," so a great effort is made to answer all questions with "yes." It is therefore tremendously helpful to ask questions in a negative way because it enables people to respond positively. "You don't want me to look into the camera?" I asked one

day on the set. "Yes!" said the director exuberantly. He meant, "Yes, I don't want you to look into the camera." Unfortunately my co-star couldn't grasp this fine point. "Do you want me looking at the camera or not?" he blustered. Red in the face and at a loss how to answer him, the director walked off the set. At the end of the day the actor was fired. He never understood why.

— Mara

Some overseas working experiences are nothing short of nightmares. There's a beaut in our chapter on Stunts. In general, we encourage you to think carefully about jobs you accept in other countries, particularly if you're going into very unfamiliar territory. Your agent should be helpful in this regard, and so should SAG. Should you accept a location job that puts you in a war zone? What are your rights as a foreigner? Do you have tourist status? Or a temporary work permit? If you're a Western woman, what rights do you have in a Moslem country? Be informed. Be wise.

PRODUCTION RELATIONSHIPS

Though all your relationships with crew members are potentially important, as an actor your most vital relationships with be with the A.D.s — the Assistant Directors.

The First A.D. works closely with the Director. All the tasks of the First A.D. are critical to the success and flow of the project. Although he or she is not specifically involved with the creative aspects of directing the film, he or she has a great deal to do with making it possible for the Director to do the job of directing without interference or delay. In pre-production, the First A.D. breaks down the script by scenes, creating a complete structure, a document that makes the entire project happen. He or she logs all items needed for each scene and creates a shooting schedule for the cast and crew.

Sometimes an actor will say to himself, "Why did the Director schedule the love scene for the first day? I haven't even said hello to my co-star yet." Well, chances are — and this is especially true in TV — the Director didn't make that decision. Most often the choice is made by the First A.D., and for purely logistical and/or financial reasons. Good First A.D.s are sensitive to the needs of actors and will try to accommodate them by scheduling scenes that aren't emotionally demanding or intimate at the top of production. But sometimes their hands are tied and your first scene is also your most emotional.

During production, the First A.D. runs the set and makes sure, minute by minute, that the director has everything he/she needs to complete the day's shooting. While being totally aware of what's happening on today's shoot, the First is also planning the next day's work, taking into consideration script revisions, weather and any other contingencies, like the rash on the lead actor's face.

The Key Second A.D. assists the First in making sure everything and everyone is on the set when needed, disperses necessary information, script revisions and changes to cast and crew. The Second does the callsheet for the next day, the production report and SAG sheet (for actor's sign out). They also check in the actors and background (extras), pass out vouchers, get everyone through make up/ hair and wardrobe and to the set as needed. They set Background (Extras) in the scenes, sign out actors and extras at the end of the day and make sure actors have their calls for the next day, pass out call sheets to crew, do the extras' pay vouchers and "skins" for accounting. They get actors' contracts signed, unlock dressing rooms doors, gaff publicity photo shoots and interviews and get cokes and coffees in their spare minutes.

On some shoots, there is also a Second Second A.D., who helps the Second do all these jobs which, as you can gather, are virtually impossible for one person to do!

As we mentioned, you'll have ongoing relationships with various crew members for the duration of the project. Respect what they do by understanding as much as you can about their work. Our experience is that you will be respected in return.

WARDROBE

Covered In This Chapter:

- First Phone Call

- Your Costumer's Credits

- Wardrobe Pre-Production

- Your Ideas & Input

- Building Character with Costume

- Communication with Wardrobe Department

- Your Fitting

- Movement

- Color

- Being a Team Player

- Budgets

- On the Set

In that first interview, be absolutely truthful. Be more truthful than you would be with your lawyer or your doctor. Your costumer is there as your collaborator, your assistant, to help you realize your goal.

— Margo Baxley
Costumer, "The Champ," "A Few Good Men"

Being late throws everyone off. Multiply the number of minutes you are late by the number of people you are keeping waiting.

— Jean-Pierre Dorleac
Costume Designer, "Buck Rogers," "Quantam Leap"

WARDROBE

FIRST PHONE CALL

After you get the job, the first person you'll hear from is the Director. Right? Wrong. The first person you're likely to hear from is someone from the Wardrobe Department. Since this may be your first link with the production company, it's important to start practicing all your wit and wisdom skills now. This business is all about people, and people talk. Be assured, the content and nature of your conversations with the Wardrobe people will be reported up and down the chain of command. As such, these conversations may as well work to your advantage.

> *There is an underground of what actors are like to work with. God forbid if you get on the blacklist.*
> — Jean-Pierre Dorleac

YOUR COSTUMER'S CREDITS

Did it ever occur to you to read the credits of your Costumer? You can be sure that he or she has read yours. It might be interesting and useful to return the favor. One way to do this is to get a guild manual, which is obtainable from the Costume Designers' Guild at 818-905-1557. It's a sign of respect — and a great conversation opener — if you know what your Costumer has done previously in his or her career. Many costumers have been in the business for years and can be a fount of wisdom and fascinating information about design and about the business in general. Perhaps most important, if you're able to make an ally — rather than an adversary — of your costumer, this will show on screen in many ways.

WARDROBE PRE-PRODUCTION

By the time the Wardrobe Department contacts you, understand that they will already have had a detailed pre-production meeting with the Director. You may not feel you're talking with the Director, but indirectly, you are. Certain broad strokes will have been decided – a general color theme, an agreement on the historical period, a sense of style and so forth – so that the Costumer and the Director know they're on the same wavelength. These decisions will affect you to greater or lesser degrees depending on your role.

In preparation for this phone call and before you have your first meeting with Wardrobe, there are certain things you must do on your own. If you haven't already read it, we refer you now to the Scripts chapter, where vital information is detailed about exactly how you deal with your script. Without repeating ourselves too much, we must emphasize again that you must lovingly and diligently read your script from start to finish in order to begin your work. That reading must take place *before* your conversation with the Wardrobe department.

During the course of reading your script you'll have gathered impressions, ideas, images and some specifics about how you see your character – and how you see that character costumed. You're expected to have these ideas and the Costumers will be looking forward to hearing from you. They will, of course, have their own ideas as well and this is where ideas from at least three sources – Director, Costumer, and Actor – start to come together for the first time.

> *The better résumé of the character the actor can bring to the fitting, the more complete that fitting will be.*
> – Margo Baxley

YOUR IDEAS & INPUT

As we outlined in the Script chapter, you'll have done a complete breakdown for yourself of each scene and you'll have made detailed notes. The Costumer will have done the same. So you can now compare notes — slacks versus a skirt, a sweater because it's night, a tie because it's a business meeting — and so forth. Have your ideas, but be prepared to be flexible as well.

> *Don't get married to a schmatta. PLEASE! It's just clothes.*
> — Jean-Pierre Dorleac

A word, now, about the line which must be drawn in every project, between doing the level of detailed work you require and going to extremes. It's generally understood that the actor will have certain costume requirements in order to make his or her part work. And generally, the Wardrobe Department takes its responsibility to support the actor very seriously.

BUILDING CHARACTER WITH COSTUME

For many actors, wardrobe elements are so important that they actually begin to build characters from them. For example, Joanne Woodward says that for her it's the hat — once she knows what hat the character wears, she begins to understand the whole psyche. For Cicely Tyson and for Joan Van Ark, the starting point is the scent — they find a different perfume for each character they play.

> *For me, the character often begins with shoes. If I play an artist, I might wear soft flats. If I play an executive, I might wear heels. When I was cast in the television Movie of the Week "Code of Vengeance," I was reaching for an understanding of my character. She was an earthy, courageous woman. It was when I found some earthy, clunky, basic desert hiking boots that the character became clear to me. It affected how I walked and helped me overcome certain refined movements which are natural to me but not to this character.*
> — Erin

COMMUNICATION WITH WARDROBE DEPARTMENT

Now you're ready for that first phone call with Wardrobe. Here we want to emphasize that communication is one key to your success and honesty is another. One thing you'll be asked for in this phone call is your sizes. BE HONEST! Yes, you meant to lose that 10 pounds after Christmas, but somehow you never did. DO NOT lie about your weight or your measurements. What will happen if you do? Wasted time at the least and murder and mayhem at the worst. One actress turned up for her fitting having given the wrong sizes — not slightly wrong, but off by four sizes — and found that before she left the building, she overheard derogatory comments being made about her on the phone to the production office. Don't put yourself in that position.

> *Be truthful about sizes and always <u>know</u> your sizes. Have a tape measure and become friends with it. We have very little time. We have to pull things from stock. If the clothes we pull don't fit you, this impedes a fitting and causes a nuisance all the way around. We have to work twice the amount of time.*
>
> *— Jean-Pierre Dorleac*

Mr. Dorleac makes an important point. When it comes to your sizes, we advocate creating a standard form for yourself, which you keep updated. Provide your agent and/or manager with multiple copies of this updated sheet on a regular basis. Include measurements, shoe size, hat size, glove size, drop measurements (example: measurement taken by dropping the tape measure from collarbone to waist), weight, height, coloring, skin tone — make it as complete as possible. DON'T be a victim of ignorance. It's not respected and it's not an excuse. We'll repeat this theme over and over again in this book. Don't use "I didn't know" as an excuse.

Depending upon the project, some of this communication between you and your Costumer will take place on the phone, some at your first fitting. When it comes time for your fitting, treat this as a golden opportunity to get off on the right foot for all your subsequent work.

YOUR FITTING

Signs written in English are often misspelled in Tokyo. A sign in a dressmaker's shop said, "Ladies Have Fits Upstairs."

It was a hilarious sign, but it brings up a point. Don't have a fit at your fitting. Be courteous, be open. This is a meeting of minds, an opportunity to develop a new relationship and work on your character.

When you go to your fitting, we cannot emphasize strongly enough: BE ON TIME. It may seem a small thing to you to keep a costumer waiting for five minutes, but aside from the basic rudeness of keeping another professional standing around waiting for you when they could be doing something else, we'll share with you a perspective on what a costumer's schedule is like.

> *We are usually booked within fifteen minutes of the last booking. We allocate 15 minutes per change of clothes, and ten minutes to decide upon alterations and markings. Being late throws everyone off. Multiply the number of minutes you are late by the number of people you are keeping waiting. If you're ten minutes late, and you keep five people waiting, you are fifty minutes late.*
> — Jean-Pierre Dorleac

The other thing to think about at your fitting is that this is your only opportunity to work one-on-one with your Costumer. As such you should consider going alone. There may be times when it's appropriate to bring along someone very close to you or close to the project. However, consider the fact that this may hamper your chance at creating a relationship with your Costumer. It's a judgment call and we leave it up to you. Based on numerous experiences, we advise against bringing children and dogs.

Remember, too, that this fitting is not only your first contact with the Wardrobe Department, it's also your first contact with the production company. So observe certain rules. For example, show up looking presentable. Don't come in with wet hair and a torn T-shirt.

In preparation for this fitting, we advocate self knowledge and preparedness. If you have a large bust and need special bras, bring them. If you wear a special athletic supporter, bring it. If you have no shoulders, bring your shoulder pads. And if you have a certain knowledge of style for yourself, be aware of it and be prepared to share it if it's applicable. For example, if you don't wear plaids or ruffles, the fitting is the place to say so — unless there's a specific reason why your character must wear something you would not normally wear.

And bring your necessities. If you need clean socks, stockings, etc., bring them. Don't hold up the schedule by forcing the assistant to search the premises for some underwear that might fit you. And bring some good basic shoes. If you're trying on a business suit and you only brought your running shoes, you won't get an accurate read on how the suit looks on you.

A word of warning here: avoid the ridiculous. It will be remembered. It's one thing to say, "I can't carry large jewelry." It's another to make a comment that goes down in the humor chapter of the annals of costuming history.

> *An actress told me she couldn't wear hoop earrings larger than a quarter because they made her rear end look big. Please.*
> *— Jean-Pierre Dorleac*

Sometimes you'll go to a fitting where the Costumer has pulled items from stock. Under some circumstances — particularly if you're doing a major role — Wardrobe may take you on a shopping expedition. Whether it's a fitting or a shopping trip, this is your opportunity to discuss ideas as you try on outfits. Don't postpone sharing your ideas, because chances are you'll not get another chance. This is when to be "creative" — not after the clothes have been purchased or altered to fit you. If you think something is great at your fitting, but two days later decide it's awful — be prepared to meet some resistance. Call and mention your idea if you feel it's necessary, but be aware you may be perceived as being indecisive, and furthermore, it may now be too late for Wardrobe to accommodate the change you're requesting. Practice the art of compromise, unless you feel this blouse or belt is a matter of life and death. Remember this business is a collaborative one, and you want to be a team player.

> *Don't be "nice" in a fitting, because you'll suffer for it later. If you have reservations about a color, a style, etc., say so. Because every insecurity will surface when you walk out onto that set. Let the costume support you, not detract from you.*
> — *Margo Baxley*

One of the most important keys to understanding wardrobe is that it is there to serve you; you are not there to serve it. If you feel subservient to your costume this will show on film and will undermine your acting work no matter how fine it may be. Realize, for example, that a man who wakes up every morning, prepares his shaving lotion, carefully lathers his face, shaves, wears a high-collared shirt complete with stays and tie pins, holds a certain image of himself, without which he would feel incomplete. You yourself may only feel comfortable throwing on a workshirt, but familiarize yourself with the intimacies of your character's clothing and make those clothes your own.

Women's clothing often starts with the inside layers, and these determine not only the shape of the outer garments, but often the attitude of the wearer as well. Wardrobe people will probably provide you with a corset if you're to wear a period gown. But they may not be so thorough when it comes to underwear from other periods of history. If you need a girdle to get the 50s look right, then ask for one. It's a legitimate request.

> *Undergarments are important. If you are coming to a fitting, bring or wear the undergarments which fit you the best. We can duplicate them. Bras are very specific. Historical underwear is so important— bloomers, corsets, etc., are vital to hang the clothes on, or you won't get the look. Same with girdles for the 50s. So if you don't like girdles but your part calls for it, don't complain.*
> — *Margo Baxley*

When I was doing the television film "Breaking Home Ties," I played a character from the 1950s. I found I had no clear idea how those women walked or sat, or how they felt about their own images, until I acquired the proper underwear. Women in the 50s didn't consider themselves to be properly dressed unless they were wearing their girdles. I got a clearer sense of my character from the moment I put a girdle on.

— Erin

MOVEMENT

One more thing to discuss is the relationship between wardrobe and movement. The degree of freedom your clothing allows or disallows affects your movements and thus how you think about your character. If you're a man, how would you feel about participating in a sword fight in trousers, as opposed to having that same fight in tights? If you're a woman, how does a tight skirt and high heels affect how you walk across a room or sit on a sofa? How would you approach that same sofa in a pair of soft wool pants? Again, think through your scenes and decide whether your clothes need to work for you without resistance, or whether you need them as a foil to inhibit what you would otherwise like to do. Perhaps your character is trying to make a good impression, but has to sit in a tight skirt in a deep, soft sofa. Suddenly you find yourself unable to sit up. This can give you a heightened sense of drama — or of comedy.

In the theatre we often find ourselves doing period pieces, and perhaps most frequently we end up doing Shakespeare. During a production of "The Merchant of Venice" at the Globe Playhouse, all the women in the cast knew enough to begin wearing long skirts almost from the very beginning of the rehearsal period. The men in the cast, however, couldn't bear the idea of wearing tights one moment before dress rehearsal. Consequently, when that fateful night came, all these men (who shall be nameless, but you can look it up) who until that moment had achieved a wonderful command over the language and customs of the day, were suddenly undone by having their bottom halves so specifically outlined and accentuated. Their dignity suddenly in

> *jeopardy, it wasn't until the second week of the run that they regained their composure. Of course, in film, you don't have time to regain that composure — you have to have it from the first day of shooting.*
> — Mara

COLOR

While shape is perhaps the most fundamental aspect of wardrobe, color is certainly a vivid element that can provide valuable keys to your character. The Director may have an overall color-concept for his film. It may be set in the Southwest and be tinged with delicate browns, pinks, pale lavenders and highlighted with turquoise. Is your character indigenous to that region and, therefore, to those colors, or in juxtaposition to them? Perhaps you play an executive from New York who wears only black, and, therefore, stands out like a sore thumb in Santa Fe.

In television work, there is another technical aspect to know about: the technology of television changes color. What appears true red in daylight will not read as exactly the same color when it appears on television. If you're making color choices about your wardrobe, you might want to ask questions of the Wardrobe experts who work with this problem constantly.

Film and video "see" and react to color differently than your eye does. To really understand the principles involved, try to have a discussion about it sometime with a Director of Photography. First of all, know there's a marked difference between film and video. The general rule is: where color is concerned, you have more leeway with film than you do with video. In either case, beware of white, black, and red. Should your Costumer and Director decide that these colors are necessary for their project, they can adjust and shoot these colors accurately. But only if they make these adjustments will the colors read properly. So for most projects, they are avoided.

> *I was recently Director of Photography on a music video. If someone had shown up in a white T-shirt for their first day of work having been asked to wear "something casual," it would have been a sure sign that*

the actor was an amateur. Unless a white garment is "teched down" — dyed or sprayed to a slightly duller shade — light bounces off the white all over the place. Black is a problem because it absorbs all available light; saturated red is a color that video doesn't handle well, because it "hallates" — creates a bizarre-looking aura around its wearer. If the costuming is up to the actor, he or she should look for pastels, jewel tones, or rich colors, but avoid anything very light or very dark. Striped or small patterns are a problem on video as well, since one part of the pattern tends to compete with the other. One other thing to bear in mind is that natural fabrics look better than most synthetics. Synthetics bounce light and create a sheen, which can interfere with the picture.

— Kieran Illes

Color and patterns on video may seem irrelevant, in that these matters are best handled by the Costumer and the Director of Photography. But an informed actor is better than an uninformed one and remember when you audition, you will often be taped. So don't wear that herringbone jacket — which will dance on the screen, overshadowing even your most dramatic scenes — and don't wear an all-white top, which will bounce light all over the screen.

Your Director may not be focused particularly on color and may leave this to Wardrobe. You may or may not be in agreement with them about the colors you're to wear. This can be sensitive ground, so do your homework before making suggestions. In some cases, the character may be wearing a uniform of some sort, and the color is, therefore, predetermined.

In playing a long-running character on "Days Of Our Lives" I'd been looking forward to developing a character with some complexity and depth. I played a nurse and was constantly frustrated by the fact that I was stuck wearing a uniform day after day. I was always in white, always wearing "sensible shoes," while every other female on the show was wearing beautifully tailored suits, designer gowns and sculpted high heels. Variety for me was confined to the few times I got to wear

> *a horrible, hospital-green uniform instead of white. What I found was, however, I made very specific choices about how I wore my hair (under the nurse's cap), what jewelry I wore and what I wore under the uniform. When I needed to spice things up, I wore interesting underwear — which only I knew about, but it showed in my attitude, however subtlely. You know how it is when you're holding a secret — everyone wants to know what it is.*
>
> *— Mara*

Your costume should always be seen as your ally, even if you have to work a little bit to make it so. You can also help your fellow actors by using your familiarity with your costumes. You can help the person opposite you in a scene to feel more easily transported to a different time and place. You can also keep him or her alert by using a bit of humor.

> *In one episode of "Silver Spoons," my character Kate was to "flash" her husband Edward. She was to greet him by opening a raincoat while wearing nothing underneath it. Of course, in real life, while the audience couldn't see me from the front, the crew could, and so could my fellow actor, so I had to wear something. To help him have something to react to, I decided to have a little fun and asked the wardrobe people to find me a burlesque outfit complete with tassels and G-string. When I opened that raincoat "Edward" got an eyeful, and so did the crew. The next trick was, we had to tape this episode twice, so I needed another surprise for "Edward." The second time I opened my raincoat, he was all set to have a front row view of my risque outfit. Instead he was greeted with a 1920s striped bathing costume, up-to-here and down-to-there and perfectly shapeless. It got as big a laugh as had my first outfit, and the crew applauded me at the dinner break. A good time was had by all.*
>
> *— Erin*

If color is something you know particularly well and something you've studied with relation to your own skin tones, apply your knowledge here, but again be open to suggestions. You may have gone to a "color consultant" who has carefully examined how individual colors relate to your skin tones and come up with palette of colors which works best for you. These palettes are divided into "seasons" – winter, spring, autumn, summer. Remember that while you may be a "winter" and may look best in black and red, your character may be an "autumn" and may look natural only in brown and beiges. If there's a color that makes you look like death-warmed-over, you may be right in insisting that you not wear it. Examine the possibility further, however, by investigating how that color is going to look under lights and on film or tape.

Also bear in mind that you are not alone in this film, and the colors you wear may have to relate to what everyone else is wearing. You may look great in blue – and the Costumer may tell you you can't wear blue in this production. It may be because another leading character is wearing blue, and the Costumer has been advised to reserve that color for that character alone. We explain this to remind you it may not be a personal issue aimed at you. Most likely it has to do with the overall production. Of course, the further along you are in your career, the more say you'll have in this and many other decisions.

BEING A TEAM PLAYER

Our feeling is that the details of costuming are incredibly important to the development and fulfillment of a role. But we also want to emphasize our constant theme: Actors must learn to be team players and remember they're part of an overall project involving many people – and a lot of money.

> Acting is a very personal and intense experience for the actor. Therefore, whatever rabbit feet they need to help create a character, is all part of our job. But it's communication between the actor and us that is vital. The costumer has to be tactful and suggest whether or not something is realistic. Actors tend to be unreasonable many times.
>
> – Margo Baxley

Margo went on to give us a good example of a case in point. The actor, who shall remain nameless in this instance, is one of the top professionals in the field and is known for detailed research on his roles, which has served him extremely well. However, in this case, he was unaware of an enormous problem he inadvertently created.

> *This actor fell in love with a certain shirt he found at a second-hand store. It was an old work shirt and may have cost only fifty cents to buy. Unfortunately that fifty-cent shirt disappeared from the set and we needed that shirt to shoot another scene. An artist had to be hired to look at a blown-up still photograph and then paint the exact pattern. We had to recreate that shirt at a tremendous cost.*
> — Margo Baxley

If you're given the opportunity to develop a character over a period of weeks or years in a series, you can really use wardrobe to sculpt and mold the finer points of characterization. The longevity of the show will almost undoubtedly convey more power to you as well and you can begin to influence your character's wardrobe more than you could in a short-term project.

> *When "Silver Spoons" first started, my character "Kate Summers" was a secretary trying to look professional on a limited budget, and I wanted her to wear inexpensive fabrics with fairly conservative lines. As the series continued, Kate took a fancy to her boss, and I then wanted her to start wearing shorter skirts and generally more flirtatious clothing. Eventually, Kate married the boss and became President of his corporation. At this point I wanted her to start wearing designer clothes. I worked with the wardrobe department throughout all these transformations, and it added a dimension and a reality to Kate that she could not otherwise have had.*
> — Erin

BUDGETS

Something we've found fascinating in talking to professional crew members is the handling of budgets in the various departments and wardrobe is no exception. As everyone does, Wardrobe people must carefully budget for their project. The more clever they are with their expenditures, the better the film will look and the more likely it is that a little pocket of money saved early in the production can be put to excellent use later on. Of course, there are times not to stint, but to spend the big money for the precise item needed. In any case, we thought some awareness of budgeting would be to your advantage.

As is usually the case, little things add up and if you're aware of this you can help more than you think. Ridiculous as it may seem, let's use pantyhose as an example. Some actresses feel they're not comfortable unless they have a new pair for every day of shooting. There are ways around this. You can alternate two pairs, washing them out every other day. Another example is cleaning and pressing. If you leave your clothes in a heap at the end of the day of shooting, the wardrobe people may have no choice but to send them out for cleaning and/or pressing. If you hang them up instead, it's possible – with a brushing and some steaming – the clothes will be fine for the next day. While cleaning may seem minor, one Costumer we spoke with said she budgets $250 to $300 per day of shooting just for cleaning.

Another place to save some money might be shoes. Shoes are sometimes extremely important to the overall look of a costume. However, in some cases, they're not. Particularly in television – where there are more medium shots and close-ups – shoes seldom show.

> Every actor should have a comfortable pair of black shoes and bring them. Eighty percent of the time your shoes do not matter because they don't show. The money could be put toward a great blouse. You're on your feet for hours. Bring your own shoes, bring black, brown, neutral, the basics. Offer your own shoes, and then there's more money

to be spent on buying some else for you.

— Margo Baxley

ON THE SET

After you've had your fitting, you may have no further contact with Wardrobe until you're on the set and at this point you'll meet a new cast of characters. Most likely, the Costumer will not be on the set and you may not see him or her again. So who are these new people and how are you expected to relate to them? The person you'll deal with the most is the Set Costumer and his or her assistants. They're on set all day and are there to make sure each actor has each piece of costume required. The Set Costumer reads the detailed notes of the Costume Supervisor and lays out your costume for you in your trailer or dressing room. These people are very busy and have very demanding jobs, but they're also there to help you.

> *If you have a particular way you want clothes laid out for you, let somebody know. If you have a superstition about putting a hat on a bed, let us know. Everyone has their idiosyncrasies. Any reasonable request is good. If I just don't have time or can't accommodate you, I'll say. The Costumer is not there to be your personal maid, but is there to answer reasonable requests.*
>
> — Margo Baxley

As with every other department, both actors and wardrobe people are responsible for doing their jobs and for getting along reasonably well while doing so. Everyone has boundaries and methods of working and you'll have to find yours. We advocate using diplomacy and awareness. After that, if you still have problems, go through the chain of command so that you don't step on people unnecessarily.

> *Any well-run costume department should work as a team. If you have a problem with the person who's on the set, go to the supervisor with your complaint. If you still have a problem, go to the designer, who is*

> the head of the show.
>
> — Margo Baxley

No doubt it has happened many times that an actor has gone over someone's head unwittingly. We again counter this by saying — ignorance is not a good excuse. Even if you intend no malice, not giving someone the opportunity to respond to your request can be hurtful at best, can certainly reflect negatively on you and can ruin your working relationship with a valued crew member. Besides which — don't forget, that crew member can make you look great — or dreadful — on film.

> This actor went over my head. He came to a costume meeting, looked at the sketches, tried on the costumes — which by then were already made — and said nothing. Immediately after the meeting I get a call from the Producer. "We have a major problem. Bring the costumes, come to my office." I was shaken. I don't like to be in this kind of situation. I go to the meeting. The actor says, "I can't act in things like this. I want something simple and black. In fact, something like this." And he pulls a sketch out of his pocket, a stick-figure drawing. I wanted to say "You _____, that's not how you work with someone." Of course I was very nice. I said, "Well, Sir, if this is what you'd like, I'll be happy to make you a black tunic." And I did. He didn't realize he'd be working against a black set. And I made it so black that on film all you see is a head floating.
>
> — Jean-Pierre Dorleac

Mr. Dorleac's story brings up another point we want to make. On some projects, particularly period pieces where historical wardrobe items are involved, the pieces may have been rented or sewn long before the actors are even hired. While you were figuring out how to audition for this role, four seamstresses may have spent sleepless nights creating the very costume you now glibly refuse to wear. So it's all well and good for you to say you can't work in a cape, but if you're playing D'Artagnon, you'd better learn how.

Part of working with the on-set costume people is deciding the extent to which you want their help. Some actors count on the costume person watching them so that a blouse isn't sticking out or crumbs aren't stuck to the front of a shirt. Others feel distracted if the costume person is in the line of sight. Think about this for yourself, and have a word with your costume people as needed.

> In "Eleanor and Franklin," Jane Alexander – who's a real pro – said, "I want to know where you are; then I won't have to worry." Some actors don't want you there unless their blouse falls off. Some actors have trouble keeping their focus. Make these ground rules early. Both ways are right! It just depends on what makes the actor feel more comfortable.
>
> – Margo Baxley

Something you may not know about is Polaroid pictures – from the very beginning, many departments will be required to take a Polaroid of you for their files. They will try to grab this picture when it's convenient for you, but try to accommodate them as well. Don't continually tell them you're busy talking with someone or eating a donut. This is part of their job. It will protect you too, because they'll have a record of exactly what your costume is supposed to include. And by the way, understand these Polaroids are for the professional use of the department in question, not for your scrapbook. It's true that the leading actors may sometimes be given Polaroids, but this is at the discretion of time and budget considerations. If you want a picture of yourself, bring your own camera and have someone snap it for you unobtrusively.

When it's time for lunch, one of your first considerations should be your costume. Will it suffer for being sat in for an hour and need to be pressed? Do you want to risk splattering it with spaghetti sauce? You may be a careful eater, but you may sit across from someone who gestures with their fork, so be warned. You may have options – cover yourself with a huge work shirt, or an oversized bathrobe provided by Wardrobe upon request. Or you can bring your own.

Sometimes the only thing to do is to change completely out of your costume for lunch, because for whatever reason, it's impossible to eat while wearing it. This is particularly true in science fiction projects where all kinds of special effects may be fastened to your body parts.

> When I was shooting "Friday the 13th Part IX – Jason Goes To Hell," some scenes required that I wear a knife protruding from between my shoulder blades. Sometimes it was funny to be at lunch with fellow actors, with our various blades sticking out, but sometimes it had been too many hours and was too uncomfortable to wear. If for any reason I did have to remove my costume, I made sure the Second A.D. gave me ample warning to get back into my costume in time for my next scene.
> – Erin

When you've finished work for the day, you will, of course, be leaving your costumes in your trailer. And here you have a choice. You can leave them piled in the middle of the floor, or you can lay them out or hang them up. Our feeling about this is "do unto others."

> When I was an apprentice at the Williamstown Festival Theatre we had to take a turn in every department. Until then I had done only leading roles, starting with my first TV series at age twelve. Suddenly I was being asked to cut flats, hang lights and sew costumes. I never became a real seamstress or a designer, but my respect for these professionals leapt forward about one light year. Not only are the hours unbelievably grueling for a wardrobe department putting a show together, but the work never stops. Getting the pancake make-up off the collars, re-stitching the seams that burst in an action scene, cleaning, pressing and perhaps most important, keeping track of all the bits and pieces and seeing to it that they end up in the right dressing room were all part of the job. I was never again able to leave my own costumes tossed over a chair or piled on the floor.
> – Mara

> *Theatre actors are usually spoken of with love and awe, because their clothes are always hung up, and their rooms are immaculate. It's not something that'll make everyone hate you if you don't, but everyone will love you if you do pick up after yourself.*
> — Margo Baxley

When the show has wrapped and you find you've been having dreams about one of the outfits you've worn in the show, is there any hope that said item of clothing can be yours forever? Yes. But there are certain procedures you MUST follow. DO NOT leave the set with your favorite suit, because you may cost someone their job. Ask the Costumer how to go about it. Sometimes you're given the opportunity to purchase the clothing at a reduced fee. Sometimes you may even have it in your contract that the clothing will be yours. Even so, don't walk away with it until you've cleared it. Make arrangements with the production office in advance, so Wardrobe is notified. Remember: there may be retakes or inserts and the production company has to be covered.

> *Many actors ask the Costumer for their wardrobe, or simply take it at the end of the show, saying that it was "in their contract" or that "the producer said it was okay." Again, this makes it difficult for the Costumer. No one wants to get into a tug of war in the parking lot.*
> — Margo Baxley

Ms. Baxley's point is well taken. Sometimes you may be able to make arrangements to borrow an item of clothing for an awards program or a talk show. By all means try to arrange it. But think carefully if it's really a good idea.

> *I once arranged to borrow a certain red sweater dress that I'd worn in an episode of "Silver Spoons." I wore it for my appearance on the Johnny Carson show and felt terrific because I looked like a million bucks. Johnny said, "Let's run a clip," and there I was, wearing exactly the same red dress. I was mortified. Johnny had a field day.*
> — Erin

A final word. Remember that when all is said and done, it's you who is going to be on film, not the wardrobe person. So, take an interest and take some responsibility for detail. It's something like what you learn in traffic school. Yes, you had the right of way. No, it wasn't your fault that the person drove into the crosswalk at that moment. But the bottom line is, if you're injured or your car is damaged, you still have to deal with it. And who wants to be an accident victim?

ARRIVING ON SET

Covered In This Chapter:

- What to Wear

- Checking In

- Sequence of Events

> "Love the art in yourself, not yourself in the art."
> – Constatin Stanislavski
> As quoted by Ving Rhames
> 1997 Golden Globe Award Ceremony

ARRIVING ON SET

You've analyzed your script, memorized your lines, and prepared yourself for this first day of shooting by going to bed early. Of course, you set three alarm clocks to make sure you wake up in time for your call, and you studied the map the night before and wrote down the directions, so you know exactly when and where you are expected. (Right??)

WHAT TO WEAR

First, a quick note, here, regarding what to wear to work. It may seem unimportant, because, of course, you'll soon be in costume. But remember, you may not be in costume all day. You, yourself, will have some clothing requirements only you can take care of.

Some suggestions: Dress simply. This is neither the time nor place for women to wear spike heels and a tight skirt, nor for men to show chest hair and bulging thighs. You're on the set to work, not to sell yourself. Wear something that's easy to get on and off so you don't interfere with hair and make-up. Leave your turtlenecks at home. Bring a jacket, especially if you're working on location. You may be there late. You may be outside longer than you expect to be. Be prepared.

Assuming you've done all this and have now shown up at the right place and at the right time, you've arrived either at a studio or at a location. If today's shooting is at a studio, you'll have a drive-on pass. Give the guard at the gate your name and the project you're working on and the guard will tell you the stage number where you're expected. You'll also be told where to park. Take these instructions seriously! People are very possessive about their parking spaces and may have worked years to earn one. DON'T park in the producer's spot. It could mean death, or what's worse – the end of the job. Even if you don't offend your producer, your car may end up being towed. You may be bused or vanned from the assigned parking lot to the set.

CHECKING IN

The first thing to do when you arrive at the set or location for the first day's shoot is to <u>check in</u>. This is VITAL.

- If you're working on a Soap, check in with the Stage Manager. On a Soap there is no Second A.D., so the Stage Manager is the key person, acting as First A.D. and Second A.D., and is also Stage Manager in the theatrical sense of the term.
- If you're working on a sitcom check in with either the Stage Manager or the Second A.D. – check to learn the protocol for the show you're working on.
- If you're working in episodic, TV movie, or feature film, check in with the Second A.D. Remember, this is probably the person you spoke to on the phone a night or two ago. Of course, you did write down his or her name, right? So now you can look up your old telephone pal and introduce yourself in person.

Remember that this person's going to be an important ally for the duration of the project. To explain the hierarchy a little – the Director is, of course, responsible for everything that gets on camera. The First A.D. never leaves the Director's side and therefore seldom leaves the immediate perimeter of the set. It's the Second A.D. who knows what scene is being shot, who's required for that shot, how much time you have before you're needed and therefore, how much time you have to go over your lines or get into make-up. You will not necessarily be kept up to date automatically. Take it upon yourself to know where you're supposed to be, and when, and in what state of readiness.

The first thing the Second A.D. will give you is your Call Sheet. If this person fails to give it to you, ask for it. This little piece of paper is your condensed encyclopedia, your itinerary for today's journey, your passport, your visa, your identification – and any other important document metaphor you can think of. We've devoted a chapter to it, in case you're not familiar with the format.

The second thing the Second A.D. will give you is your Sides for the day, probably in an extremely condensed form. These new small-sized pages are great for sliding into a back pocket, but entirely useless for those of us who can't read type that small. However, it's a good (little) reference to have.

Refer to your schedule and watch when you're needed, but this may be a good time to introduce yourself to other crew members. We find it's always good to cultivate whatever personal connections you can with people one-on-one. You may take the opportunity to talk with someone in the sound department. Again, we've devoted a chapter to this important topic. This can be the starting point – not only for a conversation, but for a relationship.

If your call is early, the Second A.D. will next probably ask you what you'd like to eat for breakfast. This may seem like a nicety, but it's practical from their point of view, because they don't want you looking around for scrambled eggs, they want you in make-up or in wardrobe getting ready.

As the day progresses, the Second A.D. will also know if there are last minute changes to the script or to the day's sequence of shots. In case you're reading this book out of sequence, we've provided detailed information on this vital document in the Scripts chapter. Be sure to refer to this.

SEQUENCE OF EVENTS

Depending upon whether you're working in a sitcom or drama or soap, the exact sequence of make-up/wardrobe/rehearsal will vary. The main thing to remember is that you must take responsibility for finding out when to get your make-up done.

Don't assume someone will always be there to give you advance warning. Indeed in soaps, there will not be anyone to warn you, because the stage manager is busy with the scene that's being shot.

Even if you have four hours before you're expected on the set – get yourself to Wardrobe (with whom you will probably already have spoken on the phone), and to Make-up and Hair. There are several good reasons for this. First of all, this will ensure that the wardrobe and make-up people know you're present and accounted for. If there're four people who need to get their make-up on for a shot previous to yours, then they will ask you to wait. That's fine. Generally, you'll wait in your trailer or dressing room, and the Trainee PA (Production Assistant), Second A.D., or Second Second A.D. will come retrieve you at the appropriate time.

Normally, your costume will be hanging in your dressing room or trailer. If you're playing a regular character, you probably will have a regular dressing room, although on Soaps the huge casts necessitate multiple use of dressing rooms, so you'll be assigned one for the day, or the portion of the day you are working.

If your costume isn't there, don't run all over the place trying to find it. Notify the Second A.D. and have him/her track it down for you. Remember that it is your job to be where you can easily be located at all times. It is his/her job to take care of all manner of details and they have the walkie-talkies to prove it.

The usual order of things is to get into wardrobe first, then make-up, then hair. This may vary somewhat depending upon the amount of time you have to wait before your scene.

> On my first day of work on my first job, when that kind-hearted make-up lady had walked by me and seen my blank and helpless expression, she tactfully recommended that if I was working in this picture, maybe I'd like to get some make-up on. I took her advice and found out that in movies you had make-up trailers, not just a make-up table at the side of the set. Once I found the trailer, I sheepishly asked if someone could do my make-up. "What's your name, honey?" one of them asked. When I told them, they then checked the call sheet. "Oh," they said. It was their turn to be sheepish. I was starring in this mini-series. Only the head make-up person was allowed to "do" me. In five minutes I'd found out there was such a thing as a make-up trailer, such a thing as

a call sheet and such a thing as a definite pecking order on the set.
— Erin

When you're all ready, you may then have a three-hour wait. You may have, therefore, removed your skirt or trousers to avoid wrinkling them; you have probably smeared some of the make-up under your eyes; and your hair may have become disheveled. You may even fall asleep.

The first television job I got was a co-starring role in "The New Twilight Zone." Since my background was in the theatre, I wasn't familiar with the way things went in television. My first dilemma was that we were going to be shooting in Calabasas. I had no idea where that was, but judging from the map, I was going to need hours to get there. I had a 7am call, so I got up at 3am, left the house at 4am, and arrived at the location three hours before the teamsters, the trucks, the crew, or anyone was there. The crew finally arrived, I was given breakfast, they got me into make-up and costume and I was all set. In the theatre, when you're ready to go on, you generally have little or no delay. You're ready, you go on stage. Well, my first shot didn't happen till 1pm. After my make-up and costume were done, I went to my trailer to wait. And wait. And wait. Having not slept much the night before in my excitement at doing my first major television role — and having gotten up in the middle of the night — I fell asleep. This wasn't just a nap. This was deep sleep. I didn't have enough experience at the time to have asked the A.D. to awaken me with any kind of advance warning. So they came to get me just moments before I went on the set. I was in a daze. I walked and talked as though I was walking through a dream. When I look at the program now, all this is obvious to me. I look exactly like I just woke up. Truth shows.
— Chuck Stransky

On soaps there's generally no waiting, because you have only one day to get through an entire show.

> *My first day on "Days Of Our Lives" my call was at 6am and we were expected to be on stage for blocking as soon as we arrived. After that I had no idea where I was supposed to be, or when. So I tried not to make a pest of myself, but I asked a lot of questions. I found out no one was going to call me for make-up. I had to figure out a schedule with the make-up department myself, making sure not to miss any rehearsals for my scenes. Sometimes it was difficult because all the other actors were doing the same, so the make-up room could get very crowded.*
>
> —Mara

Depending upon the schedule, at this point you'll probably be asked to attend rehearsal. When your rehearsal time comes, cherish the moments, which may be few. You will need to take this opportunity to familiarize yourself with the set and the furniture and think about — and ask for — whatever props you envision for your character.

This is also your chance to talk to your Director. Again, bear in mind that your moments with your Director are precious. Don't waste his or her time, or your own. Without attempting to have a long, philosophical discussion, convey your ideas about the scene and ask how he or she plans to shoot it.

The ways in which a scene can be shot may be new to you. If we use a term before we define it, you might want to refer to the glossary of terms at the end of the book. One such term is the "Master shot," which is exactly what it sounds like. The master shot encompasses all the actors and their surroundings, so that the audience understands where the action is taking place.

The Director will have already made choices about his or her shots: how much time to spend on the Master shot, for example, when to cut away from that to a "Two Shot" (a shot which includes two actors) and when to cut away to a close-up.

We want to make an important point here. We are not advocating that you assess how a Director is going to shoot a scene, and then decide where and when you'll do your "full" performance. For example, if you discover you won't even be on camera for part of the scene, but only your voice will be heard, we do not recommend you "phone in" your lines. On the contrary, everything you wish to convey in that scene will then have to be transmitted by what you do with your voice.

We simply believe an informed performer is a better performer. We're convinced that your intelligence and preparation can add immeasurably to your own work, and to the overall project in which you're involved.

In the scene you're about to do, will the camera be moving? Will the scene be shot mostly as close-ups? How much time will be spent on the master shot? Will the master shot and the close-up be done at the same time? You'll think of many other questions. Use the information to enhance your work, not to diminish it.

You'll be taking in a tremendous amount of information today. Do your best to be patient with yourself, alert, courteous to all your co-workers be they cast or crew. Be professional at all times. You'll be making a first impression today, and you can either enhance or damage your reputation.

And a final word — this is your first day at work on a professional set. You'll remember it always. Enjoy it!

CALL SHEET

Covered In This Chapter:

- Introduction

- Line-by-line Explication of Example

Call Sheet — Act Right

> *Freedom is the will to be responsible for ourselves.*
> — Friederich Nietzsche

> The call sheet is the next day's game plan. It accounts for everything going smoothly.
> — Wade Simpson
> Writer; Second A.D.

THE CALL SHEET

Generally the Second A.D. will first give you your Call Sheet, which lists all the scenes to be shot for the day, including location, personnel and all pertinent details for each department involved in creating this film or episode.

The Call Sheet is your "Bible" for the day and everyone refers to it constantly. To save space, the Call Sheet is written in abbreviations, which will look like code to you until you begin to decipher it.

> *The call sheet is the next day's game plan. It accounts for things going smoothly. It will have everything from props needed that day, to where to park. The A.D.'s job is to look ahead to the next day and plan for everything. It keeps the work day free of nasty surprises.*
> — Wade Simpson
> Writer; Second A.D.

The first thing to look for on the Call Sheet is when you will first be needed. Check the scene you're in, when and where it's to be shot and know exactly when you're expected to show up on the set, camera-ready.

Following is a call sheet example and a specific line-by-line explication of how to read it. We know it's very hard to read and we apologize for that. However, we wanted you to struggle as we had to! No, not really. We just wanted you to have the genuine article.

Call Sheet — *Act Right*

Call Sheet

Viacom Productions Inc.
Office: 818 777-5139
Beep Set: 818 973-5270

CALL SHEET — 1ST Unit — 8th Day of Shoot

Series: JAKE AND THE FATMAN
No: 3610/11
Director: Russ Mayberry / Dan Attias
Episode: "I Know That You Know" — "Let's call the whole thing off"
Date: Tues 11-27-90
Exec Producers: F. Silverman / D. Hargrove / J. Steiger / B. Kowalski
Shooting Call: 7:30A / 8:30A
Condition: R/S
Producers: K. Ringwald / D. Abromowitz / R. Madden / B. Shurley
☑ Report to Location ☐ Bus to Location

Pages	Set Description	Scene No.	Cast No.	D/N	Location
1 5/8	INT. COURTROOM (Michael on witness stand)	18 THRU 21	1,2,3,6,7,9,11,12 D2 / 13 ATMOS	D2	STAGE #27
1 5/8	INT. COURTROOM (McCabe on ...) L.A. ... tilt shot	22, 22A, 23	1,3,5,6,7,9,11,13 / 1,2	D2	
	— Company move to Stage #24 —				
1/8	INT. HOTEL CORRIDOR (She goes to A. room)	63	6, 20 ATMOS	D7	STAGE #24
1 4/8	INT. HOTEL ROOM (Jill looking for Michael)	64	2, 6, 20	D7	
	— THE ADDITIONAL — STAGE 27 — PROD. #3611 —				
4/8	INT. HAGEE'S OFFICE (Jake calls in with his trouble)	54PT	1	D2	STAGE 27
4/8	INT. McGEE'S OFFICE (Jay McCabe ...)	72PT, 78PT	1 (MAX)	D-3	
4/8	INT. McGEE'S OFFICE	109PT	1 (MAX)	D-4	
6 4/8 TOTAL PAGES	NO FORCED CALLS WITHOUT PRIOR APPROVAL OF UNIT PRODUCTION MANAGER				

Cast #	Cast	Character	S/W R/TH	Make-up	Set Call	Report To
1	William Conrad	J.L. McCabe	WF	7:30A	8:30A	Plv @ 7:00A
2	Joe Penny	Jake Styles	WF	W/N	W/N	W/N
3	Alan Campbell	Derek Mitchell	WF	7:00A	8:30A	Rpt Stg 7:00
5	Charles Frank	Michael	WF	7:00A	8:30A	Rpt Stg
6	Erin Gray	Jill	WF	6:30A	8:30A	Rpt Stg 6:30
7	Diane McBain	Abigail	WF	6:30A	8:30A	
9	Gerald Anthony	Tommy	WF	7:00A	8:30A	Rpt Stg 7:00
11	Arlene Stern	Laura	WF	6:30A	8:30A	Rpt Stg 6:30
12	Lawrence Allen	Judge	SWF	7:00A	8:30A	Rpt Stg 7:00
13	Vivian Ann	Jury Foreman	SWF	6:30A	8:30A	Rpt Stg 6:30
20	Kelly Jeans	Julie	WF	9:00A		Rpt Stg 9:00
	Ron Stein	Utility Stunt	WF	—	—	
	Tod Keller	Utility Stunt	WF	—	—	

ATMOSPHERE AND STAND-INS

	Call Time	Report To
Gaber, Gorman, Roache, Edwards + 4	7:30A	Stg #27
11 Jury Members, 2 B.A., 4 S/I's		
35 Spectators, Lawyer's Asst, Stenographer	10:00A	

ADVANCE

Wed 11-28-90 #3611
- EXT COURTHOUSE SC. 17, 118 D 2/8
- EXT COURTHOUSE SC. 1,2,3,4 D 7/8
- EXT COURTHOUSE SC. 113 D 6/8
- EXT LOADING DK SC 6-27 D 14/8
- INT LOBBY SC 90, 110 D3
- LONG BEACH / CATALINA LIMITED

Thur 11-29-90 #3611
- EXT ROAD SC. 48 D2
- EXT ROAD SC. 49 D2 1/8
- INT JAKE'S CAR MM SC. 49 D2 14/8
- SC. 110 D3 3/8
- EXT JAGGER'S STORE SC. 33 D 1/8
- INT JEWELRY STORE & RESTROOM D 5/8

17716 Sierra Hwy

Erin Gray & Mara Purl

Act Right — Call Sheet

Production Company: Viacom Productions, Inc.

CALL SHEET

Office: Phone number
Beep Set: Phone number for beeping the set

1st Unit   8th Day of Shoot
First Unit:
Since you're an actor, you're involved in the First Unit shooting. (See "First Unit" in Glossary)
Eighth Day of Shooting:
When a series episode goes into its eighth day of shooting, this usually means it's gone over by a day. You can therefore infer that today will be pressured, with everyone trying to get the shots done as quickly as possible.

Series Name: JAKE AND THE FATMAN

No: Episode Number 3610/11
Each number is assigned. In this case "10/11" refers to the 10th and 11th episodes of the season. The "6" refers to the 6th season.

Director: Russ Mayberry (1)
Director: Dan Attias (2)
Two directors because two different episodes are being shot.

Picture: (Which in this case means "episode title")
    "I Know That You Know"   "Let's Call The Whole Thing Off"
Why are there two titles listed here? This tells you that in today's shooting schedule (the 8th day of shooting as we already know) the producers are hoping to finish one episode and begin the next. You may not be appearing in the subsequent episode, but this tells you that today's schedule is a very full one.

Date:

Executive Producer: F. Silverman/ D. Hargrove/ J. Steiger/ B. Kowalski
Why so many Executive Producers? This varies from project to project. Generally the first one listed is the studio executive responsible for the show, the liaison between the production company and the studio, which in this case is Fred Silverman. Since his name is first, it is he who hired the next person in line, who in this case is Dean Hargrove.

Call Sheet   Act Right

Silverman and Hargrove are partners: one of them came up with the project, one of them sold it to the network. The two of them then hired the next person listed, this being Joel Steiger. Steiger was hired to actually get the show produced. To do so, Steiger hired Bernard Kowalski, who assists him with the day-to-day producing responsibilities.

Shooting Call Time: 7:30 – 8:30
Why such a large window? What this means is that 8:30 is when they want cameras to start rolling. As an actor you must therefore be in the make-up chair by 7:30. The Director may also require a rehearsal, and if so, you'll be called out of make-up, or you'll be notified to arrive still earlier.

Condition: R/S Rain or Shine. Meaning you shoot no matter what.

Producer: K. Ringwald/ D. Abromowitz/ R. Madden/ B. Shurley
Don't we already have enough producers? Yes. There are many routes one can take to the "producer" credit. In some cases these people are the writers on the show who are given producing credit, particularly if they are regular writers for the series. In this case you'll note that B. Shurley is at the bottom of the back page of the Call Sheet as the UPM or Unit Production Manager. Refer to Glossary.

Report to Location   Bus to Location
As we explained earlier, this will tell you exactly how you'll be transported, or transport yourself, for work today.

Pages: 1 5/8
How many pages will be covered in this shot. Generally an hour episode is sixty pages long, so at a rough estimate one page plays one minute long. If you see a shot that's only 1/8th of a page unto itself, you'll know it's probably an establishing shot with no dialogue.

Note that at the bottom of the "Pages" column the total number of pages to be shot today is tallied. In this case , even though the producers are trying to cover a lot of ground, the 6 1/8 is not a particularly ambitious number for one day's shooting. If you must shoot sisty pages in one week, you must average about eight pages a day. Why as few as 6 1/8 today? Because the company has two stage changes, and this is time-consuming.

Set Description: Int. Courtroom (Michael on witness stand)
Int. stands for Interior. This is an interior scene, taking place in a courtroom. Ext. would stand for Exterior.

Scene No.: 18 thru 21

Although this says "scenes," this should more accurately say "shots." In the 1 5/8 pages to be shot, four separate shots will be done. They are grouped together, because together these shots form one sequence and involve the same actors and same location.

Cast No.: 1,3,5,7,9,11,12,13, Atmos.
Each cast member is assigned a specific number for the duration of the episode. These are enumerated further down the page.
Atmos. stands for Atmosphere (another word for Extras)
By referring to the list below, you will find your cast number. Take a moment to key this to the list of scenes to be shot. Circle or mark each scene in which your number is listed — you'll immediately know how many shots you're in today.

D/N: D2
Day/Night — this explains whether this is a Day Shoot or a Night Shoot
The "2" is not a shooting day number. It refers to the second day <u>in the story.</u>
This is a critical reference for all departments because of continuity. On the second day of the story a character might have a bruise that he didn't have the first day. On the fourth day of the story a character might wear a red suit; that same suit might become "damaged" in an action sequence which takes place on the seventh day of the story. As we've said — nothing is shot in sequence!

Location: Stage 27
Today's work begins on Stage 27. Note that the company will be moving twice today, "time permitting" — first to another stage, then back to 27, to begin work on the next episode.

The only thing we haven't explained in this section of the call sheet is the enigmatic reference to a mysterious character named "Max." He's not listed among the cast members. Why? Because he's the dog.

NO FORCED CALLS WITHOUT PRIOR APPROVAL OF UNIT PRODUCTION MANAGER
This is a standard union regulation.

Cast No.
The number assigned to each cast member. The star is of course number 1, the next star number 2, and so forth.

Cast
Each cast member's professional name.

Character
The character that actor plays in this series or episode.

SWF
S = Start
W = Work
F = Finishes
SWF indicates that this person started work, and finished, on the same day, or in other words, that they have been hired to work for only one day.

H TR
H = Hold
This means the actor is being "Held," and is waiting to work. In some shooting schedules, a contingency is almost built in.
TR= Travel
This means the actor is travelling on this day.

Make-Up
The time you are to report to Make-Up. Make a careful note of this for yourself. Note that this really doesn't mean just make-up – it means wardrobe and hair as well. Make sure you have a sense of how much time you'll need for each.

You can actually learn quite a bit from noticing the make-up call time for each of the performers. The star (William Conrad) is called later than anyone else who appears in the first shot, in deference to the number of hours he must work each week. The next star (Joe Penny) isn't even given a make-up call time, but instead is listed as W/N which stands for "Will Notify," again in deference to his overburdened schedule. The last cast member listed, (Kelly Jones) is in the opposite situation. Her make-up call isn't until 9am, but she is on "Will Notify" status for her scene. This means the producers don't know when they'll shoot her scene, but they want her ready. She may wait for several hours before she actually works.

Set Call
The time you're due on the set. This tells you how much time they've allotted for you in Make-Up.

Report To:
P/U stands for Pick Up – this means these actors will be picked up by a studio limo, at the time listed.
Rpt. stands for Report – this means these actors must report on their own, as most performers do.

Utility Stunt
Note that stunt people are also listed in the cast section, though they are not given cast numbers, indicating their different status. Notice there is an "HF." That means they are being "Held" for a possible stunt; and they will also "Finish" that day.

Act Right   Call Sheet

Atmosphere and Stand-Ins
Gaber, Gorman, Roache, Edwards + 4

Since these names are typed, they are the regular stand-ins who work virtually every episode of this series. Hand-written are other stand-ins or atmosphere people who are needed for this episode.

Call Time
Note that this is listed as call time, rather than make-up time. This is because they are expected to do their own make-up, and are expected to be ready by their call time.

Report To: 27
Tells them where to go, in this case a certain Sound Stage.

ADVANCE
This explains what will be going on for the subsequent two days. Although some things may change, this is a projection so everyone can make plans for the rest of their week. Note that scenes, number of pages, and location are all listed.

Call Sheet — Act Right

Viacom Productions, Inc.

PRODUCTION REQUIREMENTS

Picture: "JAKE and the FATMAN"
Director: Russ Mayberry / Attias
Prod. No.: 3610
Shooting Call Time: 7:30A / 8:30A
Date: Tues. 11-27-90

NO	ITEM	TIME	NO	ITEM	TIME		
PROD			**SOUND**				
1	UNIT PROD MGR Shurley	o/c	1	MIXER Alper	7:30A		COORD
1	ASST DIR Forrest	7:30A				2	CAPTAINS Reed/Frear
1	2nd ASST DIR Schilz	7:30A	1	MIKE BOOM Baker	7:30A	1	Caterer
1	2nd ASST DIR Paul	10:12A	1	CABLE Osburn			INSERT CAR
	ADD'L 2nd AC S			SOUND PACKAGE		1	CAM SOUND TRUCK
1	Prod Coord Pytlak	o/c		RADIO MIKE			CHAPMAN CRANE
2	SCRIPT SUPR Otto/Evans	7:30A		PLY BCK OPER			FORKLIFT CONDUR
	TECH ADV			PLY BCK MACH		1	PROD VAN
1	DIR PHOTO Flinn III	7:30A	10	WALKIE TALKIES	TRK	1	Greens (as needed)
1	CAM OP McGinness		1	PROP MSTR Wilson	o/c		PROP TRUCK
1	1st ASST CAM Kowalski		1	Prop Mstr Fannon	7:30A		UTILITY TRUCK
1	2nd ASST CAM Sweeterman		1	Asst Props Picerni			SP FX TRUCK
1	EXT OP Hall		1	SET DECO Romer	o/c	1	Set Dress Van
1	EXT ASST Baum		1	SetDesign Santiago			STATION WAGONS
	STILLMAN		1	Leadman Finley	o/c		Const Trx as need
	CAMERAS		1	Swing Gang Osmond	o/c	3	MAXI VANS (for scout)
			1	Drp/Swg Pickering	o/c	1	Office car
			1	MKP ART Moschella	6:30A		BUSSES
			1	Mkp Art. Inzerella	W/N	1	Crew Cab (const)
1	KEY GRIP Ahuna	7A	1	Mkp Art. Altobelli	6:30A	2	CREW CABS
1	2nd GRIP Blair		1	Hair Styl Ferguson		1	GAS TRUCK/CREW CAB
1	DOLLY GRIP Phillips			BODY MKP Case	9:00A	1	MAKE UP TRLR
1	CO GRIPS Matthews			Add'l Hair Asst Her	6:12A		2 RM TRLR
	CRANE			CSTM Mgr. North			WARDROBE TRLR
	CRAB DOLLY		1	Set Cstm. Gilmore	o/c		CAR TRAILER
X	Pee Wee	TRK					WATER TRUCK
X	Hustler	TRK	1	Cstm. Women Sebela	o/c		HONEY WAGON
			1	SET COSTUMER Munoz	o/c		ADD GENE
1	CRAFT SERV Klein	6:30A	1	Seamstrs. Michael	o/c		SCHOOL TRLR
	GREENSMAN			MUS REP			MOTOR HOMES
2	Mlv Tables Hood	6:00A		SIDE MUS			CAST TRLRS
	PAINTER			SINGERS		1	Motor Home Conrad
1	SPEC EFFECTS Hessey	o/c				1	Motor Home Penny
				ART DIRECTOR Montejano	o/c		Set Dr Trx as need
			1	Gang Boss Thomas	o/c	1	FX Crew cabs
				CONST COORD Miyata	o/c		
1	FIRST AID Clarke			CONST FOREMAN Cordova	o/c		Picture cars
	AMBULANCE			PROPMAKERS Bahn	o/c		
				Labor Fmn. Johnson	o/c		
	GAFFER Chaidu	6:30A		Painter Fm. Osborn	o/c		
1	BEST BOY Wooten			Loc.Mgr Liuzzi/Cas	o/c		
1	Universal Elec.		X	POLICE FOOT	o/c		
3	Marshall,Stanford,		X	POLICE W/CYCLES	o/c		
2	Bateman			FIRE WARD			
	LOC 840		X	FIREMAN	o/c		
	GENERATOR		X	Watchman, Pkg Lot	o/c		
	WIND MACH			Quad Dressing on Set			TRAINER
1	CueCards Maginnis	4:00A		Security Postmus	W/N		WRANGLER
1	CueCards Tucker			Dialogue Peebles	W/N		ANIMALS
X	BRKFST RDY @	6:30A	1	Auditor Loi	o/c		
	BOX LUNCH		1	Asst.Aud Baxter	o/c		
	HOT LUNCH READY @		1	Prod Sec Aiya	o/c		OPERATORS
	DINNER READY @		1	Office PA Uzen	o/c		CAM BOAT
							SAFETY BOAT
X	CATERER	o/c					PIC BOATS

DEPARTMENT — **SPECIAL REQUIREMENTS**

Props — Stunts Tare w/ Wrangler

Note — 2 Mlv Tables hook up 6:00A
Auto br. item cooler @ 6:30A in 7

NOTE: HGX - PROD # 3611 —

Asst Director: Blevins / Schilz / Faul
Unit Manager: Bruce Shurley
Approved:

BACK PAGE – Crew Call Sheet & Production Requirements.
This page is for use by the crew, but you will find it useful to understand much of this information as well. Note that many of the terms used on this sheet are listed in the Glossary of this book, and therefore will not be explained again here.

Along the left margin written horizontally you'll note departments are separated – Camera, Production, etc. The first column gives you a numerical value which will tell you, for example, whether you have 1 or 2 captains, etc. The Item column gives you specific crew title with the names of the crew members. The Time column tells you when they must report. The last column tells you everything about transportation and animals. Some abbreviations:
W/N = Will Notify
O/C = On Call
You might find it useful to know when catering service will have breakfast ready. Look in the Meals department where it says BRKFST. RDY @ 6:30a – that of course means that breakfast will be ready at 6:30. Good to know!

Department/ Special Requirements
Every department that has anything special to bring or prepare for today's shooting is listed here. Under props, for example, a reminder is given that an "evidence table" is needed for the courtroom scene.

Note that "Max" appears again – yes it's the doggie, just so you know.

MAKE-UP & HAIR

Covered In This Chapter:

- Respecting the Hierarchy

- Arriving at Make-Up

- Your Ideas & Theirs

- Personal Behavior & Hygiene

- Nudity

- Special Effects Make-Up

- Set Protocol

Pay more attention to the acting than to the make-up and hair. Actors would rather look good than do the show! That drives the production crew crazy.

— Abby Singer
Producer

Excellent Make-up and hair can make the difference between decent pictures and phenomenal pictures.

— Lesley Bohm
— Photographer

MAKE-UP

RESPECTING THE HIERARCHY

As is the case in every department, there's a hierarchy in both Make-up and Hair. You'll want to introduce yourself to the heads of those departments and then you'll find you may or may not be working directly with those individuals.

Here's some advice which applies to every department on a shoot, but this is a good place to give it to you. Bear in mind that the crew has generally been hired before the cast has been, and many crew members have the ear of the Director, the Producers, or all of the above. As such, how you treat your crew members will almost invariably get back to the "higher-ups." So be courteous at all times, under all circumstances. We find a good rule is to treat craft services the same way you would treat the Executive Producer. And you know what? It's more fun that way. You never know who you're talking to — he or she could be a spectacular human being and your future best friend.

> *I mentioned once to a producer that a new cast member had been rude to a craft services person. The actor was fired. I felt terrible, but it seems I was not the first, but rather the fourth crew member who had mentioned the rudeness.*
> *— Anonymous Crew Member*

Your make-up person is one of the first crew members you'll be working with and many times he or she will remain a permanent liaison between you and the Director. In fact, if your relationship goes well, your make-up person can become a valuable advocate when you need extra time, or you need some help. Let's say you stayed up too late the night before and your dark circles are showing. Who is going to solve that problem for you? Your make-up artist is your only hope.

ARRIVING AT MAKE-UP

There are so many things to remember on and around a set and we don't mean to overburden you with details. But then again, details are the things that will forge – or ruin – the all-important working relationships you have with the other professionals. For example: many times the make-up room is in fact a trailer. So here's your first rule of protocol: when you enter or exit a make-up trailer, you will cause the trailer to bounce a little, even if you're an eighty-nine-pound wonder. If the make-up person is working on someone's eye at that moment, it could mean that a sharp pencil does damage. So – when you arrive, in your enthusiasm for your latest take, don't bound in. Take it easy. Announce yourself when you enter by saying: "Stepping up!" Or when you leave by saying: "Leaving!" or "Watch the eyes!" It will be appreciated – and noticed.

Once you're in the make-up room or trailer, why not stand around and make small talk? Isn't this your chance to begin to establish your popularity? Not necessarily. If you start talking with someone the make-up people are trying to work on, this can be so distracting that the make-up professionals will want to bodily throw you out.

> *If someone is going to talk while having their make-up done, I need to have them do it through the mirror. I can't have the actor turning around in my chair, even if he's talking to the Producer. In fact, recently the Executive Producer on a project was standing in my position – to the left of my chair. What happened? Well, that actor was twenty minutes late getting on the set. When the Line Producer complained about it, I pointed out that it had been the Executive Producer who had caused the delay himself.*
>   – Dee Dee Altamura

Adhere to a simple but powerful general rule: never stop the flow of work. Producing a film is a tremendously complex team effort, and each person's job is every bit as important as yours, even if you're the star. Remember that, and respect the total effort, not just your own.

When it does come time for you to have your make-up done, this is the time to begin some small talk. You may feel free to converse with everybody in the room, be it fellow actors, or make-up personnel. Again, bear in mind that you don't want to move too much while they're trying to do your eyeliner. Furthermore, you don't want to be too familiar or too open. A word to the wise — you do not yet know your fellow travelers in what may be a challenging voyage. We find a general rule in life is to listen at least twice as much as you talk.

What you do want to do, is to make your make-up person your friend if at all possible. If you're a woman, you will first have a difficult hurdle to overcome — that of allowing someone else to do for you, what you have been doing expertly yourself for several years. Treat this as a golden opportunity to learn new techniques and further explore the contours of your own face and how to enhance its best features.

YOUR IDEAS & THEIRS

Remember that your make-up person is a professional just as you are and may have prepared just as much for his or her job as you have for yours. He or she may have wonderful insights into your character and how best to bring forth your character's qualities. Ask for these ideas, and allow your make-up professional to share them with you. If you're playing a role close to yourself, these may be subtle; if you're doing science fiction or horror, these may involve complex prosthetics or unusually creative touches.

Whichever the case, take their ideas into consideration before you voice your own. You may feel that you're completely clear about your character and know exactly what shade of blush and what shape of liner is going to work. Well, you should have that kind of clarity about every aspect of your work and certainly you should come to this part very well-prepared. However, if someone were able to offer you a valuable perspective that you might not have come to yourself, wouldn't you be pleased to have it and wouldn't it be to your advantage to utilize it — whatever its source? Furthermore, here you have a chance to gain two advantages in one stroke — gain a valuable insight and make a friend.

There has to be communication about the character. Hopefully the actor will discuss with the director certain points. Communication about the character is key. Recently, I was working on a project, and two of the actors and I discussed their parts and decided that since these two had known each other since age seventeen, they would have matching tattoos. On another project, I worked with an actor and we decided to put a mole over an eyebrow and to contour his face. The thing is that make-up can be such a help to a character. Let's get into this. If you talk it through — sometimes we'll try something and decide if it works or not. You have a mouth — open it up. Tell me what's working... I want to hear your ideas. It has to be a collaborative effort.

— Dee Dee Altamura

She makes a valuable point. Acting is all about layering. You knew that. Well, here's a way to add another layer, to have a foundation meaningful to you. Those tattoos may or may not have been prominent on camera, but for the two actors, it gave them an added sense of reality and that did show on camera.

If you have a particularly strong idea about make-up for a certain part, and if you order your make-up person to make you up a certain way, no doubt he or she will comply, but you will probably have missed out on gaining an ally. Worse than that, you may have made an enemy.

This is particularly true if you happen to be working on a series, be it a day or night-time program. Remember that the make-up and hair people are there episode after episode, year after year. They've seen many a star come and go.

If you're very certain of the colors that are good for you, or have particular skin sensitivities, find a diplomatic way to share this information with your make-up person. Some actresses prepare a special make-up box or bag and offer it to the make-up person to use or incorporate with their own materials. Many times the make-up person will have excellent ideas and may know things you would not have thought of. But you may know your skin tones or skin type better than they do and if you've already done your homework on this, you can save yourself the problem of a chalky face or a skin rash by discussing this frankly with the make-up professional.

You can take this a step further if you're starring in a feature or a series. If you know you're going to need a certain base, for example, you can request that the make-up person buy this as a part of the production budget, rather than your having to supply it from your own pocket. Of course, this isn't appropriate if you're working for one day on a show — so use your own judgment about appropriate behavior.

PERSONAL BEHAVIOR & HYGIENE

If you have any allergies, take responsibility for this situation and bring your own moisturizer or base, or whatever your dermatologist has prescribed. Again, if you're going to use a lot for this shoot, you can discuss this with your make-up person and it can probably come out of the production budget.

You need to be aware of what alcohol does to your system: Alcohol shows up first on your face and your make-up artist will be the first to see it.

> *I can spot alcohol a mile away. It makes the face puffy and that's a hard thing to fix. I carry products which will help reduce the swelling under the eyes, but it can take some time. Don't drink the night before you're shooting.*
> — Dee Dee Altamura

A word about boundaries. Nothing can be more annoying to a make-up artist than an actor who walks by the make-up table and starts to use things without permission. That make-up artist may have searched the city for a particular brush or pair of tweezers and doesn't want it lost or misplaced. Have respect for their work materials, and keep your hands off.

Another critical boundary point has to do with hygiene. If you pick up a tube of blistex or a lipstick or eyeliner pencil and use it— congratulations, you now own it. Why? Because once it has touched your skin, it cannot touch the skin of another performer. So you have now caused the make-up person to search out a fresh supply, and there isn't always time or money to do so. Again, have respect for other people's property and for the production.

While we're on the subject of hygiene, there are a few things to be aware of. If a make-up person hands you some breath spray, say thank you and use it. They're not being cordial – they're doing you a favor and probably your partner in the upcoming love scene as well. And by the way, some camera operators have open boxes attached to the front of their camera dollies which contain goodies like breath mints. These are for you! Ask first, but then, help yourself.

And on the subject of bodily aromas, use deodorant, even if you are a European heart throb, or a renegade purist. In this country, your leading lady or man will expect to be concentrating on the love aspect of the scene, rather than on making his or her escape from your immediate vicinity.

Here's another important rule: **be prepared for anything**. For both men and women, this can mean shaving.

For women, be sure to shave whatever parts are going to be exposed anywhere in the script, because the shooting schedule can change and it's not up to the make-up artist to provide you with a razor, nor is it the producer's responsibility to give you the time to shave your legs, or get yourself waxed.

For men, a general rule is to be clean-shaven, unless you know specifically that a beard of some kind, or a 3-day growth is required. Being clean-shaven is the surest way to match from shot to shot, day to day. And bear in mind that if you shoot at night – either on a film, or if you're in a sitcom – shave at about 3:30 in the afternoon, so that by 11pm you're not dealing with a shadow problem. Also, of course, be aware of matching. For example, don't shave your mustache in the middle of a project. You might want to be aware of that, if you normally have a tan as well – you don't want to suddenly give yourself a white upper lip compared with the rest of your face.

Be aware that if you're doing a love scene, or a kissing scene and you're sporting a 3-day growth, it's likely that the woman you're working with is going to wind up with beard-burn. Aside from being painful and unpleasant, this can seriously interfere with the shooting schedule. She can't shoot if she has a major rash on her face. So when you're discussing the beard/no beard options with your make-up artist, think about the script and the problems which may arise.

The topic of love scenes brings up a difficult subject — herpes. There are two kinds. There's herpes simplex virus I (HSV1), which is orally transmitted and generally appears facially as a cold sore. And there's HSV2, which is sexually transmitted and usually appears as outbreaks on the derriere, or other more private parts.

We were amazed to learn how prevalent this problem has become on sets and fascinated to discover how the film & TV community is dealing with it. It has become a serious problem, because (a) a person with a herpes outbreak on their face or exposed buttocks cannot be shot — herpes cannot be successfully covered with make-up and (b) a person with a herpes outbreak cannot kiss — or have other intimate contact with — a fellow actor, without risking transmission of the virus.

Production companies have been forced to shut down for two or three days to allow actors to recover. This is not acceptable to insurance companies. So the solution at present is that actors are required to take an anti-viral drug either at the initial onset of the condition, or even before, if they're considered "high risk." If taken at the onset, all these drugs can do is shorten the course of the outbreak. If taken regularly, there is some evidence that some outbreaks can be suppressed.

Herpes outbreaks are generally brought on by stress. And as we all know, shooting can be stressful! So — if you're aware that this problem might arise for you, handle it immediately. Be prepared to get a prescription for the required medication, or work with your alternative medicine remedy right away. If possible, don't force the production to wait a day while you recover.

NUDITY

The shooting of love scenes brings up another important matter, and that is handling nudity. Some of this discussion belongs in another chapter — for example, negotiating how much nudity you will or will not agree to contractually. But for now we're focusing on make-up and we do have a couple of stories from that are humdingers to share with you.

> *Sometimes you have to protect yourself as an actor, if there are certain areas of the body you do not want exposed. I had heard horror stories where in the dailies the director says, "Oops, your breast is showing. Oh well, that's okay." It wasn't okay with me. So I took a tip from another actress and painted my buttocks with blue magic marker.*
>
> *— Kelly Bovino*

> *In Europe, nude scenes are practically routine, so it's terribly important to be clear about what you do and do not want exposed. Since most directors are not entirely trustworthy in this regard, my solution is visual. I put flaming orange tape on my penis and that means they can't include it in the shot.*
>
> *— Peter Woodward*

We found these to be an extremely inventive solutions to a tricky problem and we commend our pals for their chutzpah and creativity. What does the blue magic marker or orange tape do? It provides a specific line which the Cinematographer must avoid. He or she therefore must leave that area out of frame. Not every actor has found it necessary to resort to such measures and our hope is that you will work with people who will respect your contract, and your wishes. But the bottom line is, you're the one whose skin is up there on celluloid or video and you need to take responsibility for what shows to whatever extent you can.

Body make-up (of a more conventional kind) is also something you should know about. Both men and women will have their skin covered in pancake or a similar product if it's going to be exposed. Nude to the waist is a very common requirement for men, so your chest will have to be done. Bathing suits and strapless dresses of various descriptions are common for women.

Be aware of the sun! You may think it's a swell idea to get a suntan, but keep in mind several things. First of all, if you're in the middle of a project, you must match. Don't rely upon the Make-up department to compensate for a burn or a tan line. Secondly, if your skin is damaged you'll have a life-long problem make-up won't necessarily solve, so consider your skin an important tool for your work — and a critical investment.

And now a word about tattoos. If you have a tattoo, unless it's extremely small, and/or extremely intimate, it can be a problem. Your tattoo may be right for you, but not right for your character. This is a very personal matter, but if we have any advice at all, it is not to limit yourself in ways where you have a choice.

If it's already too late and you have a tattoo, you must bring this up in your discussion with the Make-up person, for two reasons. One, some tattoos are easier to cover than others, but in any case, he or she will need to have the right body make-up for you. And two, he or she is definitely going to need extra time to handle covering a tattoo.

> *My agenda is how long it takes me to get from point A to point B. If you come in with an angel tattooed on your ass, I need to plan accordingly.*
> *— Dee Dee Altamura*

SPECIAL EFFECTS MAKE-UP

If you're doing a science-fiction or a horror piece, chances are you'll have some extra make-up requirements, which might even include prosthetics. These require all kinds of special attention and a great deal of planning on the part of your make-up artist. If you're wearing a prosthesis, you'll have special fittings and once shooting begins, you'll have to take special care not to disturb your make-up, no matter how uncomfortable you may be.

> *The most intense make-up experience I ever had was being made up for "Star Trek." I was screen-tested to play Saavik in "Star Trek III" (it came down to Robin Curtis and myself). The great make-up artist, Wes Dawn, did our make-up, and I had to be in the chair by 4am to become a Vulcan. The edges of my eyebrows were shaved so the extreme angle could be added. My skin was given an unusual cast (including neck and hands). And, of course, there were those famous ears. It takes a long time to be made up for this kind of role. I used the time as a Vulcan meditation, going deeply into my own space. By the time the make-up was complete, I had been transformed into a Vulcan not only externally, but internally as well. As a result, I found idle chitchat was impossible. It would have been illogical.*
>
> *– Mara*

Of course, some sci-fi make-up is much more extreme, causing all kinds of problems from outbreaks to allergies. Removal of prothetics can cause terrible skin damage, so be sure to get expert advice if you find yourself playing an alien.

SET PROTOCOL

So, you've established your relationship with your make-up artist, and you're all ready to start shooting. If you need to say anything to this person, he or she will be with you on the set, right? Wrong. Or — not necessarily.

Once you've started the shooting day, you probably won't spend time in the make-up chair again until after lunch. However, you'll have continuing contact with one or more of the make-up crew members. Especially on a big shoot, there may be several make-up people, and the one assigned to you while you're on the set might not be the person in the trailer. So, take a deep breath, and start all over again, sharing the particular things you want help with.

Understand it's their job to be sure you look right before every shot, so they'll be scrutinizing you to see if you need powder, or a re-blend under the eye. You may find this annoying or distracting – here you are trying to create your moment, and people are fussing at you from head to toe. The sound man is adjusting your mike, the prop person is handing you a wallet to put in your back pocket, the hair person is spraying you and the make-up person is looking up your nose. Don't be alarmed. It's all in a day's work.

> *If we look at them, it's not to break their concentration. This is my job. What happened to me on one show was that an actress's individual false eyelash fell off and stuck to her cheek. When the Director and crew were watching Dailies, all they could see was this eyelash flapping. It cost $80,000 to reshoot that day.*
> *— Dee Dee Altamura*

If you know or think you need a touch-up, there are appropriate ways to ask for one. First of all, know your make-up artist's name. Second, don't yell "Make-up!" It's disrespectful. Ask the First A.D. or Stage Manager to find her or him for you.

> *One thing I like to do when I first encounter on-set make-up people is to review a few of my idiosyncrasies. I tell them, for example, that I have a bad habit of touching my nose and licking my lips. I ask them to help me out with these – watch out for a slightly red nose or slightly bare lips. I also hate to discover black mascara has strayed beneath my eyes, so I ask that they be diligent in watching for this problem. Lastly, I find that on a long day, powder can build up and create creases. So I ask that they go easy on the powder, or use blotting paper, or a delicate brush or some other technique to ensure this doesn't happen.*
> *— Erin*

We find asking for candid comments from both make-up and hair artists can be a great way of cultivating your relationships and immeasurably useful as the shooting continues. Wouldn't you want to be told if you were holding your head in such a way that you were giving yourself a double chin, or if your stomach was sticking out? If you've opened the door for these professionals to help you, they will. The good ones have the eyes of eagles and the hearing of canines. They don't miss a thing. They'll see and hear all kinds of details you can't because you're otherwise engaged.

At this point, we want to come back to the central theme of this book: collaboration. Remember this is a collaborative art, and as such you and all the other people working on this project are here to create something together. Each of us has a specific function and role to perform. In a race, the driver depends upon his pit crew to keep the car functioning perfectly and, indeed, without that crew, there is no race. Then too, without the driver, the car won't go anywhere. This is not the time for ego — this is the time for forging a team.

> The pit crew is what I call them. I want each department absolutely to be my eyes so when I'm intense in the scene, I can be in my character's heart and soul. My feeling about on-set make-up people — when it comes to emotional scenes is — don't say a word. Come in, clean up under my eyes and get out of my way. I am mentally jogging in place to get ready for the next take, so don't interrupt my energy. But take care of what you see that's wrong or needs fixing. In other words — always make me look fabulous.
> — Joan Van Ark

Joan always does look fabulous. And apparently one of her producers bought pink jumpsuits for her "crew" with the words "Joan's Pit Crew" printed on the back — so all of them looked fabulous too.

One of the important things you need to be aware of is correct behavior during and after lunch. Disturbing your make-up is unavoidable when you eat and your make-up artist is prepared to give you whatever touch-up you need before shooting starts again. But be considerate and don't have a food fight or intentionally smear your face or other parts of your body which are made up.

You may think you're going to need extra time to get your make-up redone after lunch. That's fine. But don't go to the make-up trailer early — that's also lunch hour for Make-up/Hair and they may need a nap or some down time. The right way to arrange for the extra time you need is to mention it to the Second A.D. and let him or her schedule it for you.

Don't have garlic during lunch! You'll annoy your cast and crew for the rest of the day. If for some reason you must, then use a product like *Breath Asure* to try to get rid of its lasting odor. Your colleagues will appreciate it, as one director told us:

> *One of the most unpleasant things an actor can do, is talk in my face with the horrible smell of garlic!*
> – Roger Cardinal

Some other gastronomic no-no's! Avoid foods that will discolor your tongue or mouth. Blue gelatto is not a good idea, for example, nor are red lollipops.

If you nap during your lunch hour, make sure not to sleep on your face! That can create a problem for make-up, for the cinematographer, and mostly for you. If you have a crease down your face, you can't shoot. We find it's not exactly a nap we need mid-day. It's quiet, meditative time. We imagine ourselves as Geisha reclining on lacquer pillows.

If you're a smoker, be very aware of both your lipstick and your breath. If you must run outside for a smoke, take your breath drops with you, and touch the cigarette lightly to your lips so your make-up person doesn't have to constantly touch you up. And if you find it necessary to sip a drink during shooting, ask for a straw. Chances are Make-up will have a stash, and will greatly appreciate that you asked.

How do you deal with lipstick during love scenes? Discuss this with the make-up artist. He or she will have a product like a pencil which will smear less than a cream lipstick. Not every kiss is scripted. If you and your co-star have suddenly decided upon a kiss, let your make-up artist know.

A final word about your lipstick — if your (real life) lover happens to be visiting you on the set that day and you think you can't resist that kiss — resist. You don't really want your kindly make-up person to have to start all over on those lips, do you? Your lover will respect you in the morning. And if he doesn't, get rid of him.

One last thing about make-up: it's an individual thing. One make-up artist told us, for example, that Shirley MacLaine does her own make-up and does it expertly. Only after the third day of the shoot did she trust the make-up artist to take over. Each performer must develop his or her own ideas. You might be surprised how much detail goes into this aspect of preparing for your role. We thought we'd share our individual approaches.

> *From years of modeling and acting, I know my face very well. I start my discussion with my make-up artist by giving my run-down. If I'm playing a role close to my own persona, I like a natural make-up with earth tones. I don't like white on my brow bone because it protrudes slightly. I don't like any brown or black eyeshadow close to the inside corner of my eyes, because it makes them look too close set. I like the eye shadow color at the outside corners. I don't need to have my nose contoured because it is naturally, and any additional contouring suddenly draws attention to it. If I'm doing a character who's under a lot of stress, I want the lip-liner to make the lips look a little pinched; if the character is sexy, I like a fatter lip-liner which makes the lips lush. Once I've gone through all this, I finish by inviting them to voice their ideas. Generally, they're very grateful for all this information, and they incorporate it into their own style of doing make-up.*
> — *Erin*

> *My make-up background comes from theatre, where you learn that an un-made-up face is a flat face. Contouring is the key to theatrical make-up and while you tone it down for film and TV, it's still basically the same technique. My sister and I are known (among other things) for the Purl nose. It's cute off camera, but on camera, it requires careful make-up. My cheekbones are so pronounced that they don't need much accentuation, I like to lift my eyebrows in the center with the slightest touch of pencil. I once found out the hard way that an orange cast foundation makes me*

look quite ill, so I know which colors work on me. I used to be timid about sharing this information, but gradually I learned that the more I opened up, the more my make-up artists opened up. So, although I shared a lot, what really happened was that I learned a lot more.

— Mara

After your make-up is done, your last job is to check it carefully in the mirror. Some make-up artists look directly at your face, but don't check the mirror — and things do look different in the mirror. It's what you see in the mirror that will be photographed — not what you see with the naked eye. If you need to, make minor adjustments yourself, or have your make-up artist make them.

If you do make an adjustment yourself, such as switching to a different shade of lipstick, be sure to offer the lipstick to the on-set make-up person so they can use it for touch-ups.

HAIR

Much of what we've said about make-up applies to hair as well — set protocol, preparation, respect for your hair artist.

Certain basics need to be mentioned. First and foremost, if you got the part wearing long hair, don't show up for your first day of work with a brand-new haircut. This can be a disaster! Your hair artist will have planned according to what he or she has been told about your hair. Don't make a change with no warning.

If you color your hair, it's best to get your own color done before you start shooting. Chances are you or your personal hair dresser know just how to get the color you want, and on the shoot, your hair artist won't necessarily have the time or budget to handle this. Of course, if this part requires a specific hair color, you must discuss this before shooting begins.

When it comes to hair, it's good to come in knowing what you want. As women, we've come to know the way our hair behaves and what products and techniques work best for us. And frankly, sometimes we know better than the hair stylist on the shoot, who's trying to take care of many people at once.

Again, communication is the golden rule here. Share your ideas, your knowledge, and your concerns. As a team you and your hair artist will come up with something wonderful for your part. If you don't communicate, the results can be disappointing.

> *When I was shooting "The Judge," the hair department put my hair in hot rollers. I mentioned several times that since my hair is naturally curly, it takes a curl in a New York minute and that if they left the rollers in too long, we'd have a curly mop head to deal with. They laughed and ignored me. When those rollers came out, my head looked twice its normal size! No amount of combing or brushing or spraying could calm it down.*
> *– Mara*

Hair requires a great deal of planning. You and your hair person must decide when and where your hair will change, and how much time these changes will require. You might want your hair straight in one shot and curly in another, but this may not be possible if your shooting schedule doesn't allow a day in between these two scenes.

You may be playing a role very close to your own type, in which case you may choose to do your hair more or less the way you normally do it. On the other hand, you may choose to do something radically different for this part, something that will enhance your sense of the character and give you a completely different look. Think about these options and discuss them with your hair person.

Some parts call for hairpieces or wigs and this is a special – and usually expensive – option. If this is what your part calls for, the piece or wig will have to be designed for you and that means color, size, style, and application. If you're using a hairpiece of any kind, be aware that it's the responsibility of the hair department to maintain it intact throughout the shoot. Don't rip it off your head! Carefully remove the pins if and when you have permission to do so. Don't fling it down on a table. Don't swirl it around your finger while you crack jokes on the set. This will not be appreciated, and will not go unnoticed. Respect the property being entrusted to you.

Every actress we know has her own techniques and her own equipment. Should you bring your bag of goodies with you on shooting day? You bet. Respect your hair person's territory, but if you understand your hair, nothing can supplant your twenty years of experience with your particular head of hair. Make your hair a collaborative effort.

Between shots, your hair may start to go south. If your hair is naturally straight, it'll tend to lose its curl or its shape. You might want to keep large Velcro rollers handy and put a few at the ends. If your hair is naturally curly, it'll tend to frizz. You might find a fat curling iron to be a perfect way to smooth it before your next take. If you have experimented with these things, and know what works, bring them and chances are you and your hair person will both be happy you did.

When your hair person has just finished doing your hair and you're ready to walk on the set, here's a good way to really annoy him or her: run your hands through your hair. There! Now you've done it!

But seriously — your hair person has structured your hair perfectly and is there to check you constantly. If you need reassurance, ask for a mirror. He or she will be happy to comply. But don't mess with your hair — let him or her do that. Even if touching your hair is a nervous habit — get over it. If you move things around, you've created problems that are time-consuming to fix.

Remember what we said about you never know who you're talking to? A whole lot of talking goes on in the make-up and hair departments. If your hair person also just happens to be sleeping with the director — it wouldn't be the first time.

Your news may go further than you intended. Don't make assumptions. Or better yet, do make one assumption: that everything you say will be repeated elsewhere, particularly the *negative* things you might have had to say.

PROPS

Covered In This Chapter:

- Hierarchy

- Property Department

- Your Input

- Props' Effect on Your Work

- Set Protocol

- Shooting with Props

I always meet with Props and Set because maybe the backdrops and surroundings say more than I could say in pages of dialogue.

— Joan Van Ark

PROPS

What's a prop? Anything you handle while working in character.

Okay, so what does an actor have to do with props? More than you might think. No, you're not in charge of finding the props for the shoot — there is, of course, an entire Property Department in charge of this. However, since you will be working with these objects, you need to know as much as possible about your interaction with them.

HIERARCHY

For starters, are you the lead in this project? Or are you a day player? If you're considered important to this piece, you'll have a proportionate amount of clout when it comes to props — and anything else. If you're lower down on the totem pole, you are not in a position to bother the Director with this level of detail. Feel your way on this.

> *If you're starring in a movie and have an idea about rolling a coin through your fingers in a certain scene, call the director and talk. No reason why not. If you're a day player with an idea about props, bring something in and talk to Props or Director, depending upon your opportunity. Understand the Director's level of focus and time. If you see the Director is "underwater" — a neophyte who's having desperate trouble keeping his act together — to introduce your prop problem is not going to go over well. In episodic or MOWs there's almost no rehearsal. Features and half-hour, you rehearse. Half-hour is like summer stock where you have a week to put it up. In half-hour, I encourage actors to start coming up with prop ideas from day one. I'm trying to figure out ideas, and appreciate the input.*
> *— Barnet Kellman*

PROPERTY DEPARTMENT

As with every other department, the Property Master and those who work with him or her have a great many responsibilities. Never assume that just because you think an object is lying around, that you may use it, move it, or even touch it. They'll have been thinking about the requirements for this project, and many objects will already have been chosen and acquired before your shoot begins.

Chances are, you won't be able to meet with someone from Props before you arrive on the set. If you've given thought to some particular props you'll need, most likely you will need to communicate with the prop department indirectly. The person to ask is your Second A.D. This might happen when you're on the phone with him or her the night before, or it might happen while you're having your Make-up done. At any point before your first take is scheduled – the sooner the better – try to discuss the plant, the briefcase, the pot-holder you think you'll need.

Remember that there are props and there are props. If you're playing a frantic executive and you feel you need a stack of messy file folders, manila envelopes, and computer print-outs, these are items the Props department probably has available. If, on the other hand, you think you require that a parrot be sitting on your shoulder in order to do your best work, the Props department may need some advance notice, and your Director may have something to say about it too.

YOUR INPUT

Of course, some props are absolutely essential, and there may be one that's central to your character or to the scene. If this is the case, most likely your Director and everyone else involved in the project has already thought of it. However, don't underestimate your own insights into your character. No one is plumbing the depths of that particular character to the extent that you are, so it's likely no one will come up with exactly what you need except you. Don't be afraid to discuss your ideas. Your Director may disagree, and your ideas may be rejected. Even if they are, the extent to which you've done your homework will show, and be remembered.

> *With Helen Hunt on "Mad About You," props feed her. It adds to the humor. I encouraged it, staged for it, and I brought in and introduced her to my favorite prop person. I gave them carte blanche."*
> — Barnet Kellman

PROPS' EFFECT ON YOUR WORK

Sometimes props can be a very important part of establishing the foundation you need to bring a sense of reality to a character. The best story we've ever heard along those lines was one told by Sam Waterston in a superb (and highly recommended) video about the Library of Congress called "Memory and Imagination." He was preparing to play the role of Abraham Lincoln and visited the Library of Congress to do some research. He approached the information desk and asked:

> *"Do you have anything here about Abraham Lincoln?" The woman at the desk looked at me like I was from Mars. And that's when I found out that the Lincoln presidential library is within the Library of Congress... (I saw) the contents of Lincoln's pockets on the night that he was assassinated. I made a list and I asked the prop department to give me facsimiles and they did...and I carried these things in my pocket, and this roots it in a kind of reality that no amount of reading could ever do.*
> — Sam Waterston

You may not find it necessary to have Abe Lincoln's glasses recreated. But you may've decided on something simple which you know your character would have. For women, almost every character has a purse, and your decision about the right purse for your character might be important. A reminder here — purses are not the responsibility of the Wardrobe department. They are considered props.

> *I give the prop person all my notes. For example, I might say "this character carries a tote which doubles as a briefcase and a purse." This is how this character organizes her things – that's why it's so important.*
>
> *– Joan Van Ark*

This is a good place to mention something about personal props. If you've done a lot of theatre, you know many times actors bring their own photographs or other personal items to give themselves a sense of reality on stage.

> *I had a long run in the two-character play "Sea Marks" by Gardner McKay – it's a very intimate love story between two people who write letters to each other over a period of time. My co-star and I each brought small framed pictures of each other to use on the set. It helped us both feel the longing our characters felt for each other and brought a sense of reality to the set. Most importantly, we had wrote the letters which became very important to our performances.*
>
> *– Mara*

This situation may come up in TV and film work as well. You may be asked for photos of yourself as a child or with family members, so the camera can make "your living room" look more realistic. Or you may decide that a certain leather briefcase is just what you need for that lawyer you're going to portray. If you do supply a production with a prop, understand that for the duration of the shoot, it's no longer yours – it's theirs. That means you don't take it home each night; you leave it in the hands of the prop department. So if you're worried about a precious antique, don't lend it to the production – show it to your prop master and have him or her replicate it, or search for something similar.

SET PROTOCOL

Once you're on the set, basic protocol – and stringent union regulations – indicate that unless you're a member of the props union, you must not move props. Remember this, because you can jeopardize someone's job if something comes up missing. There are people whose specific job it is to place props, and you must let them do their jobs. Many times prop people will in fact take Polaroid shots of a set, the moment the Director yells "Cut," so that they can match exactly to the master shot if needed.

By moving something you should not move, you'll only indicate that you're a novice. Let's say you get a phone call and ask permission to leave the set and you take the manila envelope prop with you. What if you put it down and forget where you left it? What if you spill coffee on it? Disaster.

So our advice is to establish with the Prop Master exactly what he or she would like done with your props when you've finished at the end of a scene. In some cases, he or she may be right there to collect them from you. But if not — such as in a situation where there are ten leads in a huge courtroom scene — you should agree on a location where you'll deposit the props you've used. Again, this will save time, will create a relationship between you and your prop person, and can protect his or her job.

Some actors have a very detail-oriented approach to their work, and they find that props are integral to their work. If this is important for you, all the more reason to establish a relationship with the Prop Master.

> I always meet with Props and Set because maybe the backdrops and surroundings say more than I could say in pages of dialogue. I'm a "prop actress." Let's say I'm opening a bag of groceries. I have to know where each object is. Usually when the crew is breaking to set up again, I'll take that time to do my own quick prop run through. If that's not possible, I'll do it on my own with the dialogue person. It's a dance of props and dialogue.
> — Joan Van Ark

SHOOTING WITH PROPS

Here's an interesting thing to think about when you're going from a master shot to a close-up. Let's say you have to pick up an envelope from a couch. This works fine for your master shot. However for your close-up, you'll move out of frame if you bend low enough to reach for the envelope on the couch. So — your prop person can be right there beside you, ready to hand you the envelope, so all you have to do is a slight bend, to indicate the actual move you made in the master shot (we're talking about matching — got it? Read the chapter, if not). If your prop person hasn't volunteered to do this — ask. You have a right to get that kind of help and it's very professional for you to be aware of the problem and seek the correct solution.

As a final comment we'd like to say that props are there to help you and the audience bring a scene to life. They're wonderful things! Use them respectfully; use them well.

REHEARSAL

Covered In This Chapter:

- If & When

- Relating To Your Set

- Working With Your Director

- Working With Your Producer(s)

- Working With Other Actors

- Working With Your Crew

Practice is the best of all instructors.
— *Virgil*

Actors trained in "method" sometimes expend themselves in rehearsal or in early shots. They must learn to save it.
— *Abby Singer*
Producer

REHEARSAL

By now you've completed your own private preparation and are ready to begin the collaborative preparation known as rehearsal. This should be one of the most joyful and creative periods of the entire project. Sadly, under certain circumstances – particularly when it comes to TV work – rehearsal may scarcely exist. Rehearsal is one of the things that varies tremendously from project to project.

As you prepare for this very important and thrilling first job, your mind is on all the things you've studied for years – character elements and choices, focus, professionalism. Your expectation may be that you'll have the opportunity to have a meaningful discussion with your Director, and develop important character choices during the course of the rehearsal period.

IF & WHEN

If you're about to work in a feature film, this may all come true, and if so, revel in the opportunity. Unfortunately, when it comes to television work, time is generally much more critical. You may never even see the Director until you meet him or her face to face during your first take.

Here's a tidbit of information you might not have a chance to learn elsewhere. Mention to your agent that you love to rehearse and that you're willing to rehearse without pay. As we said, you won't always get the chance. But sometimes the Director is willing, but is not aware that you are too.

> Actors may not realize why they're not getting a chance to rehearse. So, if you'd like the opportunity to rehearse, call and let the Director know it. Say you'd love a chance to go over the scene and you understand you're not going to be paid, but you'd just like to make yourself available. Most often the Director will be delighted.
> – Barnet Kellman

Assuming you do get to rehearse, one of the first considerations is the all-important process of memorizing your lines, and there are various philosophies. There are also varying situations. In the theatre, sometimes you're learning blocking while still working "on book" (with a script), so the process of line memorization happens concurrently with the process of memorizing movement — a situation we consider to be ideal.

> When I studied with Bobby Lewis, in a way his entire master class was about the rehearsal process. His sense of structure is lucid — and very clearly outlined in his seminal work "Advice to the Player." Whenever I start a project, I always return to his step by step outline of the rehearsal process, because that process allows me to lay my foundation. Otherwise, you're trying to build a house in thin air.
> — Mara

Feature film work generally also respects the rehearsal process and a certain amount of time is allotted for it to happen. For some directors rehearsal is the most important period.

> Sidney Lumet rehearses for two weeks, with all the scenes in sequence and if you're not available for these rehearsals, you don't have the part. It's that important.
> — Joy Todd

However, when it comes to TV, there's so little time that it's sometimes important to have your lines memorized before you get to rehearsal, which is not the time to fumble through your lines and try to vaguely remember them. It's possible that if you're working on an episodic show and are in a scene with the star, you may know your line and he or she may not. Remember that the star is in practically every shot and may have an excuse that you do not have. Learn the rules of the particular situation in which you're working. When the time comes, know your lines, know your cues, and this will help you and everyone else on the set. Everyone will remember how professional and well-prepared you were.

Whenever your rehearsal time comes, cherish the moments, which may be few. You'll need to take this opportunity to familiarize yourself with the set and furniture and to ask for whatever props you envision for your character.

RELATING TO YOUR SET

As a professional actor, you already have specific ideas about how to relate to your set, so we won't presume to tell you how to approach this aspect of your work. We'll simply say that since this is the space in which you'll be doing your work, you'll want to have made specific choices about how to relate to the set.

Is this set a room in your own house? Is it a stranger's office? Do you know exactly how much clearance you have between the sofa and the coffee table? Ask yourself all the questions you can think of.

> As a guest star on "The New Lassie," I once played a character who was on crutches. I was to enter a room that was my office — obviously a room in which I spent a lot of time. I had to have a routine already established for how I put my crutches down, against which wall I leaned them and how I maneuvered in and out of my desk chair. Because I was completely familiar with the set from the very first day of shooting, it was believable that this woman on crutches actually lived in this space.
> — Erin

An important thing to know about is what's known as a "Hot Set." If you see a Hot Set sign on a sofa or posted on a flat, this means that everything on that set is in a specific position and must not be touched or moved in any way.

WORKING WITH YOUR DIRECTOR

Rehearsal is also your chance to talk to your director. Again, bear in mind that your moments with your director are few and far between, so don't waste his or her time. Without attempting to have a long, philosophical discussion, convey your ideas about the scene and ask how he or she plans to shoot it.

One of the key things about rehearsal is going to be communication between you and your Director. You'll find some directors are better communicators than others.

> Unique about directing in this country, versus the U.K., for example, is the different schools of training and the different languages that actors speak. One of the toughest parts of a director's job is knowing how to speak to each actor, individually, in his or her own tongue, in terms of communicating what he or she wants or needs.
> — Barnet Kellman

Of course, all communication is a two-way street. Assuming you get the chance — you must also be willing to share your thoughts openly with your director. For some actors, this is not only a conversation about the emotions, but also about the technicalities of a scene.

> I get "married" to my directors. We talk and communicate all the time. I usually ask how they're going to cover a scene. In the 90s, they're trying to get as much as they can in one shot. I ask, "Where are we heightening this?" I want to know where the camera is. Is this shot all eyes? Or are my arms showing?
> — Joan Van Ark

Of course, your ideas are important, but we encourage you to see from the director's point view as well. We asked a director what he needs to accomplish in rehearsal:

> From my point of view, the rehearsal process is to ensure all elements come together — the several performances with scenic visual elements — to create the point of the scene, to tell the story to the audience. It's not just about all the actors feeling comfortable.
> — Barnet Kellman

You may sometimes feel strongly about your character, or about a specific choice. We don't want you to squelch your creative spirit. But we have to emphasize the larger picture.

> *I'll take all the time in the world to re-do, re-design, re-block, whatever it takes to tell the story. This is my prerogative as the director, not the actor's prerogative. I'll have to make up that cost somewhere else. I'm responsible for all the parties. This is why the actor should not insist. He is not responsible for the day. I am. This is where you get reports that say, "We didn't make the day because the actor was a pain in the ass."*
> — Barnet Kellman

You didn't know that reports get written about your behavior? Then we'll tell you. You thought you were out of school, but in fact you're still getting Report Cards. You just never see them or hear about them. Don't be naive.

To interject a bit of personal philosophy about directors, we feel there are various ways to arrive at the position of Director and perhaps the route one has taken to achieve this important position to a large extent determines his or her method of working. Of these approaches, the two most obvious are what could be called external and internal. Does the Director work from the point of view of the final, visual product, as is likely to be the case if he or she began as a Cinematographer or Editor? Or, did he or she begin work as an actor, where it was the motivations, the emotions, the characters which drove the scenes and determined the action?

Our feeling is that the better a director is, the less you see of the direction.

> *A good director allows the actor to be better than he is.*
> — Uta Hagen

Ultimately, a good Director must understand both kinds of disciplines and have the sensitivity to understand the emotion that would, for example, drive an actor to walk from point A to point B, and at the same time have the objectivity to realize he/she's going to need three quick cuts at this point in the film, and will therefore not want his actors moving out of frame. If you think about this for even a few seconds, you'll begin to appreciate the complexities your Director is dealing with from moment to moment.

In any case, chances are you'll know within minutes which orientation your Director works from and you'll have to adjust accordingly. Most actors love to work with Directors who are former actors, or who worked in the theatre, because of their complete understanding of the actor's process and, of course, the ever-present possibility that "magic" can happen.

> I don't know where the camera is. I don't know where I'm going to put it. I didn't go to film school. I'm an actor who became a Director. Besides, I don't know what magic is going to happen on the set. I want to see what the actors come up with. I want to let them feel the lines. Then when I see magic happen, then I know where to put the camera. There's an important exposition scene in "Big" with Tom Hanks. This kind of scene has to be included, but tends to be boring. What I did was to give Tom a prop, a spray canister of something sticky, something for him to work with. What Tom came up with was funnier than anything I could have devised.
>
> — Penny Marshall
> from a talk given at AFI, after the release of "Big"

If magic is going to happen, it's going to be up to you, so the clearer an idea you have about the character you're playing, the better. If you're fortunate enough to have a Director who wants your input, be prepared to offer something. This isn't an opportunity you want to waste.

> On an episode of "Murder She Wrote" the Director had set aside several minutes for rehearsal. He approached me and asked, "So, what do you want to do with this scene?" If I'd been smart, I would've used the time I had before that rehearsal to think and walk through some ideas, but I hadn't. When he saw I really didn't have any ideas to put forward, he quickly said, "Never mind. Let's do this." I had missed a

chance not only to express myself, but to make a better impression on the Director.

— Erin

A completely different, but equally valid, style of directing is that practiced by visually oriented directors. Alfred Hitchcock, for example, was disparaged as a Director who used actors as furniture, but admired because he knew precisely what each shot would contain, frame by frame.

Many Directors today work with story boards and they're smart to do so in many instances, because of extreme time and budget constraints. Also, they must often incorporate special effects, which have to be visualized before the actor does his performance.

Most often you'll find some combination of these approaches when you work, and, of course, it will depend upon whether you're doing a science fiction feature, or a sitcom taped in front of an audience. What you can do — in addition to being flexible and receptive to your Director's methodology — is to come up with ideas that work for your character and try them in rehearsal. If you and a fellow actor come up with something that enhances the development of your characters, discuss this with the Director, because he or she may decide to incorporate these ideas into the next day's shooting.

In "The Princess and the Dwarf" my co-star Kathleen Freeman played a nosey busybody, listening at every keyhole and I played the Duchess. Something happened by accident one day: I slammed the door and caught her skirt. She then opened the door, picked up her skirt in a huff and then slammed the door in my face. This moment had not been in the script, but it worked. We went to the Director, when she was not busy, and told her that we'd like to make this a running battle between our two characters and asked what she thought. She liked it; it added humor and spark to our scenes, so we as the actors worked out moves and moments for each of our upcoming scenes.

— Erin

We usually find that in some scenes, the Director uses what we come up with, and in some cases he or she can't, because other needs predominate. But basically, what we come up with as actors adds to the film.

WORKING WITH YOUR PRODUCER(S)

We don't mean to be harsh — but we're not even sure some producers would agree they work WITH actors. In the established hierarchy, actors work FOR producers.

We've mentioned several possible scenarios where you, as an actor, might get to share your ideas. We'd be less than candid if we didn't also tell you there may be lots of times when your ideas are NOT welcome.

We've said this is a collaborative business. True. But collaboration is not necessarily going to happen when and where you might think it will. From a technical standpoint, your efforts to place a prop correctly and deal with makeup appropriately will be greatly appreciated by the crew.

However, if you think your ideas will always be welcomed by your director or producer, you're probably in for a nasty surprise. Time and again, we've heard stories about stars who are cordially invited to keep their mouths shut. The stars of one well-known television series were invited to a meeting. When they were seated the producers said, "We just want you to know, we don't want to hear your ideas." Tempting though it must have been for these professionals to walk off the set, they sat tight.

From a producer's point of view, he or she has fought long and hard to achieve a position of Power and authority. Actors are the hired help. When does it change for actors? If and when they become bankable, and start getting producing credits of their own, then, and only then, they too are invited to the bargaining table. Lee Majors, Tom Selleck, Robert Urich, (notice how many women we're mentioning?) eventually achieved these positions, at least temporarily.

The business uses a pyramid as its basic shape. That means there's lots of room on the bottom and less and less space at the top. If a project is written by three writers, who then attract the interest of two producers, who then go to a production company with three executive producers — even before they approach a network, there are eight people all wanting equal shares of power and money and the first scene hasn't even been shot yet. The last thing this group of people needs, is one more person who wants to offer their two cents — even if their ideas are valid. If their ideas *are* valid, they might have to be paid attention to! And they might have to be paid! Heaven forbid! You begin to see the problem.

Remember, too, that you are working from an actor's point of view. Other people involved in the project have their own points of view, and they are equally valid.

> Actors are not aware of and not responsible for, the business considerations of a project. Producers are up against time and budget constraints actors don't even know about. Always remember — this is a business.
>
> — Linda Purl

This is a good moment to use that well-worn phrase "timing is everything." If you *are* going to bring up ideas, rehearsal is about your only chance to do so. Don't save your ideas for the actual shoot — that's a good way to get shot (and we mean with bullets) — or at least to get shot down.

As cast and crew prepare for a shoot, there is a flow of activities, information and communication. If you have some awareness of this flow, you'll be able to sync yourself better to the overall production considerations.

In a worst case scenario, sometimes actors get so frustrated that they have to be "handled." What that meas is, the actor has been perceived as being "difficult," and the producers "assign" one of the group to go talk to the actor, to give the actor the impression (or the illusion) that someone cares about their ideas.

In a situation like this, though it may appear to you as an actor that you've made headway, it's quite possible it's just a matter of insult being added to injury. We think the best defense against all this is probably deep breathing, a philosophical approach to life, and so much longevity in the biz that eventually you yourself become a producer. Who knows? Perhaps then you can improve the business and create situations where real talent is nurtured. Till then, at least you won't be naive..

In a more positive scenario, we heard a story about a series star who was getting increasingly frustrated that her ideas were never being considered. In her case, one of the producers realized that all she wanted was to be heard, so he began talking with her. It came to light that decisions were being made without her because she didn't offer her feedback fast enough. When she found out about the time constraints, she responded more quickly. She wasn't trying to be 'difficult." She just wanted to be part of the creative process in her daily work.

WORKING WITH OTHER ACTORS

Throughout the book we've been talking quite a bit about your working with crew members. You will, of course, also be working with other actors. The dynamics of your interaction with fellow actors is one thing in class. It's another thing when you're on the set, preparing to shoot. Yes, you need to take your moment and do your own best work. But no, this entire project does not revolve around you, even if you're the lead.

> *I do not insist that an actor have total sensitivity to my needs, or the crew needs. I do insist that an actor not infringe upon other actors. There's no prettier sight than actors working well as an ensemble. And nothing's an uglier sight than seeing the flip side of that process, where an actor only feels they're working when all the attention is on them, where people don't make eye contact, where they denigrate the other person's lines or attitudes, or constantly have "inspirations" for their characters which subvert the other guy. Like, "What if I play this whole scene sitting at her desk." It's a situation which paralyzes everybody.*

Or the piece de resistance of telling other actors how to do a line reading or directing them to read a line a certain way because it will "help them." I jump in with both feet and send the fighters back to their corners and straighten out the offending party. I feel comfortable doing that now after twenty-five years of directing. I did not always feel comfortable doing that. Common decency is the only thing that works. I've stood up to the star sometimes, only to be sandbagged by the producer. It's a dysfunctional family situation in which everybody's walking on eggs. It's important to respect other actors' needs.
— Barnet Kellman

He makes several good points. One is about giving a fellow actor a line reading. Of course, you know that this is a cardinal sin. Right? In case you didn't know, **giving a fellow actor a line reading is a cardinal sin.** You expect your creative process to be respected. You must respect it in others.

If you as an actor are having a problem doing your work because of the behavior of another actor, bring it to the attention of the Director and request his/her help in resolving it. They may have noticed a problem, but been hesitant to say something, not being sure of what's going on. Your telling them may be just the catalyst they need.

WORKING WITH YOUR CREW

As is the case with every form of theatrical or cinematic presentation, rehearsal is the time to try any and everything you're going to try. This is the time to ask questions, experiment and work out all the details of your performance, both emotional and technical. Bear in mind that the crew is using this time the same way you are and are step by step discovering what they will need to do to make this scene work.

Once you've set something in rehearsal, remember it's going to stay that way. Why? Because this is a collaborative project you're working on. And all of you must agree about what you're going to do before you commit it to film or tape.

If your blocking indicates you'll be sitting at a particular spot on the sofa, understand the lighting will be set for that spot; the boom operator will have worked out a way to mike you from that spot; the camera operator will have positioned his camera for that spot, and so forth. It will definitely not be appropriate to make a change during a take. You can imagine what kind of havoc it would mean for everyone involved. Know this going in and take full advantage of the rehearsal period to make whatever changes you think you'll require.

One thing both you and the crew will probably need at some point is one complete run-through. We also cover this in our "Shooting" chapter, but we'll mention it here. The crew calls this a "May Day Rehearsal" — that means no stops, no interruptions, come hell or highwater. Actors usually call this an actor's rehearsal. Sometimes you just can't concentrate when the boom operator is yelling, or a prop is being moved in your sight lines. If you need an actor's rehearsal, ask for it. You may only get one — so make it count.

All departments of the crew are going to be taking notes during rehearsal — script supervisor, props, wardrobe, etc. Even if they have to erase these notes later, this is giving them a head start on a very complex series of tasks they will have to do. Be aware, then, that decisions are probably happening quickly and that things you may still feel are liquid, are in fact setting like quick-set cement.

Nowhere is this more evident than in shooting Soaps, where the work schedule is faster than in any other form of cinematic shooting.

> *The basic schedule on "Days" ["Days Of Our Lives," NBC] was highly compressed. Each soap is shot differently, but on "Days" we ran through the text in sequence four times through the course of the day. It was a wonderful way to work — it was very much like doing a complete play each day.*
>
> *— Mara*

A word about emotional scenes. Each actor has his or her own approach when it comes to choosing how far to go in rehearsal. We find this varies from project to project. Sometimes you need to find out for yourself how far you'll go, and give the sound tech a chance to mike for high volume, for example. Sometimes you need to conserve your energy for the take.

> *On an emotional scene, during rehearsal I just like to mark it, rather than giving a full out performance.*
> — Joan Van Ark

In summary, when it comes to rehearsal, two things are important — have ideas, and be flexible. Nothing is more valuable than an actor who is so spontaneous, so open, so ingenious, that even with poor material, their performance has life and interest. Some actors are hired again and again because directors know they can be relied upon to rescue "dead" scenes, bring life to any project and make fellow actors look great.

SHOOTING

Covered In This Chapter:

- Punctuality & Patience
- Structural Differences:
- Features, Episodic, Sitcoms, & Soaps
- Personal Preparation
- Set Protocol: Whose Chair Is It Anyway?
- Run-Throughs & Final Rehearsals
- Shooting Sequence
- Second Team
- "May Day"
- Performance
- Close-ups
- Terminology
- Hitting Your Mark
- Behavior On The Set
- Lines – Letter-Perfect & Not
- Stopping & Starting
- Do's & Don'ts

Actors in this country have a lack of desire to learn the technical aspects of this business. I hear actors say, "Technical? That's up to the crew!" What they don't know is that if they don't know the technical, they're not going to have any close-ups. That's what I teach in my classes.
— Jim Kelly Durgin
The Cinema Academy

Unless an actor has a firm and clear idea of his character before he presents himself on the set, he is lost. Never rely on help being at hand on the day.
—Malcolm Taylor
Director, "East Enders," "Coronation Street"

SHOOTING

You've taken many steps and overcome many obstacles to get to this moment. All this preparation and struggle has brought you to this opportunity to be in front of the camera.

Because by now you've probably studied with the finest teachers you can find, performed in show cases and theatrical productions and have your character down pat, you feel you're ready for whatever happens on the set. However – strange but true – many professionals have been told by their acting gurus that the technical stuff they're about to encounter is irrelevant to their work, or at most, secondary. But that's a bit like telling a first-time flyer it's not important which terminal they go to. In fact it *is* important to clear security, have the right boarding pass and board the right plane. Only then can you fly to the intended destination. The following story is from a consummate professional with over twenty years of theatre experience

> *I was doing a guest appearance on the TV series "Power Rangers." I got to the location at the required 5 am and put on my regalia to play the part of the eccentric art teacher. After an entire day of waiting around, I performed my two scenes and was heading toward my dressing room when the Second A.D. said, "Amity! Where are you going?" "I'm going to change," I said. "What do you mean? We haven't done your close-up!" "Oh," I said sheepishly, trying desperately to cover the fact that I hadn't known the actual procedure of shooting.*
> *— Amity Janow*

Picture the following ideal shooting situation: you were hired to do a starring role with eight weeks to prepare. Linda Hamilton trained for months to prepare for "Terminator II;" Meryl Streep took the time she needed to study accents for "Sohpie's Choice" and "Out Of Africa;" Jon Voight spent weeks in a wheelchair preparing for "Coming Home;" Dustin Hoffman interviewed scores of women in preparing to do "Tootsie." To us, this is the best of all possible worlds. Like them, you have immersed yourself in the milieu you're about to portray, and create of yourself a new person. Lots of time. Lots of money. No pressure.

And now back to reality. The star they hired hasn't worked out and you're their second choice. Or fourth or fifth. You have two days to change your hair, learn to sky dive, find a kennel for your dog, rent your house, get your passport renewed, and show up with your lines learned in Madagascar. You meet the director for the first time when you arrive on the set, and he has no time to say more than "Thanks for coming" before you start to shoot your first scene, which takes place in bed with your co-star. Welcome to the business.

PUNCTUALITY & PATIENCE

In discussing the best order to present this material, again we realized it's all about time — how much there is, or isn't. In the currency of the realm, time is money. One aspect of time is punctuality. We've said it before and we'll say it again: the first, the cardinal rule of working in this business, is to BE ON TIME.

> If you're late it shows a lack of respect and shows you don't think much of your co-workers. Now more than ever — time is money.
> — Joan Van Ark

Another aspect of time in this business is the "hurry up and wait" factor. You will rush around getting yourself ready. And then, you will wait. This is unavoidable because of the complexity of creating this art form. The crew is dealing with set-ups, weather, lighting shifts, and many other technicalities. So — you have the difficult task of being ready... and staying ready.

Jet pilots often spend the largest portion of their flights sitting at the controls while the automatic instruments actually fly the plane. However, pilots are paid to do the tough job of being ready to respond on one second's notice, even if they've been sitting still for hours. When it's time to respond, they have to be fully alert. You must do the same. You have to plan for the preparation time you'll need and see to it that you're ready when the crew is ready for you. One of the most common delays on a set is – what? Actors. Why? Because no one can find you.

> As an A.D., I would love it if actors would make a point of letting us know where they are going to be. We spend so much time on our feet running around it can be very irritating when you leave an actor in their room and go back to get them, thinking that's where they are, only to find they have left to go who knows where and you spend the next 20 minutes walking around looking for them. They may have gone to craft service or to the restroom or to the set or to some other stage on the lot to visit a friend or to mail a letter.... It would be great if they could just take a moment to find an A.D. (any one of us will do as we normally have radios and can communicate with each other) to let us know where we can find them when we need them. Sometimes, after looking forever, when we do locate them and tell them we've been looking for them, they respond with, "Oh, I've been right here." not realizing that we don't know where "Right here" is.
> — B.C. Cameron

STRUCTURAL DIFFERENCES

Each kind of project has its own schedule and rhythm – feature films of various budgets, television movies, dramatic series, sitcoms, and soaps. Each have their own time and budget constraints and these dictate differing requirements.

- **Feature Films** generally involve more money than television projects, which does two things to the project: it makes it possible to take more time with each scene and each detail. It also places an even heavier burden upon producers, directors, actors, and everyone involved to make each moment on film all that it can be. There's more time devoted to rehearsal and to shooting, which can seem luxurious compared to television. But each moment is weighted just as heavily.

- **Low-Budget and/or Independent Feature Films** are yet another kettle of fish. They can be wonderfully creative and a dynamic medium in which to work. They can also be disorganized and maddening. As an actor, you need to be aware that you may have less union protection on a low-budget feature shoot, because some of the rules are not as specific as they are for other forms. Be as clear as you can about your contractual obligations, and be aware that you may have to intervene in your own behalf, if no one else is there to protect your interests. Watch for meal times, sign-outs, overtime, any penalties owed you for turn-arounds, and so forth. Under no circumstances should you sign blank production reports. We even heard of one actor who created his own daily journal. When he was asked to sign out each evening, he replied, "I'll sign yours if you sign mine."

Television tends to be a frantic business.

- **Television Movies** generally have a shooting schedule weeks or even months shorter than it would be if the same picture were being released as a feature. They have a crew hired long before you (the actor) were hired, so it can be very much like working as a temp in a corporate office where everyone else knows each other and is used to working together. They have an inexorable schedule where a certain number of pages must be completed each day.
- **Television Series** have a product which must be completed, no matter what, during a six or seven day period. Again, the series stars are generally used to their roles and are also beaten down to some extent by the rigors of a series star schedule. As a guest star, you must make the most of every moment. You'll be in and out of the show, while the show will roll on (they hope) long after you're gone.
- **Sitcoms** must create a live show almost as though they were completing an entire piece of theatre in five days. The first four days of the week is rehearsal and the show is shot on the fifth day. To be more specific: Day one is a talk-through or read-through. This often generates writers' revisions, which are implemented and rehearsed on day two. By day three, the show is on its feet, the actors are off book, and the network execs are there to watch. Day four is the tech day, so you're at the service of the crew and all its departments, so be prepared for a long one. Day five begins with one more run-through before shooting.

- *Soaps* have only one day to complete an entire one-hour program. There are basically two ways of shooting a soap and they both work very well, with each form having its advantages and disadvantages. The first way is also very much like live theatre and very much like sitcoms, although it's done in a day, not a week. The second way is more like feature film shooting.

    "Live Theatre" or "Chronological" Style: These shows ("Days Of Our Lives" for example) are shot chronologically. You start at about 6am with a read-through on book for the actors. At about 10am you do a camera blocking, which includes both cast and crew. At about 2pm you start a dress rehearsal, going through the show top to bottom. And at about 4pm you start to tape. By the time you tape, you have progressed chronologically through the entire day's script three times, and the taping is your fourth time.

    "Film" or "Set-up" Style: These shows ("As The World Turns" for example) are shot one set-up at a time. Lighting is done for that scene, the actors rehearse on that set, then that scene is shot. The production doesn't leave that particular set until shooting is completed. The whole production then moves on to the next set-up. This may or may not be chronological according to the script.

As you can imagine, each of these final products determines the amount of time spent on each component and it'll be important for you as a performer to know which you're working in and to adjust accordingly. If, for example, you're used to working in feature films and suddenly find yourself doing two weeks on a soap, you'll either develop a nervous twitch...or find a new rhythm for preparation and performance.

Because of these different demands, you'll have to be flexible. In fact, flexibility and adaptability will be your keys to surviving and thriving in this business. Don't complain – just adapt. Each individual movie or film becomes a world unto itself as it's created. We've attempted to give you an idea how features or series or soaps or sitcoms are done. You will have to adapt the information to a particular situation in which you find yourself.

What we'll give you here is some good, general information about shooting, whichever form you're working in. Remember: when it comes to capturing you on film, you're the one who has to make it work. It's your face up there, not the director's or the art director's, or the prop person's. You have the ultimate responsibility to infuse your character with life, to bring the truth, to make it play.

Captured on celluloid, forever and for always, will be the essence of your work. All that you are able to bring to this particular piece at this time and place will now be recorded for all to see – yourself included.

PERSONAL PREPARATION

When it comes to working in front of the camera, we're amazed at how few "acting" schools ever really tell you what to expect – or give you the opportunity to develop the techniques needed in working with the camera.

Our hope is that after you've rehearsed the scene – and before you're about to shoot – you've checked over your preparations, you're confident of your lines, you're clear on your choices and those of your director, and most importantly, as you've waited you've been able to maintain the delicate balance between staying revved and conserving your energy.

> As part of my preparation for the "take," I often do a few minutes routine of Tai Chi. It's something I find keeps me centered, strengthens my ability to focus, helps relieve me of stress and tension, and gives me energy. And I always make sure I've allowed enough time to get my make-up and hair adjusted before the take.
>
> – Erin

> The most important thing for me to do before I perform, is to get centered. For years, I've done Yoga breathing exercises, as well as vocal exercises, which help me to depart from the "efficiency tapes" running through the intellectual part of my brain and get me to "tune in" to the instinctive, intuitive side of myself. It's from this center that the actual performance comes.
>
> – Mara

Sometimes there can be quite a length of time between the initial rehearsal period and when you begin shooting. If the master shot incorporates a large area it could take hours to light. You could even be brought in to rehearse before you go to Hair and Make-up, especially if you're in the first shot of the day. So how you fill this time is important. Every actor has to choose what works best. Mia Farrow sometimes likes to knit. Franklyn Seales of "Silver Spoons" liked to read periodicals. Jon Anniston of "Days Of Our Lives" likes to do crossword puzzles. Henry Fonda liked to do pencil sketches. You need to find what works best for you.

If you're working on a Soap, there's no Second A.D. There's only a Stage Manager who does the jobs of several people.

> *The Stage Manager on "Young & Restless" works as a First A.D. and a Second A.D. — he (or she) does it all. She/He's "the man." Stage Managers on Soaps get Emmys when the Directors do, because they're the floor directors.*
> *— Granville Van Dusen*

Because of this, the Stage Manager has no time to find you and give you advance warning you're about to be needed on the set. You must be listening to the backstage/dressing rooms speakers to follow what's going on, and appear at the right moment.

If, however, you're working in other forms of TV or film, we recommend asking your Second A.D. to give you a few minutes warning before you're wanted on the set.

> *I always tell the Second A.D. to constantly keep me posted. I want a five-minute warning for everything I'm doing. I have to pace myself both emotionally and physically. I have to be ready for the moment.*
> *— Joan Van Ark*

There are many reasons why an early warning can work well for you, and for the whole production. Sometimes it's fairly obvious why you need the extra time.

> In the movie "Jason Goes To Hell," I spent one day with a dagger protruding from my back. It was a little difficult relaxing – I couldn't lean against the back of a chair. So I'd have the harness removed between long set-ups, therefore needing a 10-minute warning before being called back to the set.
>
> – Erin

You might need to partially redress, since it may not be a good idea to lie around in wardrobe, or you might simply wish to touch up your hair and make-up, or want to review your notes one last time. Whatever the amount of time you'll need, requesting will protect you and your co-workers. No one is amused by having to halt production while you get your eyebrows retouched, or rememorize your lines.

> As an actor dealing with technical details, if you anticipate, you're very much appreciated.
>
> – Joan Van Ark

Let's say you've just been told by the Second A.D. that you're wanted on the set. Do you finish your phone call to your agent? Do you finish reading your magazine article? No. You are expected to stop whatever you're doing and immediately go to the set.

> One day I was having an important meeting with Scott Bakula, the leading man on my series "Quantum Leap." The A.D. knocked on his door, calling him to the set. In mid-sentence, the actor immediately excused himself and walked out the door. At first, I was a little miffed, but then I realized just how lucky I was to have hired such a conscientious actor. This was an actor who didn't allow his ego or self-importance to change the way in which he worked.
>
> – Don Bellisario

It warms our hearts to hear a producer speak highly of a fellow actor. Believe us, this is rare. Most of the quotations we received from our interviews were along the lines of "I wish actors wouldn't be such babies" or "actors are all like spoiled children."

> I wish actors wouldn't place such importance on where their parking space is, or on the size of their trailer.
> – Abby Singer

There's one actress, who shall remain nameless here, who actually has it written in her contract that no fellow actor is allowed to have a trailer larger than hers, even if that actor has a family of nine and will be on location for a month. Suffice it to say, we don't believe she has her priorities in order.

And now a word from our philosophical mountaintop. We all know when life throws you challenges, you have the choice of either complaining, or of making the most of the situation. Our experience is that if you spend your time complaining – either to others or just to yourself – you actually miss out on what's happening in your life at that moment. There are people who enjoy working, and there are people who can hardly wait till the work is over. We are workers. We find our joy in the work itself. We highly recommend this attitude, for it yields a life full of treasures.

SET PROTOCOL (or Whose Chair Is It Anyway?)

When you arrive on the set, there's a certain protocol to be observed. The prop department will have set up folding director's chairs. Your rank of importance – star, guest star, day player, etc. – will dictate how tall your chair will be, and whether or not your name is on it, or indeed, whether you have a chair at all. (If you're hired for background work or a non-speaking part, you will probably have to supply your own chair, or just make do with a step, a curb, or whatever you can find to make yourself comfortable. You will also not have a dressing room, but will have to share some facility or rest room.)

Having a chair of your own is a coveted thing. More importantly, it's an earned thing. Chairs are only brought out for a few key people: Director, D.P., stars, etc. Everyone else – make-up, hair, grips, etc. – have to fend for themselves. There's an unwritten rule on the set. NEVER sit in someone's chair without permission. And our advice is be very careful about asking permission to use anyone's chair. People who have their own chair feels they earned it, and it's their one haven on the set. Don't take it away from them under any circumstances. The set is a beehive of activity and one's chair is an island of refuge – a place for your script, a place to rest, a place to drink coffee or water, a place to wait between set-ups.

If there's absolutely no appropriate place to sit and you need to – and you're performing with lines in the scene – you are certainly within your rights to ask one of the ADs for a chair. Under special circumstances your costume might not permit you to sit, and if you're a big enough star, special arrangements will be made. We heard a great story about Bette Davis which is a bit of film history. In portraying Queen Elizabeth, her costume was so complex and cumbersome she couldn't sit down, so a special device was constructed for her to rest between takes. It looked like an upright, open coffin, a tall wooden box which leaned back at a 70-degree angle, with special arm and neck rests. Such an apparatus might be also necessary if you're performing in a sci-fi production, for example.

We've mentioned this before, but again we encourage you to think about your own energy while you wait between takes. Yes, there are times to schmooze. However, in our opinion, waiting for your take is not one of them. Conserve your energy, maintain your focus. This may mean retreating to your trailer. This may mean staying on the sound stage somewhere. You'll find what works for you.

> I don't hang with others on the set when I'm working. I stay by myself. I need to keep my own thoughts and not be distracted. But there have been times where, if it's very intense, I want to stay connected to the set. I will find a corner behind the set, listening to everything, yet staying in that space, so when they say "First Team," I haven't lost energy. I'm already at "speed." When you're in the flow, sometimes you don't want to break it.
>
> – Joan Van Ark

RUN-THROUGHS & FINAL REHEARSALS

Once you're back on the set, you will then do a run-through. Just to keep things confusing, this is often called "rehearsal," although this is not the full rehearsal process we described earlier. We'll call them "run-throughs."

You'll run through the scene from the top. This gives the camera crew a chance to synchronize their movements, the D.P. a chance to review his/her lighting, the script supervisor a chance to make some preliminary notes, and the director the opportunity to see the scene brought up to speed, allowing him or her a chance to focus on making some final adjustments.

Usually the first few times you run through a scene, you will be forced to stop and start a lot. As the camera crew is finalizing some of their intricate technical moves or as the lights are adjusted, people will be calling out, asking questions and it's very disconcerting. Here you are, trying to find the connected energy through the scene, and — just as the energy is building and finding its flow — someone yells in your ear. It's much like coitus interruptus. And in both cases — it's important not to let it get to you.

Another word of warning here. It's possible that you never did get a rehearsal for this scene, and that the run-through is all you get. The camera blocking has been done with your stand-in. This isn't great for you, but you're good; you're professional; you can deal with it. Remember what we said — be flexible.

An essential part of an actor's job is not letting outside problems or surrounding energy interfere with the emotion that's needed for the scene at hand. However, at the same time, if something happens that makes you angry and anger is what is needed for the scene, then the old adage is: "use it."

> It was the final day of shooting an episode of "Silk Stalkings." It was 11:40pm, and the crew knew that in twenty minutes they'd be reaching for their beer. They even went so far as to start blasting rock and roll music while they reset the lights. I, however, had to summon tears during a scene where I was being interrogated in a police station. Surrounded by all this exuberance, it seemed my original preparation

wasn't going to do a thing for me. So instead, I got angry at the crew for their disregard of my needs. I got angry, and I got hurt, and I used all those feelings. When the camera rolled, the hot angry tears came down my cheeks and the scene worked very well.

– Erin

SHOOTING SEQUENCE

"Shooting Sequence" can mean two things.

First, we'll use it to describe the flow leading up to that all-important word "Action."

There's a specific sequence, where each department indicates their readiness. It's the job of the First A.D. to determine whether or not everyone is ready for the scene. Once she does, she'll tell the Director of Photography to "Roll 'Em." Next, the sound recordist waits for his equipment to start up then says "Speed." (See SOUND chapter) When the Director knows Camera and Sound are ready, he'll say "Action." You as the actor will be responding only to that word "Action" – not to anyone or anything else.

"Shooting Sequence" can also refer to the order in which scenes are shot. As you know by now, the sequence of shooting scenes can be anything but logical, in terms of the chronology of the piece itself, depending upon the kind of project you're doing.

In soaps and sitcoms, you do, for the most part, stick with the chronology of the script. In episodic, and in feature and TV movies, an entirely different logic governs the shooting sequence, having to do with budgets, locations, lighting and many other factors.

While shooting the end of the picture may make sense to the crew, it's rough on the actor. In a feature film you may find yourself divorcing someone before you've married them, sending a child off to college before they're born, or jumping into bed with someone you haven't met yet!

> *We had the use of a set on a studio lot for only a certain day, and this was the location the producers had chosen for the naked love scene. Unfortunately, this had to be shot on the first day of shooting.*
> — Kelly Bovino

SECOND TEAM

There's another aspect to this process, having to do with Stand-Ins. Actors are referred to as the "First Team." There is, logically, also a "Second Team." These wonderful and indispensable people take the actors' places during the sometimes torturously long lighting process, allowing the actors to regroup, run lines and prepare for shooting.

Members of the Second Team adjust their own appearances as much as necessary to match the actors — they will stand on boxes, wear wigs and make other appropriate adjustments. They sometimes request items of clothing from wardrobe if their color or shape will affect the lighting.

You may wonder how could any one else stand in for you. You might want to think again.

> *On my first job on the first day I was told, "You're excused; it's time for the Second Team." "What's that?" I asked. "They're the people who will stand in for your lighting." I thought to myself, I've worked with Avedon, Irving Penn and Horst, each of whom has lit me meticulously. "No one stands in for my lighting." Of course coming from the world of modeling, where the only thing being lit is the model's face, I failed to understand that they had to light an entire set. After three hours of standing still in my high heels, I asked if I could be excused. There were quite a few snickers on the set that day.*
> — Erin

EXTRAS

There's a whole separate arena of work about which there's some confusion, and that is "Extra" work which also goes by the name of "Background" or "Atmosphere."

Extra work is not acting work and it may not necessarily lead to acting work. But it is an interesting, honorable profession of its own and it can be a superb way to figure out correct set behavior.

In the early days of Hollywood, extras were generally hired because they had a certain look, or could perform certain specific physical activities: members of motorcycle clubs had the right clothes and knew how to ride bikes; members of dance clubs were adept at ballroom dancing and had the right shoes. This made them extremely hirable.

A company called Central Casting was eventually established and those who wanted to work as extras signed up under the appropriate categories. Eventually this work was unionized under Screen Extras Guild (SEG) which was entirely separate from SAG or any other union. This changed, however, a few years ago when SEG and SAG joined forces, making it possible for a would-be actor to get a coveted SAG card not by doing acting work, but by doing extra work and thus facilitating the actor's professional career.

Even if you're not a member of some elite group with its own uniforms, doing extra work can require some interesting skills — dancing without music, speaking in animated conversations silently, to give a couple of examples.

As an Extra — like everyone else on the set — you are a valuable part of the overall team and you may be able to support the actors in a way that improves the entire energy on the set.

> While shooting a very emotional scene in "Heaven Help Us," I had to look into an audience of extras. I greatly appreciated finding those few who had committed to the moment. What was annoying was seeing the

many who weren't committed. They would either be "watching" me perform, or they would get nervous if I looked them in the eye, both of which were disconcerting. After the long hours and endless takes, it was a relief to know I could count on those who were totally there with me, equally full of emotion, even though the camera wasn't on them.
— Erin

Extra work can be hardest of all for an actor, because in many cases it requires that the actor NOT act: that is, not be aware of the camera, not make eye contact, not have motivation, not have something interesting going on behind the eyes. Why? Because all these qualities "steal focus" and your job as an extra is to blend in, disappear and make the background more plausible for the actors.

Working as an extra can also be the hardest work you'll ever do because of the hours of standing — hours without being spoken to, or asked an opinion, hours where you're not allowed to ask for a chair or speak to the actors. It takes great stamina. And occasionally provides tremendous comic relief for the whole cast and crew.

While working as 1st A.D. on Deep Space Nine, I was setting the background in a scene on the bridge of a Jem Ha'dar ship. The background were characters called "Breen" who were originally only supposed to be minimal characters but in our final episodes became key players in the war with the Dominion. Since they were not intended to be main characters the costumes were not designed for mobility or convenience. Consequently, the outfits, which were similar to an armadillo's layered shell with full helmets and beak-like face pieces, made movement, breathing and seeing very difficult. As we were setting up our last shot of the day, under the gun, timewise, as always, I quickly set some "Breen" background, asking one in particular to walk across the bridge and exit out of a door — forgetting his limited vision and awkward mobility. I "rolled" the camera and at the appropriate time called "background" for their cue to start acting and suddenly realized my error — too late!! The director had called action for the actors and

> my "Breen" began his dutiful trek across the bridge. Trying subtly to "feel" his way across the room with extended hands, he bumped into the center console, clunked into an extended set piece along the floor, noisily ricocheted off both sides of the doorjamb and tripped over the threshold as he finally made his exit. I kept hoping he would just stop but he was determined to do as I had asked him. We were all trying to be quiet but we were laughing so hard it was impossible. It didn't matter, though, because the "Breen" had made so much noise the director cut the take prematurely (fortunately, he was laughing too) and we had to go again, this time with the "Breen" working quietly at their stations.
>
> — B.C. Cameron

Occasionally extra work can lead one step further into what would be called a non-speaking role, that is an actual part where you are doing everything you do as an actor except actually speak. Even if you don't have a speaking role, your understanding of set protocol is critical! A remarkable actor who now is an ACTRA (Canadian actors' guild) board member, created his own seminars similar to our own. When he shared his story with us, we could certainly relate!

> When I was in theatre school, there was a film being shot in Ottowa. They came to the school to cast some of the smaller roles and I got the part of a waiter. It was a non-speaking role, but since much of the film took place in a restaurant, I was on camera almost all the time. A lot of physical action was required — carrying, placing, turning, walking. What that meant was this role was loaded with technical details which were part of something called "continuity." There were all kinds of things I'd never heard of. Someone was calling for the "First Team," someone said I should "hit my mark." The Director called me to the set and she expected me to know all this. When she realized I didn't understand the terminology and didn't know how to hit my mark, she was very upset. She took all her frustration out on me, and it made my experience very unpleasant. She didn't feel she should be teaching and directing at the same time. And since I was in so many scenes, I

became a burden to her. Had she known I was so inexperienced technically, I would not have gotten the part. Later I created the workshop "Acting for Film and Television" for ACTRA. I didn't want other beginners to have the same experience.

– Gilles Plouffe, actor, ACTRA Board member

"MAY DAY"

As you go through your final rehearsals just before the camera rolls, this is the time to make your own technical adjustments, to lock in your movements, see where you may have trouble hitting your mark, at what point you may look up or away, and how you'll use your props. Unless you're shooting a soap, remember that once the master shot is in the can, you will have to repeat your performance, every hand gesture, every head turn, every ear scratching, again and again, at exactly the same moment for every angle the director wants for coverage.

At this point we must pause for emphasis about something extremely important in the career of an actor: **matching**. It is, in fact, so important that we have devoted an entire chapter to it, and we refer you there for some information and stories. The real test of your technical ability as an actor comes when you must repeat an action time and again, perfectly matching what you've done in all the previous takes.

In most cases, just before the camera rolls, you'll have a chance to run through the scene from top to bottom. Sometimes if you're working in a low-budget film, or a 1-hour episodic when they're trying to shoot in four days instead of seven, such as "Silk Stalkings," or the sun is setting and you have five minutes to get it in the can, then you may not get the opportunity. Sometimes, for no particular reason, the actor's need is just overlooked.

Remember most of the people you'll be working with have no idea of the inner process and work you're doing. And, of course, if you're doing your work properly, the old Spencer Tracy line about acting – "Just don't let them catch you at it" – makes everyone think that what you're doing is effortless. It's not your job to educate them, and more than likely, they don't really want to know.

If you need to run through the scene, then ask for it. You may need to take the Director aside where your conversation cannot be overheard, and tell him or her that it's necessary for you to run through the scene without technical interruptions. Most often this will not be a problem. As we mentioned in the "Rehearsal" chapter, you may only get one, so make it count. The crew may need one too — they call it a "May Day" rehearsal.

In this book, we're generally making it a point to avoid giving you acting notes per se, because many masters deal with this subject in many books and classes, and you have access to these excellent sources. We do want to say a word about how the various forms of film and TV affect your acting work, however, as this can be very useful information.

On the matter of spontaneity, we find it's very important to be prepared, and it's equally important to let your ideas and energy flow when it comes time to shoot.

> When I act, I don't always want to know exactly how a scene will come out. I know what the scene is about, I've made my choices and like connecting the dots in a puzzle, I know where I'm going, yet at the same time, I don't. When I add the emotion and let it flow through me, I hope for what we call the "accident" — that special something, that unknown element that makes it special. Just as when a ceramicist throws a pot and paints a design on it, everything up until then had been carefully crafted. At the point when the pot is placed in the kiln and fired, the final product will have obtained its own uniqueness, something totally unplanned and divine.
> — Erin

Some actors don't like to rehearse because they want to be fresh and spontaneous. Shirley MacLaine's last book about "Postcards From the Edge" told a story of how Meryl Streep didn't want to rehearse and just wanted to see what happened, which can be very viable. However, if it's your first job, it can be very unsettling. Although it wasn't the way Shirley was used to working, she wasn't thrown by it and enjoyed the challenge.

Another actor may prefer to rehearse so much that the work seems to become encased in cement, having lost any spontaneity and freshness. As you can tell, we're not in favor of rehearsing something into the ground, but we also feel that good preparation is the key to most good performances.

PERFORMANCE

Don't be interesting. Be interested in.
— Warren Robertson

We share this quotation with you because we find it to be full of meaning both from the micro and from the macro point of view. We constantly emphasize collaboration, and so, let this quotation remind you to be interested in the overall project of which you're now a part. And of course this also applies to your acting work, in the sense that you are not here to be the center of attention, even if you're the star. You're here to listen, to react, to collaborate.

To work for an involvement for its own sake on stage, bogs down the movement of the play, disconnects you from the play, makes you blind and deaf to the play. Beware.
— Uta Hagen

Ultimately, your job here is to forget the ego entirely — to move into the action of the piece so deeply — that the actor is no more. You're now faced with one of the paradoxes of the business: you must be conscious and unconscious of what you're doing. You must have that part of you which watches, but does not judge. Yet you must also have that part of you which loses itself in the creative flow of the moment, without sacrificing control.

As we've said before, we're avoiding giving actual acting advice in this book. There's something we want to share with you that's one part experience, one part observation, one part technique and one part pure metaphysics. The basic thought here is this: **the camera will see what you are thinking.** We're not sure why this is, but we do know this is true. It's a law of the universe, and you'll experience it every time you work in front of a camera.

This can be a fearsome thing. But in fact, when you harness this thought, and allow it to inform your work, you will possess a grace and a power that will allow you to communicate in astounding new ways.

When you think about this, you'll realize that, although you're working with text, you are primarily working with *subtext* and film is the medium of *subtext*, because it focuses on the eye, the window of the soul. If you let them, the viewers in the audience will see right in.

The eye is so important in film, that you'll notice in vital close-ups, many actors choose not to blink. Think about powerful leading men in key scenes: Jack Nicholson and Tom Cruise in the courtroom scene in "A Few Good Men"; Alec Baldwin, John Travolta, Paul Newman, and many others. One friend of ours calls a blink a "mental stutter." A blink is so important – and so large – on film, that it becomes a punctuation, and so must be chosen carefully.

Movement is also something that must be chosen carefully on film. Too much movement can be harmful, because you can lose the attention of the audience. You can, in effect, upstage yourself, causing the viewer to be more interested in what you're doing than in what you're thinking. Of course, if the text is a real bore, you can rescue the scene by creating an action which expresses the subtext. And sometimes in-action is the most powerful action of all.

> *Stillness is probably the most important quality an actor needs to possess if he or she is to be successful in the craft of acting for the camera; stillness not only of the mind and eye, but also of the body.*
> *– Malcolm Taylor*

Just a side note – the next time you watch a film, think about text versus sub-text. Some films have so much sub-text there's barely a plot: "Scenes From a Marriage," for example, and many other of Bergman's movies. Some films are all action and sub-text is utterly missing, leaving the film completely flat: "Hollow Man" being a good example. In our opinion, the mega-hits – no matter their genre – have plenty of both. "Cliffhanger" was a big hit not just because people were hanging off the edges of cliffs, but because we cared about them.

What you're really doing when you perform on film, is you're working with energy. Your energy needs to be contained, focused, and directed. In fact, it needs to be harnessed, and this brings us to some horse metaphors. This may sound strange, but we both have done some riding through the years and have found there's a tangible communication between horse and rider that translates itself kinetically.

> An advanced rider friend of mine took a master class where she was asked to direct her horse without the use of a bridle. Great, she thought, I have a hard enough time using the reins! However, she found that when she got her mind clear enough to have one thought, like "go to that tree," the horse immediately went there. I've been using this technique ever since and it completely changed my riding, because I realized I can trust the connection I have with the horse. If we trusted this in all our activities, we'd know a thought communicates itself.
> – Mara

The philosopher Gurdjieff makes the analogy that our emotions are like a horse and our thoughts are like the rider. To pull a carriage and arrive at a specific destination, a horse needs to have a driver – that driver is the mind. Yes, we need access to our emotions, we must be emotionally available and those emotions need to be powerful. But we also need the ability to harness those emotions and govern where and how we'll use them.

Sometimes actors worry about expressing their emotions. Remember that – particularly on camera – sometimes concealing those emotions can be just as interesting, if not more so. In terms, again, of working with energy, we must learn to feel, and to contain.

> *Less is more... It is more interesting to watch an actor struggling not to show his feelings.*
> — Michael Caine

In his invaluable work, "Advice To The Players," Bobby Lewis shares notes he has given to students in class.

> [After the final Nina Treplev scene from "The Seagull" by Anton Chekhov:] Don't try to cry. If anything, try *not* to cry....If you're working right, in your situation, the proper emotion will be there. If not, we examine the work. But don't fool around with the problem of "feeling" or it will either go away altogether or just be simulated.
> — Robert Lewis

Another thing about working with energy — most scenes are an exchange of energy between you and another actor. So you need to develop your skill at both sending and receiving the energy that is moving back and forth. Many times your most interesting work on film will not so much be action, as it will be reaction.

> *It is reaction that gives every moment its potency.*
> —Michael Caine

Talking is easy. It's listening that takes discipline. Don't be trying to remember your next line while your acting partner speaks. Actually listen to what they're saying. This is your time to gather the energy being sent to you. Accept it, respond to it from the depth of your character's understanding. You will form your response from the energy you receive; if you don't receive that energy — which you can only do by listening — you won't have anything to give back.

In the best of all possible worlds, all your preparation will help you move into that magic place we call "flow." It's the "effortless effort" place where you feel connected to your character, to your fellow actors, to your director and you feel you're simply in the right place at the right time doing the right thing.

Of course, your director is working hard to realize his/her vision as well. Some directors describe this process of directing as the Mise-en-Scène — literally the "Putting Into the Scene" in French — but the literal translation misses the deeper point. Our director friend Roger puts it eloquently:

> Le mot mise-en scène is a very noble word. Most of the actors of all nationalities knows its signification. I use it all the time in my English productions. For actors it's a divine word, a warm human way of directing actors, it means more of guiding coaching, taking care of, it's a far better expression than the cold and almost technical" directing."
> – Roger Cardinal

Now we want to shift your attention to the camera. As we've said before, the camera's point of view is what it's all about in this business. For starters, always find out how a scene is being shot. Another term for this is how a scene is being "covered." Do you have two, three, four cameras running? If so – yippee – you don't have to remember what you did in the master when you do a close-up. Find out which segments are going to be shot in close-up. Find out where the camera is "holding" on you: Mid-waist? Mid-chest? Cheekbone? (There are names for these shots listed in the glossary, such as Clint Eastwood shot, Cowboy shot, Sophia Loren shot, etc.) You need to know this for many reasons, one of the most important being movement. If you make a large move while the camera is focused on your eyeball, you'll be out of frame literally in the blink of an eye. Know how the scene is being shot.

Actors sometimes believe they shouldn't talk to crew members. While there is indeed a hierarchy, it's also true the crew are there to create a good show, just as you are, and you are all on the same team. Sometimes the best thing you can do for the project – and for yourself – is to ask questions and get help.

> As First Assistant Camera, I'm responsible for the camera itself and for keeping the shot in focus. When I'm the Camera Operator, I'm also responsible for framing the shot. I was amazed on a recent shoot of a hit episodic show that one of the stars had no clue I was doing her

close-up. She was worried about the master shot, but I was right down her tonsils. Had she asked me, I could have helped her. On another show, a sit-com, one of the guest actors looked around and began to figure out which camera was getting what. "Do you have my close-up?" she asked. Once she knew, she was able to adjust her movements, and I was able to film her optimally.

— Jim Lewis

The previous story alludes to the point that some actors don't believe they're supposed to know anything about the camera. We disagree! We feel the more you know, the better your work can be. A well-known actor friend of ours from London agrees:

One of the earliest lessons I learned as an actor was when I was working on Michael Winners "The Wicked Lady" and Jack Cardiff was our DOP [Director of Photography]. I had the presence of mind to ask him about the lenses he was using and from then on I was very aware of which lens was on, how to read which it was and to adjust my performance accordingly. Overall, apart from the advice given to me by Laurence Olivier when he was directing me for my first West End performance — "Never pause when the audience knows what you are going to say next" (brilliant) — the most important thing to remember whenever you're working in this crazy business is always to keep your sense of humour. Don't slag off [disrespect] the techies. They are trying to do their job as well as you and you would not look as good without them.

— Marc Sinden

You also need to make choices about which lines you deliver to your acting partner and which lines you say looking elsewhere. This is an issue in the energy exchange, but also becomes more of a technical matter when it comes to matching, for which we refer you to the Matching chapter.

Some actors hold back their energy on the master, and don't give a full performance, wanting to save it for their close-ups. If you end up shooting your close-up first and base your performances on what the other actor gave you in the master, then it can be quite annoying having your fellow actor change the rhythm and interpretation of the scene by changing his or her level of intensity on their close-up. It's not fair, it's not right, but it happens.

Soaps have their own unique problems. Some of them have to do with the critical time element.

> One day on "Days Of Our Lives" an actor missed his entrance completely. We had rehearsed it a certain way, but when it came to the take, he didn't appear. I improvised some lines, which covered the gap and completed the scene. The Director decided she liked the improv and that the scene still worked, so she didn't have to reshoot. That saved her precious time and money and she thanked me for it.
> — Mara

Some of the situations that come up for actors in Soaps have to do with the unique open-ended structure of an ongoing drama.

> In creating a new character on "Young & Restless" something was bothering me, and it wouldn't go away. I finally figured it out. It was a simple but important thing — any time you do a part in the theatre or in TV, you have a script and it has a beginning, middle, and end. Based on that, you create an arc. In a Soap you can't do that. You don't know where you're going. One day I opened the script and I had two teenage daughters. That informs your performance! There's no "Bible" for a new character.
> — Granville Van Dusen

In episodic TV or features, you may sometimes have to deal with someone being ill and unavailable to shoot on time.

> Once when I was working on "Jake and the Fatman," William Conrad was quite ill and unable to make it to the set, so the Producers decided to have another much younger actor stand in for him during my close-up.

> I shot my close-up opposite Alan Campbell, and he had his own approach to the scene. Later that week Mr. Conrad was feeling better and they shot his close-up, in which his approach was entirely different than the one I had responded to. Later they edited the footage together – my response to Campbell, opposite Conrad's close-up. Although the audience probably never sensed anything wrong, I cringe whenever I see that scene.
>
> – Erin

CLOSE-UPS

This brings us to the important matter of close-ups. As we've explained, you don't often have a choice about the order in which shooting occurs. If you do, take advantage of it and protect your work by doing your emotional close-ups first.

> During the "Heaven Help Us" shoot, as the crew was preparing for my farewell speech, Jerry the D.P. noticed that at rehearsal I gave a full performance, tears and all. He asked me if I'd prefer to have my close-ups first. I hesitated at first, noticing the camera was already pointed in the other direction, and that it would be easier for them to shoot the other half of the room first. But then I said, yes. I was very grateful, because had we done the master shot first, I would've been completely spent before we ever got around to shooting my close-up.
>
> – Erin

It's possible you'll have to do your close-ups to a stand-in, or even to thin air. Sometimes your fellow actor is needed in make-up for another scene, or is being used in a Second Unit shooting, or it might just be that he or she is the lead in the series, and is just too tired, and has already gone home. Whatever the reason, you have to make the most of your own close-up.

> There are many awkward things an actor may have to do. In "Murphy Brown" I always keep the master going when all six people are talking... let's say in terms of coverage, [you may have to] talk to a person's ear,

pretend... so imbue that ear with life, because then you'll show up on camera.

— Barnet Kellman

One important rule: make sure you have something specific to look at. If, for example, you're doing a science fiction piece and you're supposed to be looking into the Gamma Quadrant — but in fact are looking at the far end of Studio H23 — request a flag be attached to a pole or request that a piece of tape be attached to the screen you're staring at, so that your eyes don't wind up with a drifty, far-away look.

But, of course, if you had your choice, you'd prefer to be looking into your acting partner's eyes. Our advice, therefore, is to offer your acting partner the same courtesy, and be there for them.

I like to be there for the other actor's close-up, and I like the other actor to be there for me.

— Joan Van Ark

Most actors are there for the other guy during close-ups and give full performances. Even if you've been released and are off the clock, out of your own generosity if you can choose to stay, it's noticed and appreciated, and someday you may wish to have the action reciprocated.

— Barnet Kellman

We love hearing stories of generosity and consideration between performers. Unfortunately, such is not always the case. We want to point out some pitfalls to you, and we give you this information from a position that ethics are more important than anything else — more important than power or ego or fleeting moments of success. We trust you won't abuse what we give you.

Let's say you're ready to do your close-up, and sure enough, your fellow actor has graciously agreed to stand off-camera so you can look at him/her while you do your lines. Of course, that person must stand directly beside the camera – which is called "hugging the camera." The idea is that your eye will go just past the lens, but will almost be looking into the lens. This is what the Director needs on film/video. So. "Action." You look into your partner's eyes and all is going well, when you notice your partner is drifting away from the lens, moving further and further away from the camera. What do you do? Follow the person you're supposed to be looking at and lose the lens? Stop? Whatever the case, you're greatly disadvantaged because you're no longer thinking of the emotional content of the scene! You're worrying about a technical detail which should've been irrelevant. Don't do this to fellow actors. Be wary if it's done to you.

A similar situation can arise if someone other than your acting partner in some way interferes with your sight lines, particularly during a close-up. We need to emphasize here that this is a major no-no. It truly is one of the rudest things one actor can do to another.

> *During the shooting of an episode for the series "Hotel," I was ready to do my close-up. This was a flirtatious scene, and my leading man was terrific, and was very much there for me. So he was hugging the camera. But then something bizarre happened. Another face appeared above his. It was his co-star, and she, too, had decided to hug the camera. She was staring at me, scrutinizing my every word, my every move. Needless to say, I couldn't remember my lines with this going on in front of me. The Director didn't realize this was all happening, and asked why I couldn't remember the lines I had remembered perfectly a moment before. "If you want a performance out of me, I suggest you remove <u>her</u>." "Aha", he said, and asked her to leave.*
> — Erin

Here's an area where you do have a perfectly good reason to request help. Any time anyone is in your line of sight in such a way that it's distracting to you, you may request the person move. We recommend saying this kind of thing quietly to your Director, rather than intentionally embarrassing someone. Whether or not their intentions are malicious, yours don't need to be.

TERMINOLOGY

You'll hear a lot of new words on the set. Many of these are covered in our Glossary, so have a look. We'll cover a few of them here as well.

"Places" is what the Director will say when he or she is ready for you to walk onto the set and stand where you should be when shooting begins. The First A.D. may then say, "Final Checks?" and this is an opportunity for Make-Up and Hair to take a final look at you. Then the First A.D. will start to ask if each department is ready. "Camera ready?" he or she may ask. You may find sometimes that although everyone else is asked, you are not. Our experience is that good First A. D.s generally _do_ ask if the actor is ready. If you don't get that courtesy, you might want to ask for it.

When you're shifting from rehearsal to shooting, the First A.D. will say, "This is a take." After the master shot is done, sometimes you'll shoot parts of scenes, which is called a "pick up." In such a case, you'll need your "cue" or "feed line." You'll sometimes want to ask to "go back" and "pick it up from" a previous line, so that you can get enough momentum to deliver your lines well.

In the Sound chapter we explain the word "speed" — you'll hear it as the beginning of a sequence of important words in the following order: "Speed" (sound is ready), "Camera" or "Rolling" (camera is ready), "Action" — that is your cue to begin the scene. Don't do or say anything until you hear that famous and all-important word. Only the Director can say it. It is the only word you are to use as permission to start.

There are some important words which refer to the movements you'll be asked to make as an actor. If, for example, you're asked to "banana" into a shot, it means you are not to approach the camera in a straight line, but rather, to use a curved arc as your approach.

You may be asked to "rock into" or to "turn into" a shot. The idea here is that you're suggesting a sense of movement which will match with a master or another shot. To "rock into" the shot means to rock on your feet, which will look as though you're completing a previously started movement. This looks much more realistic than starting from a stock-still position. To "turn into" a shot accomplishes the same thing, suggesting the completion of a turn previously started.

> I once had an important close-up in a film where I was to deliver the single most powerful and shocking plot point. Just before the cameras rolled, the director came up to me and said, "Before you say the first line just turn into the shot." I was focused on emotional preparation and nodded my head as though I understood — but I didn't, so a few minutes later, I asked my leading man what the director meant. He told me, "Don't worry about it; just plant your feet firmly and anchor yourself to me." I did just that. And it was one of my best performances. The director was elated. I had done it in one take. However, as we were preparing to exit the set, he came up to me and asked why I hadn't turned into the shot as he'd asked, and I mentioned what my leading man had said to me. He chuckled and said, "You do know, of course, that I can't cut to you." So it was my leading man who got the close-up.
>
> — Erin

We cover some of this ground again in the next chapter, "Matching." But the point made in this story is so important that we want to explain it at the risk of boring you. Technically, what happened here was that in the master shot, Erin was moving just as she spoke the all-important line. Therefore in order for the close-up to match the master, she would've had to "cheat" at least a small sense of movement in order for the Director to use her close-up on that line. Once the first line was spoken they could cut back to her — and did. But meanwhile, the most powerful and emotionally charged line in the film — which should have been her close-up — was not.

HITTING YOUR MARK

> *The point is that on Monday morning you have to be there and hit your mark.*
> — Joan Van Ark

This is such a well-known phrase in this business, that it was the original title of our book and our seminar. Those who know what it means have worked in the business. Those who don't, haven't.

> *We were on location in Honolulu shooting an episode of "Magnum P.I." The night before, the First A.D. had hired some extras to do a couple of non-speaking roles. Tom Selleck and I are being chased by these beefy men in fatigues who're shooting at us with M-16s. The Director says to the lead extra, "It's real important here that you hit your mark." Of course, the Extra completely misses his mark. The Director tries again. "I know you're running at full speed, but it's really important that you hit your mark." He misses it again. Now the sun is setting, and the Director is pulling his hair. He says, "Listen, you see this mark on the ground? I want you to <u>hit this mark</u>. Okay. Roll 'em. Action." The Extra was determined this time. He ran up to the X the Director had drawn on the ground, aimed his M-16 at it and shot it. Even though there were blanks in the gun, he obliterated it. The entire crew fell over and rolled down the hill in gales of laughter. Tom was completely out of control, holding his sides, and so was I. No one had bothered to explain to the poor man what the heck "hitting your mark" meant.*
>
> *– Erin*

Hitting your mark isn't as easy as it may seem. What's the point of hitting your mark? The point is to show up on film. The camera is set, and is expecting you to be at a certain place. If you're not there, the camera may get your ear or your left elbow, or it may miss you altogether. Even if it gets you perfectly in frame, you might be out of focus. The focus-puller isn't looking through the lens, he or she is looking at numbers and lines. So as you can see, this is about as basic a skill as you will need in this business.

So, you'll need to develop some techniques for arriving at that all-important spot, without glancing down. Imagine that you come into a room; see the long lost love of your life; say "Oh Johnny!"; rush toward him; look down at your feet; then hug him. We don't think so. So here are some tricks.

One thing we've often done is to stand at the mark (a piece of tape on the floor, or a little tiny sandbag usually), then walk backwards from the mark to the place where you begin to walk. If you're working with a sandbag, be careful. They can be terrific because they stick up and you can feel them with your toe. But they can also trip you, so you need to have your own little rehearsal for dealing with them.

Another way of hitting your mark is to choose places and/or objects on the set which become your own personal landmarks. You can figure out that as your elbow clears the refrigerator, it's time for you to stop, or when your hand brushes the top of the desk, that's when you turn left into the camera. Figure these things out for yourself, and do an excellent job of it. Don't improvise on hitting your mark! Be professional.

To complete the task of hitting your mark correctly, you must be able to do it unconsciously, or at least to make it appear so.

> When I hit a ball in tennis, I don't think, "Do I have my racket back far enough?" It just goes there. It has to be that way in acting. You can't be worrying about hitting your mark. It has to be "muscle memory." You have to own certain habits. And there are many of these kinds of things that you need to know as an actor that are not intuitive.
> — Don Uehling

So take the time to get the skill of hitting your marks so perfectly that it ceases to be an issue when you're doing your work.

BEHAVIOR ON THE SET

There are some things not to do on the set. Avoid mugging, upstaging, scene stealing, or bit-stealing. This should all be self-evident, but just in case it isn't, we'll spell it out. If you see someone do a clever piece of business, don't steal it. Appreciate it, allow it to inspire you to pull something equally original from a deeper place, but be careful about appropriating it for yourself.

A "piece of business" or a "bit" is usually a gesture (or a series of gestures) someone makes. It can either be funny, or just extremely telling. In "Rosemary's Baby" – a scary film – Ruth Gordon plays a character who doesn't seem to notice anything unusual about people giving birth to devils. When a guest at her dinner table throws a knife into her dining room floor, she simply pulls it out, wets her finger and repairs the damaged floor. That simple gesture said everything about the character and thus became a "signature." Had anyone tried to steal this gesture, they would simply have been quoting Ruth Gordon. That's the danger of stealing someone else's "bit."

We'll take a brief tangent, here, and share some philosophy about how an actor learns. Most acting teachers advise watching any and everything to learn as much as possible about acting. Watch great actors, watch not-so-great actors, watch comedians, watch singers... and this has great value. We want to emphasize that it is equally important to watch "regular people" instead of actors, because possibly this will offer you richer source material. However valuable it may be to understand a choice made by Robert DeNiro or Meryl Streep, never underestimate your own ability to notice and assimilate human behavior which may not be your own. The more you attune yourself to noticing, hearing, and feeling the nuances of body language, facial expression, vocal melody, light and shade, silence and sound, the more you'll be aware of the extraordinary dynamics of our complex species even under the most mundane circumstances. Let these observations inform your work.

> My acting teacher Tad Danielewski recommended that, if we were going to watch TV, we watch "real" shows, the best known one at the time being "Candid Camera." I watched an episode where a man puts a suitcase in the bottom locker, in a wall of lockers at a train station. As he inserts his bag, it disappears out the back of the locker. Of course this in itself was funny, but it was the man's reaction which I wouldn't have predicted. He simply stared. He stared and stared at the open, empty locker. The longer he stared, the funnier it was. Next, he apparently decided he must test reality, so he placed his second bag in the locker. This, too, disappeared. This time his reaction was completely different. Without so much as a tenth of a second's

> hesitation, he dove into the locker after his bag. Of course this was hysterically funny and the audience members were falling out of their chairs laughing. I have never forgotten this episode, because of its unpredictability, and its simplicity. The "real" man's responses included no posturing, no mugging. Because he didn't "act," he was much funnier.
> — Mara

When it comes to mugging, know that even if you think you're having fun, it can be very distracting, annoying, or even damaging.

> When I was screen-tested for the feature film "Star Trek III," I worked opposite a young actor (who shall be nameless) who'd already been signed for his part. He had already screen-tested with two previous actresses and I was the third. He couldn't have cared less which one of us got the part. For him, this was just another boring day in a Starfleet uniform costume. For me it was my first professional screen test. I'd done a superb audition lasting five hours; I'd signed a three-film deal with Paramount; I'd waited for this for years. During my entire screen test, this actor mugged for the camera, joked with the crew, and even went so far as to scoop me up and dance me out of frame just before the cameras were to roll. He may have thought he was just having fun. But his antics may have lost me the job, because I couldn't concentrate. When I told my acting coach about this experience, his first question was, "Did you use it??" I hadn't. I was too much of a novice at the time and too worried that a Vulcan mustn't show emotion. Had I been older and wiser, I'd have understood that a Vulcan just sits on emotion with extreme control and it could have made my performance powerful. I wish I'd been given one more take. That's why we're writing this book.
> — Mara

If you're an actor – or even an extra – and you're in a scene, be fully committed to that scene. Don't mentally drift or wander. Be in the moment, and use your intuition, or your good old common sense, to figure out what's appropriate behavior. As you can see, sometimes it's right to remain serious, and focused.

There are also times when the opposite situation is true. If you've been working on a series for two years with the same cast and crew, you may find you'll do just about anything to keep the energy up and the spirits high.

> *During the shooting of "Buck Rogers," there were days when going to work was really a grind. My co-star Gil Gerard loved to play practical jokes and I was always "Miss Serious." One day I decided it was time to change that. I warned the camera operator to keep rolling after the director said "Cut." My character Wilma was about to be thrown into a volcano. My scene-mate said "Oh Wilma, this is the end!" I looked at her and said, "You know, it's really tough being an egg. You only get laid once, eaten once and it takes ten minutes to get hard." She fell over backwards, and the entire cast and crew clutched their bellies and laughed. The camera shook, the props fell to the ground. That changed the spirit of the set. From then on, we all took turns trying to crack each other up. Some days it was the only way to keep the energy going after sixteen hours of shooting.*
> — Erin

So, as you can tell, we're not saying you should always be polite and reserved on the set! Sometimes it's appropriate to have fun at work, as we all know. Sometimes, it's appropriate to stay focused, as a well-known Canadian director points out.

> *Here's my pet peeve. It's when, between set-ups, an actor smokes, and fools around with the crew, instead of concentrating on his character and learning his lines.*
> — Roger Cardinal

What we're saying is — be committed, be aware.

LINES – LETTER-PERFECT & NOT

A word about words. When it comes to shooting, you'll be expected to say the lines you've rehearsed, which of course, are the lines the writers wrote. Some actors take liberties with the lines as written, and approximate what's on the page. Some actors go a great deal further than that, and take the liberty of completely rewriting scenes. This is really a separate discussion, because extensive rewriting with an actor's participation does not happen at the beginning level, and in fact only happens under certain circumstances.

Returning, however, to the point in the process where you're about to shoot – this is certainly not the time to think of changes to the script. You may encounter Directors, Producers, or fellow actors who don't mind the occasional word change. However, thinking always from the perspective of being a team player, we find that choosing not to really know your lines is disrespectful.

It's disrespectful to the writers not to work hard to learn their words. They worked hard to write them and may have torn their hair out over a certain sentence. Even if you feel you're a better writer than the person who wrote the script you're performing, do your best to find the logic behind the lines, and incorporate the through-line of your character's choices and actions in your learning process. This will be an invaluable tool to memorization. If you feel bored or distressed about the material, remember that you're dealing not only with text, but with subtext, which is the real depth of the piece. If, somehow, you're working with a script that has no subtext, you have the opportunity to create your own.

If you change lines, you'll be changing cues your acting partner is listening for. Furthermore, you'll be changing cues numerous crew members will also be listening for. If you transpose a line, or add something minor, you may think most people won't mind. But remember you have a director who's trying to keep writers happy, and you have crew members who are trying to find their place on a page. It's our recommendation that you take memorization seriously and treat your lines very professionally.

We feel this way even if you're working several days a week on a Soap. There are, however, many actors who don't feel the same.

> *A lot of people use cue cards. It's weird! There you are working with someone and your fellow actor is not connected to you. You basically have to learn to talk to a wall.*
> — Granville Van Dusen

The cue cards on Soaps are to address the time problem again, because there literally is no time to deal with actors who don't know their lines. We think you'll agree with us, however, and realize that working from cue cards is not the same as working from the heart.

There are times in any form of shooting where lines can spontaneously arise and sometimes this works, depending upon the form in which you're working, and the individual responses you get from your Director and fellow actors. Soaps may be the most fluid in this regard, because they are an ongoing process, where writers are writing for specific actors, picking up their rhythms.

> *When I first started writing the scripts for my soap "Milford-Haven," I had certain cast members in mind. As those cast members actually began performing in the show, I became more and more familiar with their speech patterns, their idiosyncrasies and their dynamics. More and more I would write specifically for them, and more and more they would find themselves performing lines that sounded and felt natural to them. This was the ideal situation. It's one of the things that made the show such a success and it's one of the great advantages to working in Soaps.*
> — Mara

> *When I first started on "Young & Restless," I added occasional idioms to my lines. At first the producers would stop me and I'd apologize, and do the line as written. However, eventually, the writers started adding those idioms to my lines. To some extent you can also steer your story. You have to be careful not to be a "problem" actor. But on*

> a good show, the Directors and Producers will listen to your ideas. This show stays pretty "human" in the things that happen. And it's the number one rated Soap.
> — Granville Van Dusen

Sometimes rather gloriously spontaneous things happen in this business. When they do, be flexible, go with the flow, and enjoy!

> John Houseman guest-starred on "Silver Spoons." He was, of course, the consummate actor, and we were thrilled to have him. He rarely said anything, but when he did, it was fascinating. When it came time to shoot, he surprised us by never saying what was written. He proceeded to rewrite every scene he was in. We, of course, never knew where our cues were, but it did force us to give him our full attention. And what he spoke was far more eloquent than what had originally been scripted. He was eighty-three years old at the time and one of the giants of the industry. It was a privilege to have worked with him.
> — Erin

STOPPING & STARTING

Remember back in the Audition chapter where we gave you that good advice about stopping yourself if the scene is going badly? Well, here's where the advice changes 180 degrees.

In shooting, when you've started your scene, it's up to the Director — not you — to stop the scene. Under no circumstances should you ever say the word "Cut." That is not your word, it's the Director's word. If you've gone up in your lines and simply can't go any further, the Director will notice, never fear. And if you've genuinely lost your lines, don't worry about the fact that you'll have to start over, just stay in the moment.

> If actors "cut" themselves because they're uncomfortable with the crux of a scene, I'll get on them. But if it's clearly going wrong and he cuts himself, I'm not going to be a prima donna about it. The protocol is, if

an actor says, "I'm sorry, I went up" – fine, but if he were to say "cut" that would make me upset.

– Barnet Kellman

A word to the wise: don't abuse your position by manipulating the Director – or at least, don't do it too often. If, for example, you can't stand the way the scene is going and really want to stop, our advice is to stop. Some internal process is telling you to stop and fix things. Fine. But don't intentionally ruin a take if you think the other actor is doing a better job than you are, or you think you'll get more focus by creating a problem. Professionals can see through this pretty quickly, and they won't appreciate it. There are better ways to build a career.

DO'S & DON'TS

- Do know your hours are going to be long and/or erratic
- Don't expect meal breaks
- Do learn to pace yourself regarding eating
- Do watch what you eat, and don't gain weight during a shoot
- Do learn to keep relaxed yet attentive
- Don't waste energy
- Don't get dehydrated
- Don't allow your blood sugar level to drop too low
- Do give your best under the worst conditions
- Don't complain
- Do know your lines
- Do make the most of rehearsing; don't expect much rehearsal time
- Don't leave the set without telling the appropriate person
- Don't upstage your fellow actors
- Do give your partner the same energy or reading in both master and close-up
- Don't steal focus and energy by joking around – unless it's appropriate
- Don't lose focus – stay with the energy of the scene you're doing
- Do be mindful of your fellow actors
- Don't be thinking of your next line when the other actor is speaking
- Do prepare in detail
- Don't just hang around

- Do anticipate when you'll be needed on set
- Don't anticipate your performance
- Do keep it fresh in take after take
- Don't dirty your wardrobe at lunch
- Don't make plans for your days off without getting approval
- Do make sure the production office has a contact number for you at all times
- Don't plan on a dangerous activity during the shooting period – this includes a ski trip or a motorcycle ride

As we've said many times, this is a collaborative endeavor. Not one of the many disciplines within this business can function in a vacuum. We all need each other and we each must fulfill our respective tasks. We might be tempted to think that we'll look better by making someone else look bad. In fact, just the opposite is true. The better you make your co-workers look, the better you'll look.

If you talk to a lighting person, he'll say that without proper lighting you simply don't have a project. If you talk to a casting person, he/she will say that without the right cast, you simply don't have a project. If you talk with actors, directors, writers, costumers, or anyone else involved in this complex process, each of them will say the same thing.

We have only one thing to say about all these opinions, and it is at the heart of shooting. They are all right. So make your own indispensable contribution by loving what you're doing, and giving it your all. Happy shooting.

MATCHING

Covered In This Chapter:

- The Editor's Job
- The Script Supervisor's Job
- The Editing Process
- Learning to Match

It is circumstance and proper measure that give an action its character.
— Plutarch

Acting demands that you bring total attention and awareness to yourself — mind, body, and emotions.
— Warren Robertson
Acting Teacher, Author, "Free To Act"

MATCHING

On my first job, on the first day, the first scene took place at a restaurant. I was working opposite Glenn Ford, who said, "Just hold your wine glass through the whole scene and you'll be fine." I thought to myself, "Well, no one is going to tell ME how to act." And I proceeded to add every possible detail of movement I could think of. I cut my food, I took bites, I sipped my wine, I wiped my mouth. Then I did a few more unconscious gestures — I touched my chin, I leaned on my chin, I rubbed my earlobe. I touched my nose, and generally filled the scene with movement. The script supervisor came up to me afterwards and said, "You're new in the business, aren't you?" I was devastated — and defensive. "Is my work that bad?" "Oh no," she said, "but you do realize you'll have to match." I said, "Match what?"
— Erin

"Matching" may seem to be one of those irrelevant technical terms that has something to do with the editing process, which is completely beyond the control or the purview of the actor. Not true.

Although you may never get fired for not matching, it's quite possible that your fate could end up being just as ignominious, because you will likely end up on the cutting room floor. To understand what we're talking about, here's a brief explanation of the editing process.

THE EDITOR'S JOB

If you could ever visit an editor still working with celluloid, you'd learn more in two minutes than we could explain in a chapter. Since these working methods are quickly being replaced with digital ones, we ask you to visualize the following. What you'd have seen in the editor's room was strip after strip of film hanging in a carefully organized and arranged order. It was — and still is

— the editor's job literally to piece the film together from all the footage on which the director yelled "Print!"

To vastly oversimplify things, the editor must cut from one thing to the next, adhering to the script, of course, but also making judicious choices based upon what best illuminates the plot, the emotional subtext and the action the film must deliver.

In order to accomplish this, he or she must use a combination of shots. For example, if you had nothing but close-ups, you wouldn't know where the characters were. If, on the other hand, you had nothing but master shots, you wouldn't see the all-important detail in the face and eyes. The editor artfully moves from long shot to medium shot to close-up.

While the editor's doing this, he/she must pay close attention to the continuity of the story as it is expressed visually. This is where every detail counts. If the characters are driving a car that later gets banged up in a chase scene, the car can't be unblemished, then banged up, then perfect again. (Take a look at a couple of low, low budget films and see if you can catch where they goofed. And for one classic example of a big-budget film — and a good one at that — which had a major matching flaw, check "48 Hours." Eddie Murphy is wearing the cuffs, then he isn't, then he is. Oops.) If the actor is wearing a scarf when he walks through the door — and isn't wearing it by the time the editor cuts back to him — it looks like a science fiction time-fluctuation and is jarring to the audience, even if they're not quite sure why. To smooth this out, the editor needs the option of cutting to a shot of the actor removing that scarf. The other choice is even simpler: cut the actor out of the shot completely.

So. It's as simple as this. If you want to stay in the film — learn how to match.

> David Carradine was a guest at my acting class at NBC. We all asked him various questions about his career. When we asked him what he considered to be one of the most important things about his acting

work, he said, "Oh, that's easy. It's matching. And it's something I'm really good at." He went on to describe how complex this could get in an action piece like "Kung Fu." He knew that he was saving the producers hours and even days of wasted time by matching his own action shots. This may have been one of the things that allowed the series to continue for as long as it did.

— Mara

When the editors go into their editing room, they don't start by reviewing every shot. In fact, you may be chagrined to discover, they do their best not to look at shots at all. Instead they work from a "bible," and that bible is the script supervisor's notes. They save the editor a great deal of time, because they're very detailed, more so than you might imagine.

THE SCRIPT SUPERVISOR'S JOB

Here's a basic list of the different kinds of detailed record-keeping a script supervisor keeps. One, she or he keeps a daily log, which includes the camera roll, the duration of the shot, what set they're working on, the scene number, the lens being used, which takes are "prints," any delays and what (or who) caused them, the crew call, lunch and so forth. This daily log, by the way, becomes the basis for production reports by the script supervisor herself, but also for the A.D., and for other crew members.

There is also the "lining" of the script itself. Red lines indicate what action is on camera. Squiggly lines indicate that this action is not covered on camera, and so forth. This "lined" script is an all-important tool for the editors, because when they are in the rhythm of cutting, they don't want to break their concentration. They don't even want to have to go to the detail page unless they need to. But, they must know exactly what the D.P. saw.

In addition to the daily log and the production report, the script supervisor also takes detailed descriptive notes. There are various formats for these notes, and generally, the editors and script supers will agree upon what works best for them. Since this becomes the "bible" for the editors, often the first thing they want to see are the scene number, the take, the time, and if it's a print or no print, and a description. After that every shot is meticulously described — the position of the actors, which way they're crossing, which way they're looking, who crosses in front of whom. Some script supers — depending upon the relationship with the director — will also write down comments like "the director liked that" or "sound person heard a plane." The editor looks at that script page, using it as a map. If there's something he doesn't understand, then he goes to the description page with complete detail. The basic idea is to give the editors as much information as possible, so they don't have to look at the shot.

What does this say about you, the actor, and your relationship with the Script Supervisor? It means you need to pay attention to what he or she has to say, and count yourself blessed if you have a diligent script super on your crew. Sadly, some actors fail to realize that his or her information can save a performance from being unusable, even if you've done your best emotional work.

There's a great deal to be said about set protocol, and we hope we've said it in the Shooting chapter. Briefly, as with every on-set job, there's a certain hierarchy that must be acknowledged. The Script Super has valuable information that can help the actor to match himself, but how is that information to be delivered? Each situation is different. Sometimes the Super approaches the actor directly; sometimes she or he goes to the Director; and there are times when the First A.D. is the one to talk to the actor. Here's a story about a Script Super who had the Director's permission to speak directly to the actor — she did her job properly, though it was, unfortunately, not appreciated.

> This one actor continuously smoked in this scene, so I had to constantly go to the Director. He got tired of it, and told me to start going to the actor directly. So I went up to the actor right before a close-up, and whispered to him, "The cigarette needs to be in your mouth." This is the kind of thing you want to do as discreetly as possible. You don't want to point out what may be perceived as a

> mistake, and yell it across the set. You also don't want to disturb the actor's emotional work. Well, the actor blew up. He had a temper tantrum in front of everyone. "I'm trying to concentrate on the scene!" he said. "Do I have to listen to her? Can't I just do this the way I feel?!" The Director was glaring at me. I quietly said to the Director, "If you don't want to match, then just know that you won't be able to cut to him." The editor later said that in this crucial scene, he was unable to use any of this actor's close-ups.
> – Melisa Sanchez

The same Script Super had a much more positive story to tell about a different film project and it involved an actor who turned out to be a bit better known than the one mentioned above:

> I went to Kevin Costner right before a scene. There were various things to keep track of because he was wearing a tie which kept flipping over and also he was smoking a pipe. As the scene was being shot the pipe was in, the pipe was out. I went up to him and quietly said, "The pipe needs to be in your mouth." He smiled and said, "Thanks!" He probably already knew that, because he's very good at matching. But in any case he was nice about it.
> – Melisa Sanchez

Blake Edwards understood the importance of matching and underscored it in his brilliantly comedic way in the now classic film "The Party." Peter Sellers plays an actor who gets caught wearing a modern-day watch in a period film and the director wants nothing more than to fire him for it – and thus begins one of the great comedy films of all time.

Some Script Supers do extensive wardrobe breakdown in their notes, including not only the lists provided by the wardrobe department, but also everything the actor has brought to the character. For example, Wardrobe may have provided a picture of a jacket with the sleeves down, but you may have made the choice to roll the sleeves up. Or you may have decided that your character drinks Jack Daniels and smokes Camel cigarettes. You can, of course, trust the Wardrobe and Script Super to pick up on these details themselves. But you can also do them – and yourself – a favor by sharing this information with the Script Super before he or she has to figure it out. It'll end up in their notes and you'll have help in keeping your choices consistent.

THE EDITING PROCESS

As we mentioned earlier, the editors choose from a variety of shots. Normally, they cut away from the master shot after the first couple of lines. Then they'll go to close-ups, or to what might be called sub-masters, such as a two-shot, a high-angle, or an over-the-shoulder shot. What you need to be conscious of is that the more you match what you did in the master, the more of your close-ups and other shots can be used in the film.

If all your shots match, you'll succeed in giving the editors what they most need: the greatest number of options, so they can use your best performance, rather than having to eliminate good takes because they don't match.

Here's another aspect of editing, which theoretically should never be your problem to solve, but it's an important thing to be aware of. It's called "crossing the line." We like to think of it as an old-fashioned Saturday afternoon matinee where the cowboys and Indians are chasing each other from Oklahoma to Colorado. If this is the story line, then you want to see those horses going East to West (right to left.) You don't want to see them suddenly change direction and go West to East (left to right)!

> *I was shooting a commercial for Kansas City Power and Light in Kansas City which involved filming an emergency vehicle leaving the station. What we had to do was draw a mental line through the middle of the truck from the front grill, to the rear bumper, then work on one side of the line or the other. On one side of the line, the truck moves right to left and on the other side, left to right. It is simple, just pick one side of the line or the other, and stay there for proper screen direction. If you don't, it's confusing to the audience. In our commercial, it would*

have looked as if the truck was leaving the station, but then returning immediately. The only exception to the rule is if you include the audience in the process of showing the change in direction. For example, in KC, if we'd had a master shot or a dolly shot showing an overview of the vehicle from all directions, we could have gotten away with crossing the line. In most cases, you can't.

— Jim Lewis

The basic rule the Director follows in shooting is first to establish direction. After that — don't show them going in the opposite direction. Directors can only get away with changing direction in complex car chase sequences if they first cut to a neutral shot, say one coming toward the camera.

All this gets increasingly complicated when it comes to close-ups, and this is where your matching can once again come into play. If you're looking camera left in the master, you'll have to be looking camera left in the close-up. Sometimes you may have to "cheat" the look, because the camera may now be on your other side. In any case, you can't afford to reverse yourself in the close-up. As you can see, you have to keep your wits about you. As we said before, you're blessed if you have a good Script Super. We should also tell you that crossing the line can end up being so complicated that sometimes the D.P., the Director, and the Script Super even argue amongst themselves as to what's correct. Let them work it out and advise you. It's really not up to you to figure out these complexities. It is your job to sell it — that is to make it work, even if it feels backwards to you.

LEARNING TO MATCH

We find a good, solid technique for getting your own matching clearly in mind is to marry your action to your words specifically. This process takes shape in rehearsal, which we discuss in more detail in the Rehearsal chapter. Even if you have to beg, steal, or borrow rehearsal time, we feel it's important to make your decisions about "On this word I'll pick up the cereal box." Once you've got that on film, you must stick with the choice. You can't decide that next time you'll pick up an apple instead.

While we have the utmost faith in the Script Super, remember he or she may be watching three actors and must, of course, look up and then look down to make notes. So make your own mental notes as well, and master your own techniques for matching.

When you think about shooting, you probably assume your master and your close-up will be shot on the same day. And in most productions every effort is made to do just that. However, sometimes the D.P. is losing the light, and must quickly move on to another set-up, with the intention of getting back to you for your close-up. Sometimes he or she just runs out of time. If this happens, do your best to memorize your state of mind, your emotional state and as many of the details of your movements as you possibly can.

A word to the wise: in the theatre there's a term every actor knows – "upstaging." The term derives from the days when stages were raked – slanted downwards toward the audience. If an actor wanted to eclipse someone, he had only to walk upstage, forcing his colleague to turn his back on the audience. Obviously, this is a No No. Unfortunately, many performers have used this to good effect.

Here's a theatre story about upstaging which we can't resist telling you. Apparently Talulah Bankhead was trying to one-up her co-star one evening and she did so by intermittently exposing herself to him, subtly moving her leg. The audience couldn't see, but he could see plenty. He was lucky to remember a single line. The following night, during that same scene, he worked hard to balance a glass full of liquid while Miss Bankhead spoke. Of course, the audience didn't hear a word, worrying only as to when and if the glass would fall. We figure that actor stayed up a whole night to think up such a wickedly perfect revenge. In film and TV, upstaging can be a little different, but it's the same principle.

> In "Silver Spoons" we were, of course, working in comedy. In one of my first episodes, I was doing my best to "keep alive" in the scene, so I wanted to be physically active while I was listening. My co-star was busy giving me a joke, but I was busy with a physical action, twirling a

> *piece of ribbon around my finger. He finally said, "stop moving on my joke!" He was right — I was upstaging him. I learned something more, though: the audience would never laugh unless I gave them permission to do so, by having a reaction myself to the joke being given on stage. So long as I was too busy to react, the audience would never find the joke.*
>
> *— Erin*

There's one more way that you can upstage a fellow performer in comedy, and that is by stepping on his or her laugh. You understand here we're not talking about interrupting the actual lines your colleague is saying; we're talking about the audience reaction to it. Audience laughter has an arc — you must allow that arc to complete itself before beginning your next line. This is part of the all-important timing of comedy. Laughter is the bread and butter of comedy — don't squash it.

This is easy to understand in live theatre, or in sitcom, which in many ways is the same as live theatre. When it comes to feature film comedy, you can see that editing is critical. The editor has to leave room for audience reaction and not squash the laughs by cutting too quickly to the next shot. If the editor is not adept at cutting the film for comedy, he or she can ruin a good project. The audience has to have time to laugh, finish laughing, then hear the next joke.

> *I first saw the feature film "M.A.S.H." in Tokyo, where it was subtitled. The Japanese audience needed time to read each joke. By the time they laughed, they covered the next joke, which I was trying to hear. I missed half of the humor of the film.*
>
> *— Mara*

When it comes to working in film, naturally, you want to keep your work fresh, no matter how many takes you have to do. We understand only too well that inner dialogue which goes something like: "Pardon me, but I was trained in the theatre. I never repeat a performance! Every moment lives in its own time, creates its own space, has a vibrancy all its own!" Basically, what we have to say to this is: Vibrancy, schmibrancy. If you want to stay in the film, you gotta learn to match.

> *Recently I was working on a feature film of the "Karate Kid" genre called "A Dangerous Place." After work one day, the Script Supervisor came up to me and told me my matching was great. She said, "I put a note to the Editors on the script, which said, "Of the three actors in this scene, Erin matches perfectly so you can always cut to her.""*
> *— Erin*

We'll end this chapter with a success story, a story about an actor whose skill at matching is so advanced that editors who work with him compare him to the master actors from the old studio days, who were trained and expert at matching. This one was told to us by the editor of "Friends" and the actor whose skill is so noteworthy is Elliott Gould. Remember what we said about eating scenes and how difficult it is to "match?" Well, a real pro can pull it off brilliantly.

> *I started the edit on the eating scene, and Elliott is amazing — he eats spaghetti, and mops up the sauce at the end of the scene. He did it the same way each time. You see him do it and it looks natural. You see it in the medium shot and it is identical. Take after take, he had the identical amount of spaghetti on the fork, moved his arm at the same spot in the dialogue. The really magical thing was that his performances were slightly varied emotionally. What that meant was, we could use any one of the takes, because they were all perfect technically. We were, therefore, free to choose the one which best served the emotional content of the story.*
> *— Andy Zoll*

SOUND

Covered In This Chapter:

- Sound Design – an Overview

- Voice

- Sound On The Set

- Looping

- Voice-Over Work

- Walla & Loop Groups

One way to see how sound affects your consciousness is to turn down the sound track of the next video you watch — whether it's a thriller or a romance — and note how your level of engagement changes. In fact, it is often the sound tracks of films, more than the images, that influence our emotional responses.

— Andrew Weil
"Sound Healing," <u>Self Healing Newsletter</u>

SOUND

Sound is something most of us take for granted in life, and this sometimes extends to our work in film and television as well. But sound is as colorful, complex and vital an element of your overall work as any other aspect of your performance.

> I was invited to a NASA launch from Cape Kennedy. There was a great deal of excitement leading up to the moment of lift off, as I sat with other VIPs and guests in bleachers looking across the Florida landscape at a distant rocket. But when the rocket actually lifted, I felt a curious sense of detachment. At the edge of the horizon, plumes of smoke billowed, and a toy rocket began to move away from the ground. It seemed surprisingly anti-climactic. Then something hit me in the chest full force. It was the sound of the engines. I burst into tears — as did almost everyone around me — and really understood for the first time the emotional impact of sound.
> — Mara

SOUND DESIGN

Sound in a motion picture or television program doesn't just "happen," any more than the images on the screen just happen. More than most of us realize, there is a tremendously complex and layered process that goes into the creation of every sound we hear while we enjoy the moving pictures we're watching.

Sound design has a fascinating history of its own and if you're interested, please delve into the subject by reading, or even better, go to one of the broadcast museums — the Museum of Broadcast Communication in Chicago, or the Museum of TV & Radio in New York or Beverly Hills — where there are fantastic collections of early broadcasts.

Even when the early silent films were shown, it was understood they had very little impact without some sort of sound, so pianists, organists and sometimes full orchestras were hired to accompany what was happening on screen. Imagine the Keystone Cops racing around corners without their signature "do-dee-oo-dee-oo" music! Something would be missing.

Murray Spivak pioneered the "moving sound effect," creating all his sounds simultaneously with the actors. Among his other inventions was a giant drum filled with beans which, when rotated, sounded like rain. You can imagine what a frantic business it was trying to match the motions of actors while also creating background sounds. By the time the original "King Kong" came along, a breakthrough was possible because multi-track recording had by then been invented. To create Kong's mighty roar, the sound engineer recorded a tiger's roar, lowered it an octave, then mixed in other sounds to create something unique and terrifying believable. Imagine what that film would have been without Kong's threatening sound.

To this day, one of the problems producers encounter while shooting a film is the interference of extraneous sound. To address the problem, Jack Foley invented the "sound stage." The motion picture scene, already shot, would be projected and missing sounds would be added. Foley invented the technique of synchronized footsteps. By wearing particular shoes and carrying a cane, Foley could create the sounds of more than one person walking at the same time. He went on to perfect many other sound techniques as well, lending his name to a whole new field of endeavor.

Some Foley jobs are fairly simple – footsteps, or doors opening. Even these make all the difference to the realism of a moment. Some foley jobs are particularly challenging:

> *I wrote an episode for my radio drama Milford-Haven in which a tanker goes aground. (Ironically, the Exxon Valdez disaster had not yet happened.) In the many sound libraries there was no such thing as "Tanker Goes Aground," so my ingenious foley artist David L. Krebs had to create the sound from scratch. Using a metal bucket filled with water, some pieces of metal and a secret technique known only to him,*

he came up with the basic sounds. Then our engineer Bill Berkuta added some studio sound adjustments. They created the most harrowing sound effect sequence in all of the sixty episodes. Listeners were convinced we went out and taped the sound on location during a real-life disaster.

— Mara

The creation of Foley techniques and the use of real sounds recorded live gave rise to the paradigm we still work with today — the field recording taken documentary-fashion where the natural sound is occurring, and the Foley recording, created by Foley artists on a sound stage. It's the blending of these recordings which creates most sounds we hear in productions. A sound designer named Berkus, who won an Oscar for his sound design of "The Hindenberg," had to come up with an engine sound for the dirigible and did so by mixing together diesels and several other kinds of engines. He then created the sound of St. Elmo's Fire, a particular electrical phenomenon, by mixing in the sound made as foley artists snapped off pieces of carpet padding. To create the sound of the "Star Wars" light saber, sound designer Ben Burrt layered scores of sounds, among them that of a coin operated marking meter. For the 1997 re-release of his film "Das Boot," director Wolfgang Peterson had foley artists bang on metal canoes in a pool, capturing the sound with underwater mikes.

As the producer of a radio drama, one of the most fascinating things I learned was that we experience sound as layers and therefore must create it that way. For example, at any given moment there is first an "ambience." This may sound like silence to us, but in sound-drama we call this "room tone" and that same term applies on the set. (See GLOSSARY) Every room has its own. Next there will be distant ambiences — birds singing, or traffic going by. Next there may be a closer ambience — say the sound of a restaurant. These sounds can be pre-recorded. But unless you add foley none of it works. The sound equivalent of a close-up is foley, which is the personally created sound done right next to the mike. If my characters are in a restaurant but there's no close-up sound of their own cups and spoons, they will seem

> *disconnected from the scene. Foley is the critical element for realism.*
> — Mara

Not only is sound important in film and TV work, but the dimension of sound brings with it another dimension of work for actors including radio, audio books, narration, animation, voice-over, and walla work. One or more of these areas might prove to be a wonderful niche for you as your career develops. But whether you become a sound specialist or not, you'll need to know as much as possible about sound, beginning with your own voice.

VOICE

> *Speak up! I never want to interfere with an actor's character, what they're trying to bring to the screen. But if it's possible, I would ask an actor to give me as much voice as possible. Then we can work in unity together. Because this is a sound and visual medium.*
> — Vince Garcia

As any actor who does voice-over work knows, your voice — its melody, its textures, its variety — can be your fortune. Anything you can do to enhance and improve your vocal variety and range will be all to the good. But whether or not you've been gifted with a gorgeous set of vocal cords, there are technical things to know that will improve your work and your working relationship with not only the sound person, but the director and the editor.

One thing to be aware of is accents. Having a specialized accent can be an asset in certain parts. However, to be as hireable as possible, you <u>must</u> get rid of any accent you have and cultivate what is called "Mid-Western speech." This is as close to "no accent" as Americans come. What this enables you to do is work from a neutral position, and from there you can, theoretically, go in any direction. To accomplish this you can do several things: work with a dialogue coach, listen to tapes, listen to yourself and most of all, practice, practice, practice.

There's also the matter of working on your voice itself. Through working with good teachers, you can increase your range, vocal power and control. This is a routine part of the training British actors receive but Americans have to work a little harder to find good people with whom to study. Consider this an important part of your personal homework. Your voice is an important aspect of your "tool box."

Your local university might be a place to find a teacher. And many books have been written on this subject, one of the best being Kristen Linklater's "Freeing The Natural Voice." We will leave it to experts to describe the process in detail.

To describe it briefly: you need to "find" your voice and find a way to connect your emotions to your voice. You have probably yelled at a football game or raised your voice to a loved one. Chances are you've not done so "correctly" — that is, by using the full power of your voice. Most people squeeze off their voices in the fever pitch of emotions. This works against you when you're performing an emotional scene.

We'd actually be better off if we did what babies do. They scream "correctly" — with vocal cords open, not constricted. That's why they can scream for long periods. They learn the wrong way eventually, by mimicking adults.

Have you ever watched a gorgeous, glamorous woman and anticipated what she would sound like? Have you ever laughed out loud to discover that either she talks with a mousy squeak or delivers a Brooklyn accent that would stop a Mack truck? Use the squeak and the accent when you want to, not because you have to.

SOUND ON THE SET

Sound on the set is managed by the sound person, officially called a Sound Mixer, and by his or her mike operators.

The sound crew include:
- Sound Mixer – in charge of Sound
- Boom Person – places the mike, be it the boom or the body mike, and handles all the moves the boom makes, in concert with the actors he or she is miking.
- Cable Person – makes sure all the wiring is correct, and that the cables are coiled and handled properly.

Generally, the sound person works with a top quality reel-to-reel machine. Because it takes a moment for the reels to reach the proper speed, the sound person will never risk getting what's called a "wow" effect. This can happen if a sound is recorded while the machine is still running a tad too slowly. For this reason, the sound person yells "SPEED" before the Director calls for action, letting the director know that sound is ready.

We'll say again here of what we mentioned in the SHOOTING chapter. There's a specific sequence, where each department indicates their readiness. You as the actor will be responding to the word "Action," but many things happened before you hear that word. The sequence is: "Rolling," "Speed," "Action."

> *First-time actors are inundated with "don't do this" and "don't do that." They must be terrified.*
> *– Vince Garcia*

There is a lot of information to know about sound, and our aim is not to so overburden you with technical details that you can't remember what your performance is all about. However, we feel actors should be as informed as possible.

Along those lines, we encourage you to introduce yourself to your sound mixer and ask for his or her help. Remember you're on the same team. Tell him or her that your aim is to get it right the first time, not have to fix things later. You might go so far as to say, "I hate to loop." (What's looping? We'll tell you in a minute.) The ideal situation always is to get it right in production, not in post-production. Many things can be fixed later. But why create problems if they can be avoided?

Here are some things to avoid. Don't interfere with your mike. Find out first of all how you're being miked. If the crew is using a boom (a mike suspended from a large movable pole) all you really need to do is avoid hitting it. Problems include standing up too quickly and banging your head into the mike; and also not hitting your marks as you move through a scene. All moves on a set are choreographed and it's a dance in which you are not the only dancer.

> *I don't want an actor to hit his head when he stands, but I don't want to interfere with an actor's work. That's what rehearsals are for. We have to coordinate our movements. If an actor has done the moves a certain way four times, let's say, in the rehearsals and in the master, we assume he'll do it the same way in the close-up.*
> *— Vince Garcia*

Pay close attention to what Mr. Garcia has said here. There are many reasons why you do things the same way in rehearsal and once you begin shooting. One of those important reasons includes the movements the boom operator must make in concert with you. We refer you to our Rehearsal chapter for further details.

If you're being miked with a small contact mike, you'll be wearing four things: the mike, the wire, the antenna and the battery pack.

Here are the exact terms:
- transmitter — the battery pack, which goes on the body
- first cable — the antenna
- second cable — goes to the mike
- the mike — usually a small half-inch square, which attaches to your clothing with a "vampire clip." One type commonly used is a "tram."

Somehow the crew has to find a place to anchor all these bits and pieces so they can't be seen. Sometimes you'll be handed a belt with a Velcro closure with a pouch for the pack, and most often, the pack rests in the area of your lower back; sometimes you'll be handed a thigh belt; and there are many variations on the theme. In theatre, it's not uncommon to place a mike in a wig. In any case, the crew can't always find a place where extraneous sounds can't be heard, however, and this is where you'll need to be careful.

You need to make sure, for example, that you don't move in ways that cause fabric to drag across the mike. Be aware that crossing your arms might not be an option, nor patting yourself on the chest. Wardrobe should help you with this, but certain fabrics and certain kinds of jewelry are a nightmare for sound. Rustling fabrics like silk, charm bracelets and bangles, dangling earrings, all can create problems, so be aware.

We want to say a word here about attitude as well.

> *I worked on a seventeen-week shoot recently with an actress (who shall remain nameless). She kept complaining about wearing the mike, saying, "Why do I have to wear this? I have to walk and talk and wear this thing?" This was an action picture, we were running three cameras at once, so there was no room for a boom. Eventually, I had to go to the Director. "Can we go talk to her together?" I asked. He said, "Yes." He sat down with her very politely, and said, "We have to hear you. You have three pages of dialogue." She reluctantly agreed to wear the mike.*
>
> *— Vince Garcia*

We think this story says it all, but in case you're not clear about the point we're making, we strongly advise that you not create a problem for your crew. If you spend your time complaining, think about the ripple effect this will generate on the set. Let's say you complain to the Boom Operator first, who will sometimes be in charge of placing your body mike. Then the Boom Operator goes to the Sound Mixer. If you're still complaining, this then goes to the Director. What do you think the topic of conversation will be around the catering table when you've gone back to your trailer?

Save your complaints for something truly dangerous or genuinely interfering with your work. We think any good actor can, in fact, walk, talk, and wear a pack, a wire and a mike.

> *I've been miked between my breasts, in my pocket, between my thighs, at my neck, on my lower back, you name it. The worst was between my thighs.*
>
> *— Erin*

We think these situations are excellent opportunities to learn a new skill, and incorporate it smoothly into your work. Wouldn't you feel terrific about yourself, knowing you could deliver an emotional scene and never let your discomfort with a mike interfere?

By the same token, it's the ultimate goal of your sound crew to do their job, and then get out of your way. They want to enhance your work, not prevent you from doing it well.

> *Sometimes the lens is so wide that there's no way to get a boom in. If you happen to have two pages of dialogue, we don't want you to sound like you're in the next county. We want your sound to be good. And we want to do our job so well that you hardly notice us. Our job is not to distract you.*
>
> *— Vince Garcia*

We appreciate Mr. Garcia's attitude, and we're sure you will too, should you ever be fortunate enough to work with him.

Remember what we said about "room tone"? Don't disappear from the set too quickly. The sound recordist may need to capture some "room tone" — and that means that for a few more moments, the room you're in must stay exactly as it is — and that includes your being there.

When there's a break, or you're finished working for a while, there are important things to know about removing — or not removing — your mike. First of all, if you have a pack on, let the crew member remove it, unless you've been shown how to do it correctly yourself.

> *I don't mind if actors remove their own mikes. I show them how and it makes my job easier. If I'm doing a series, the leads usually do that anyway, and we get used to working together.*
> — Vince Garcia

If you're a woman and you're uncomfortable having a male sound crew member remove equipment from sensitive areas, you have the right to request that a female crew member, either from sound or from wardrobe, do the removal for you. These pieces of equipment are very delicate and expensive. Many times it's their own equipment crew members are leasing back to the production. So respect that and ask them to deal with it.

> *We're one of the few departments where part of the job is actually personally touching the actor — Make-up, Hair and Wardrobe being the others. I try to be sensitive to the actor's needs.*
> — Vince Garcia

Then there's the matter of making sure you're not miked during private moments. Some Sound Mixers make a point of not eavesdropping.

> *I always keep the radio mike turned off when we're not working, because I don't want to overhear actors. What they're saying is none of my business. I always tell an actor, you're on or you're off. It's a courtesy.*
> — Vince Garcia

However, not all Sound Mixers are so aware, nor so polite. So — a word to the wise: don't go to the bathroom — or start telling personal stories — until you know your sound is turned off.

> *During the filming of "Evening In Byzantium," I was in the middle of a scene when the Director was called away to shoot a pick-up scene with Glenn Ford. The Director said he'd get back to us as soon as possible.*

Gloria de Haven and I were freezing, trying to keep warm on the beach in Santa Monica, so we decided to tell dirty jokes. They got dirtier and dirtier and we laughed harder and harder. Eventually, we progressed to describing penises in all their shapes and sizes. After half an hour of this, Jimmy Rogers, our sound man, took off his headset and said, "Girls, that was the best half hour I ever spent in my life." We turned eight shades of red and purple and I never forgot about my mike after that.

— Erin

Believe it or not, things can get even worse.

An actress went to the restroom, then came to me and said, "I don't know how to tell you this, but it fell in." I said, "No problem." Of course we washed it and we had to open it up to make sure it still worked. But it did.

— Vince Garcia

Now that's a true gent. We're not so sure every sound mixer would respond so graciously to that embarrassing moment.

And now a note about how sound can affect your performance. One thing to be aware of in certain scenes is overlapping dialogue. If a scene calls for you and another actor to interrupt each other a few times, you might want to check with your Director to make sure overlapping won't make editing impossible later. It's not really your job to make sure the sound editors can get their "scissors" between one take and another, but then again an ounce of awareness is worth a pound of problem-solving.

In overlap situations, I mike the off-camera actor for dialogue as well. Otherwise you have to get each actor in the clear for editing purposes.
—Vince Garcia

Mr. Garcia is protecting the Director and the actors by using this technique. Where one actor is on camera and one is off camera, you need to understand that you might be asked to perform this scene two different ways — once where your dialogue overlaps, once where it does not. This will give the editor the maximum flexibility in post-production.

Here's another word to the wise: you might assume that if you're off camera you can have a little fun when you throw your fellow actor his or her cues. Oh, what the heck, you'll throw in an "f" word instead of saying "darn." Well, guess what. You might still be miked. So watch your language, stay in professional mode, and don't just say your lines, perform them as if you were on camera.

LOOPING

What is looping? As our Glossary says, it's replacing dialogue previously recorded, usually for some technical reason.

> *A lot of actors don't do well on the looping stage. It's better to capture it as we go.*
> — Vince Garcia

The first bit of bad news about looping is that you'll usually be doing this months after the picture wrapped. Needless to say, you'll probably have a challenging task remembering the emotional content of what you performed so long ago.

Second, you'll be recording this in a special recording studio equipped with a large viewing screen. You will not be in an environment anything like the one you were in when creating the scenes — for that, you'll have to use your memory and your imagination.

Generally, whatever you do correctly in your performance now, you won't have to do later in looping. Sometimes it's beyond your control. You might be in a period piece from 1898 and you've got 1998 background sound like airplanes intruding so you have no choice but to re-do your whole performance.

> *My sister Linda Purl had starred in a TV movie called "The Adventures of Nellie Bly." When they got into post-production it turned out the sounds of planes flying overhead were mixed in with a great deal of the original dialogue. This wouldn't work at all for Nellie's time period, but Linda was by then out of the country, filming her next project. Suddenly, her manager realized our voices were very similar. He recommended me, and the Director had me come in to loop Linda's part. By raising the pitch of my voice just slightly, I found I could match her uncannily well. Of course, it meant actually doing the performance — running, breathing, gasping, shouting, emoting — whatever the part required. The producers ended up with a combination of our two performances — but it worked, and it saved their project.*
>
> *— Mara*

Having the chance to do full scenes, as in the above example, is rare by the usual looping standards practiced in the U.S. Usually you'll be asked to loop only a phrase or a sentence at a time. That's not the case in Europe, however, should you ever find yourself in production overseas.

> *When I was shooting "The Myth That Wouldn't Die" we had an international cast, and the film was to be released both in English and in French. I was the only cast member who didn't speak French, so I did my French close-ups phonetically. Months later I had to fly back to France to loop some of my scenes. It was wonderful to discover their looping technique. Instead of just looking at the shot on the big screen in front of you, you also have a special dialogue and movement visual running along beneath the scene, like a kind of musical score. You can look at your lines; and you can also look at a drawing of a wave form which describes the rhythms of what you need to say. Having the chance to do complete scenes, and having this kind of visual score, made the looping process much easier because it enabled me to stay in the flow.*
>
> *— Erin*

If you're doing a heavy emotional scene, it may be very important to you not to loop it. In such a case, we recommend talking to your sound man and asking that he or she pay particular attention to sound, and not accept a take which has any kind of sound interference.

Looping emotional scenes – and all kinds of scenes – is, however, sometimes unavoidable.

If you have to loop some scenes, you'll be notified by the Second A.D. or another crew member, and be told when and where to report for work. You'll work in what's called a sound stage, which essentially will consist of a large screen, a mike, and a control booth. You'll sit or stand at your mike and watch yourself on screen. Your mission – and sometimes it does seem like an impossible one – is to lip-synch yourself.

The footage will be shown in black and white and will have code printed across it. It will also be shown to you in brief segments, which are useful to the editors, but not so useful to you, in that they're truncated segments that may not make sense emotionally. You'll be given a series of three beeps – you're to begin speaking (or gasping, laughing, crying, etc.) on the fourth beat.

Because you must watch the screen, you can't also be looking at your script. So you'll have to memorize at least one line at a time in order to do your job. Of course, you must match the timing of the words as you originally spoke them.

As we said, you also must match the emotional content as you originally performed it. It can be very challenging to remember and/or re-create the love/hatred/fear/terror/compassion/inspiration you delivered several weeks or months earlier. On a good note, you might be able to take this opportunity actually to improve your original performance.

Our experience is that even though producers sometimes promise you'll be able to hear a critical moment of your previous work, somehow they can't, or don't, always deliver, and the sound bite you needed can't be found, or isn't cued up in time. So – do your own homework. Your own preparation for a part can include audio taping yourself, for example.

This can be especially important if you're doing a part with an accent. If you've mastered a special accent for a part, do record yourself so if you need to refer to it, you can.

When you arrive at your looping session, chances are you'll be dealing with a series of surprises and unexpected changes. You may think you're going to re-create the drug-crazed haze you performed in this role, only to discover the Director has now decided your character is stone-cold sober. Some things are impossible to prepare for. But be as prepared as you can be.

> *I had to loop a part I had performed in a small feature film recently and there were a lot of surprises. The first time you see yourself on screen for a certain part, you have all these things to deal with. Sometimes it was flattering, sometimes it was disturbing. Meanwhile, you're listening to the three beeps and making sure you start to speak on "four." You don't want to look, but you have to look. Also when I got there they had actually changed some of the dialogue, some of which felt really unnatural to me. And they had me change some of the emotion I had originally used, so I had to make some new acting choices. Also I didn't realize they give you only phrases – you don't get a chance to do whole sentences. I wish I had known more about looping before the session. I'll be better prepared next time.*
> *– Kelly Bovino*

VOICE-OVER WORK

This is a large category that includes: radio commercials, providing voice for animated characters; announcing or narrating documentaries, movie trailers; audio book reading; radio drama performance; and many other projects.

Breaking into this kind of work can be difficult, as much of it is cast on a referral basis, but few things are impossible. If this kind of work interests you, look in the trades for workshops and classes, preferably those which include actual work in a recording studio where you'll get the practical experience of hearing yourself on tape.

There are vocal techniques that differ in the audio versus the visual media, and voice workshops of various kinds can be indispensable to making yourself hireable for this kind of work.

> When I first started producing "Milford-Haven," most of us had a background in television – not radio – and we had to train ourselves to use this "new" medium correctly. For example, what works as a pregnant pause on film becomes a black hole of silence on radio, so we had to learn to vocalize emotions and thoughts in new ways. Actually it made our work richer not only in audio performances but in other media as well.
> – Mara

Essentially, voice work divides itself into two large categories – dialogue and narration. And within the dialogue category, there's: "natural" and "character." If you're doing commercials, most of the time, you'll need to cultivate a "natural" or "normal" voice.

> In radio spots, it is very important that you are natural in all your readings. One-on-one is the common technique used in voiceovers. You learn to talk to that one person instead of a whole audience. It is known as a "no read," the "vanilla" voice, and the "voice next door."
> – Alan K. Lohr, "Voiceover Bootcamp" Workshop

If you're doing "character" parts, there are many ways to create marvelous things with the use of your voice. For example, with different accents you can play several characters in one show.

Voice-over work requires an innate sense of timing. Many times you'll be asked to read some ad copy, for example, and to do it in exactly 10 seconds. The Director may then want a slightly different interpretation, while the Producer needs you to shave two seconds off the time. If you're good at judging and adjusting the time of your performances, you'll almost certainly be hired again.

Doing voices for animation is a skill unto itself. In this case it's not a matter of timing your performance to an existing image, but rather of defining what the image will be by what you do with your voice.

From an acting point of view, playing animated characters requires the gift of playfulness and the ability to translate this into your voice. If you have an unusual voice, or can do unusual things with your voice, you might think about this avenue of work and again, look for workshops which can get you started.

> *Don't underestimate the value of working at a Theme Park. I worked at Disney World in Orlando performing as characters and began to perfect some character voices. Ultimately, I developed these voices as my specialty and now I work regularly doing a number of well-established cartoon characters like the "Tazmanian Devil" for Warner Brothers and other production companies.*
> — Dee Baker

WALLA & LOOP GROUPS

So far we've talked about performing actual characters with your voice, but there's another whole realm of voice work we'll briefly mention here, because it can be an excellent source of income and experience.

"Walla" is the background sound required in virtually every film and TV project. A team of experienced walla artists can create the atmosphere of a busy train station, an intimate café, a fight in a crowded high school hallway, a full subway car, or any place you can imagine.

People who do this work generally work in teams, becoming very familiar with one another's skills and timing. These teams are called Loop Groups, and there are several that work regularly on film and TV projects. This work requires a particular skill — quite different from "principal acting" — and those who are good at it are a marvel to watch.

> I'm sometimes asked to perform with loop groups because of my language abilities – I speak Japanese and French. One show included a scene which took place in the United Nations. I was to voice the female delegates from Japan and France. The footage appeared on the screen. The three beeps went by. I found one of the Japanese ladies I was to voice and improvised a line for her. I was very proud of myself because I'd gotten it on the first take. Only when we stopped did I realize the other five people in the room had each voiced three or four characters – all in that one take. They worked that fast. I realized they had a skill I would probably never perfect. I'm just lucky I speak languages which continue to be needed.
>
> – Mara

SUMMARY

Sound is just one of the many dimensions in which you'll be working in this business, and our experience has been that it's increased our awareness of sound and all its qualities in many ways.

Just in case you're starting to feel overwhelmed with all the information we're giving you, take a deep breath and remember you'll always be learning. That's part of the joy.

All in all, it's a great business.

> I'm so fortunate to be in this business. The long hours can be killers, but the people I've met, the places I've traveled… I wouldn't want to be doing anything else. When I was doing the series "Matt Houston," the star Lee Horsley – what a great guy he is. He and I were sitting in his trailer late at night after a long day's shooting. I looked at Lee and said, "Aren't we lucky?" "Yeah," he said, "This really beats roofing."
>
> – Vince Garcia

STUNT WORK

Covered In This Chapter:

- Definition

- Hierarchy

- Expertise & Safety

- Stunt Coordinator's Blueprint

- CYA (Cover Your Ass)

A man's actions show his character.

— Anonymous

STUNT PEOPLE

As is the case with many of the disciplines in this complex business, stunt work is on the one hand extraordinarily important, and on the other hand, grossly under-appreciated.

DEFINITION

First it's important to define terms. A stunt person, or stunt double, is not at all the same as a stand-in. A stand-in stands on the set in place of a lead actor, so the Director of Photography can properly focus and adjust lighting.

A stunt person works — as you do — on camera. He or she doubles actors during action sequences. Stunt work requires every bit as much training as acting, but — unlike you — many stunt workers risk their lives every day they work.

> Actors don't realize we are also members of SAG (Screen Actors Guild). Most think that the Stuntman's Association or Stunts Unlimited is our union. That's not the case. We perform on camera, just as the actors do.
> — Terry James

When you think about it, this may be your closest collaboration — it's you who creates the dialogue-delivering portion of your character. But it may be your stunt double who creates most of the action-delivering portion of that same character. Through the wizardry of all the technologies this business now has to offer, these two performances, yours and that of your stunt double, will be blended together into a seamless whole, a character your audience will find believable. If the work is done well, your audience won't know where your work left off and your stunt double's began. Since your ultimate result is collaboration at this level, it should begin with collaboration as well. So begin with appreciating what a stunt person does.

While you're busy taking elocution and Shakespeare and method and dance lessons, the stunt person is learning to sky dive, scuba dive, ski, water ski, fence, fall out of buildings, dangle from helicopters, be jerked off a motorcycle while it flies through flames, crash through plate glass windows, tumble out of moving cars, fall from a horse, and flip an automobile doing 60 miles per hour — and do it in the same way, in the same place, on take after take.

To the tremendous frustration of many of the stunt professionals we've spoken with or worked with, the actual skill involved in this line of work is still not widely recognized, even within the business itself. In fact, it was only fairly recently that the Screen Actors Guild recognized Stunt Coordinator as a separate category. And the Taurus Awards, a separate awards ceremony by and for Stunt People, took place for the first time in May, 2001.

You may find you have something in common with stunt people with regard to lack of appreciation for your credits. Actors who have done "just soaps," for example, are often not taken seriously, although their schedule, memorization, and grueling hours make it difficult to keep their work believable. Similarly, stunt people may be taken lightly because they've done "just TV," whereas in fact, if you can deal with the rigors of a TV schedule and complete stunts on an action series, chances are you can handle a feature film with ease.

If stunt people have a pet peeve, it's probably that they seldom feel their work is understood for what it really is. Many feel they're perceived as daredevils who risk everything for the thrill of it all. The reality is that their work involves extraordinary discipline, hard physical work, a talent for translating words on a page into performable action, and all this must be done cheaply and safely.

> Stunt people are not thrill-seekers. Where a daredevil might jump a motorcycle over the Grand Canyon, I'd rather do that in front of a blue screen. It's not the thrill I'm looking for. It's the skill.
> — Diamond Farnsworth

What's true is that this work can be dangerous, and even with the best-laid plans, one sometimes must improvise. Stunt people are often asked to take falls, and of course, they always have a plan for where and how they'll land.

> *On one show I was supposed to land on an airbag, but we were shooting in Wisconsin and by the time I made my landing, half the airbag was frozen. That was a <u>hard</u> landing. Sometimes there's no budget for an airbag, so I'll build a stack of cardboard boxes, and tie them off. Then I cover it with cardboard flats, then cover that with packing blankets. As I land, I fall through the collapsing boxes.*
> *— Diamond Farnsworth*

A word to the wise: don't try this at home!

HIERARCHY

There's a hierarchy within the discipline of stunt work. The Stunt Coordinator is the individual who's responsible for choreographing the stunt itself, whether it's a fight or a fall. He or she is also responsible for the safety of all stunt people, and all actors. And this part of the job is taken very seriously.

The Stunt Coordinator may choreograph an activity which involves stunt people some distance from the camera. And he or she may also choreograph a stunt for you to perform yourself — a fight, for example, where your face will be seen in close-up. The ability to teach you how to look believable in an action sequence is an extraordinary talent, and you should do your best to take advantage of this opportunity to learn and to collaborate. If you let them, your Stunt Coordinators can make you look terrific on camera, and everyone gains — you, the stunt person, and ultimately, the project itself. You may think you can throw a punch with the best of them, but can you do it without knocking out a tooth? Or can you take a punch without getting bruised? Let a professional show you how.

> *If an actor has a problem with a stunt, who does he go to? To me. To the stunt coordinator. If Scott Bakula says, "I'd rather do a kick here*

than throw a punch" — fine. Two heads are better than one. It's also okay to go to your director. But if you don't want to bother the director, or if you're scared — I'll find a way to help you with it.
— Diamond Farnsworth

Usually the Stunt Coordinator is also a stunt person, and usually is working alongside other stunt people in the project. What exactly do stunt people do when they come to work? They double one specific character (a "utility stunt" person doubles more than one character), wearing the same wardrobe, wearing a wig if necessary, and generally doing everything necessary to make him- or herself look indistinguishable from the actor who is performing the part. The stunt person cannot survive the scrutiny of a close-up — for that they need you. And for this reason you may find that you yourself must occasionally do something you may consider a stunt — and we'll get into that in a moment.

EXPERTISE & SAFETY

When the script calls for scaling a sheer rock face or doing a 360 in a car, it almost certainly won't be you who performs this feat; it'll be your stunt double. You may think riding as a passenger in a car isn't much of a stunt. You're wrong. People have been injured or lost their lives on less complicated stunts.

There's a line between the responsibilities of an actor and those of a stunt person, and they should be clear. Unfortunately, this isn't always the case. We'll try to help you find your way through what may sometimes be a maze.

First of all, the production company isn't interested in losing time or losing money. In their efforts to stay on time and on budget, arguments may be won or lost in favor of safety. Theoretically, your safety is important to them for financial, if for no other, reasons. But what if the stunt seems simple? What if hiring a stunt double is more expensive than what they're prepared to pay? What if you're only being asked to stand still on a bridge — which happens to be 500 feet above a ravine?

Under the press of circumstances and the pressure to keep your job, you may feel that the best thing to do is just agree to do this "simple stunt" — whatever it is. Although there are no hard-and-fast rules in this business, generally our advice would be — don't do it. There are professional stunt people. They're trained. They're terrific. They need the work.

"Oh, this stunt is easy!" someone may tell you. Well, if you've seen professional stunt people do this on screen, you may be convinced it's easy. Why? Because they're so good, they've made it *look* easy. That's their job and most of them are really good at it. You don't need your leg broken or your hair singed. Think about the fact that even a scratch on your face might shut down production for three days, and then where would their budget be?

> When I was working on "Perry Mason," on location in Denver, Colorado, I was told that they needed me and William Katt in the foreground while an explosion took place in the background. We were told the explosion would happen so far away from us that we had nothing to worry about. They showed me the distant hill where the helicopter would be, and it looked far enough away to me. We were in the middle of nowhere, far away from the Stunt Coordinator. I wanted to be agreeable. Thank God William Katz threw me to the ground the instant the explosion happened. Shrapnel flew past us. As a matter of fact, shrapnel flew past the cameras, and past the group of people standing behind the cameras. They had been completely wrong in judging the distance the explosion would carry flying objects. We were all very lucky.
> – Erin

If you find yourself in a situation like this, who do you go to? What if there's no phone for miles? If your fellow actors have already agreed to the stunt? If your Director has assured you you'll be "safe" but you're not so sure, who do you go to next? Go to the Stunt Coordinator and ask his or her frank opinion on the safety of the stunt and the wisdom of your doing it yourself. He or she'll know, and tell you. That's his/her job.

What if you're miles away from your stunt coordinator? Well, you shouldn't be, on an action sequence, and that's an indication something is amiss. Take it as a cue to investigate further before continuing. You may feel extremely worried about making a pain of yourself at this point. But if you do not have access to your Stunt Coordinator we feel you may be in a compromising situation. Whether you *do* feel comfortable doing this particular stunt (you're a great rider and you're being asked to gallop across a field) or you *do not* feel comfortable (you're being asked to hang off a balcony), you still have a right to ask questions and get the full reassurance and involvement of the Stunt Coordinator. Accidents happen! Don't be a statistic.

> *It's all about money. If you don't feel safe doing the stunt, ask for the stunt person. If they give you a hard time remind the Producer that the stunt man can be replaced at this point – you can't. Since you've already worked a number of days it'll cost them more money if you get injured. And keep this in mind – if you do the stunt, you're denying someone else employment. Remember a good U.P.M. always has extra money stashed just for situations like this. Believe he or she is well-aware that they may have to hire someone. It's been discussed. Sure, they may not like to use up their spare money, but there are a lot of ways they can save money. Risking your life or limb or eye shouldn't be one of them and you'll not be thought of badly.*
>
> *— Terry James*

Now we'll address the opposite scenario – the one in which you want to do a stunt and may not feel you're getting the support of the production company. First of all, as we've already pointed out, the production company has invested in you as an actor, not as a stunt person. If you've already shot several days, that investment is substantial and to replace you might cost them a tremendous amount of money, or worse, might cost them the show itself.

What if you're an excellent horseback rider and are being asked to do something simple which you routinely do on your own horse? It's a judgment call, of course, and it might benefit the production tremendously to be able to get a close-up of you during an action sequence. Our advice, again, is to take as responsible an attitude as possible and consider the fact you are part of a larger whole. Ask the advice of your Stunt Coordinator and listen to what he or she has to say.

Fortunately, things have continued to improve in the film business as people have learned from their mistakes. When it comes to safety standards for both humans and animals, you may find things are not at all the same in other countries. Along those lines, we heard one from our friend Marc in London which we hesitated to share with you because it's so horrendous on so many levels. But then we decided it brings up so many important points that we should share it with you after all. Here goes.

> *Never do a stunt unless it is demonstrated to you first and never, ever do a stunt on the last day of filming. I was filming "Clash of Loyalties" with Oliver Reed in Baghdad during the height of the Iran-Iraq war, not a wonderful time spending 6 weeks in a war-zone but as the film was financed by Saddam Hussein and was set in 1920's Mesopotamia, it proved quite illuminating. A sequence required me to, whilst under attack from screaming (but curiously heroic) Arab forces, shoot a man off his horse. He was to fly past me and the horse was to land at my feet. The only way to achieve this was by using an invention from the greatest ever stuntman, Yak Cannut, who I met just afterwards, shortly before he died, in which an axle from a car is buried in the sand with a given length of wire hauser attached to it, coiled on the ground and via a special contraption suspended under the saddle, is then attached to the two front fetlocks of the horse. This is known as a "Running W" and the stunt has been banned since the 1960's in the U.S. and the U.K.. But this is Iraq! The rider then gallops the horse, the wire suddenly tightens, the horses legs are jerked up causing it to nose dive straight into the desert sand and the rider flies forwards. I was shown my mark and given my revolver. A fine sight in full English Officers uniform at high noon in the middle of the desert! I had a gut feeling and said I don't believe that the horse will stop where you say it will and I pointed to where I thought the mark should be. They said no,*

so I insisted on a demonstration first. Eventually, after a lot of arguing, they agreed. The stuntman galloped the horse off and I fired into the air at the right time. The wire tightened. The horse's legs jerked up. It nose dived and we all heard a dreadful crack as its neck broke. The body of the dead horse shot up into the air, somersaulted and landed with full force and deadweight right on my mark. The stuntman meanwhile was catapulted forward at a much greater velocity than he expected, slammed straight into the camera dolly and broke his collar bone. They moved my mark to where I had suggested. When I told Yak what had happened, he said that was what had always happened, which is why it was banned. They now use the "falling-horse" technique worldwide. So I seem to be the only person left who has ever used a "Running W," and this technique was one of the reasons that the animal cruelty lobby was able to call the shots in Hollywood. It was a dubious honour, but for the above incident I was made an Honourary Member of Stunts Inc. in the UK.

— Marc Sinden

We hate to think how many times incidents like this must have happened before some brave souls took a stand against cruelty and for safety.

Here's another thing to consider strictly from the acting point of view. Let's say there's a scene where your character has to drive a car. Yes, you may have driven a stick shift car most of your life and know perfectly well how to make a left turn into a driveway. However, let's say you're now asked to run out of a burning building and jump into the "Magnum" Ferrari, start it up, and tear into a driveway. You're in a car with more horsepower than you've ever driven. The Director shouts, "Action!" Fifty crew people are watching. Are these normal circumstances? No. Is your adrenaline pumping? Yes. Is Murphy's Law about to take over? You decide. We think, given a choice, this is a good opportunity to let your stunt double do the job, while you prepare for your next shot.

STUNT COORDINATOR'S BLUEPRINT

The Stunt Coordinator may be recommended for a job any number of ways. An actor may request him or her, or the recommendation may come from the Director, the Producer, or in some cases from a friend or colleague from any one of the departments — one person we talked to was recommended by Transportation for one job.

Generally, his or her first meeting is with the First Assistant Director, by which time he has read the script, and carefully looked over the First A.D.'s storyboard. The storyboard tells the Coordinator exactly what stunts need to be done and the number of days he'll have for completing them. Also present at this meeting is the Production Manager, whose job it is to argue against cost overruns. It's the Stunt Coordinator's job to present realistic dollar amounts for accomplishing each stunt written in the script.

> *When I get a script it's like a blueprint for building a house. I have to tell the Production Manager if you want this wall, it will cost you X. If you can't pay X, that wall has to be removed. Let's say they want a car turnover. Not only do I have to tell them it's going to cost $5000, but I have to explain why it's going to cost $5000, and perhaps come up with alternatives.*
>
> *— Diamond Farnsworth*

Once a Coordinator has bid and won a job, he remains in close contact with the First A.D., who's in charge of any set. The Coordinator's job is to advise the First whether or not something is safe.

In order to do this, he must first translate what the writer has written into a do-able stunt. Sticking as closely as possible to what the writer intended, he or she must visualize, strategize, and choreograph, the specific moves to be made by people, vehicles, flames, and anything else that must appear on screen. The trick is to design this sequence so that it can be shot — and shot again. So it must be repeatable. It can sometimes be an almost impossible task, to control the uncontrollable. But this is what the Stunt Coordinator has signed on to do.

Two things stunt people often work with – but over which they have no jurisdiction – are guns and explosives. Props are in charge of guns. Special Effects people are in charge of explosives. However – stunt people often have expertise in these areas and will work collaboratively with the other departments. The issue of safety on the set is so important we will mention it under all three headings.

It's the Effects department who will design explosions, but most Coordinators know their explosives pretty well and may have valuable suggestions.

> We know about explosives and we know when the Special Effects guy knows what he is doing. We can see how the explosives are rigged and we're able to figure what will happen. It is our job to know what is safe.
> – Terry James

Similarly, Coordinators will often know which angles will enhance and which will detract from an action sequence, and so will have suggestions for the D.P.

> If he asks me, I'll recommend to a D.P. that a car shot will look better from this angle, because I've done so many. In working out a fight, for example, it's up to me and the cameraman to work it out together. I won't know where the camera's going to be without his help. And the D.P. won't know how to shoot the scene without discussing it with me.
> – Diamond Farnsworth

We keep saying this, but here we go again: this business is about collaboration. It's a series of cooperative efforts, which make or break a moment, a scene, a film. Or as Diamond Farnsworth put it, "It all comes down to communication. If you don't have communication, you don't have jack diddly."

Are all stunt people equally talented in all physical skills? Almost. But not quite. Howard Curtis, who was, until he died, one of the most respected stunt men in the industry, spent much of his free time keeping a high polish on every one of his skills. If he wasn't doubling Roger Moore on one of the James Bond films, he was jumping out of a plane at 20,000 feet just to make sure he still had that skill finely tuned. This was a man who took his work so seriously that he was later killed while preparing for a complicated parachuting stunt and he is sorely missed.

However, everyone has the special areas in which they excel. If a Stunt Coordinator finds himself in charge of a scene involving mountain climbing, and he himself isn't a mountain climber, what does he do? "If we're doing mountain scenes, I'd hire the best mountain climber I could find." And this is the general rule.

CYA (Cover Your Ass)

On the subject of hiring experts – you may find yourself in a situation where you need to do the same. Sometimes a scene requiring some sort of physical expertise on your part is written into the script. Trusting that someone will show up at the right moment to train you may not work. The day arrives to shoot that scene and guess what? They're ready to shoot – and you're not.

No, it's not in your job description to hire a stunt person, a physical coach, or a dance teacher. But our advice in this situation is to ask questions and take the initiative if you need to in hiring someone yourself to work with privately.

> *One of the scenes I had to do in "Days" was a fight scene involving myself and two other women. Perhaps because this wasn't a fight scene between men where fists would be used, but was "only women" fighting, no stunt coordinator was on the set that day. So the other women and I worked out something for ourselves in one of our dressing rooms. It was only fair, because we weren't experts. We didn't know*

where the cameras would be, we didn't know what questions to ask. Who ended up looking bad? We did.

— Mara

In "Dark Justice," my character had to do a scene that was virtually a strip tease. Although I've studied dancing, I spent days worrying about how this would be shot and I knew the production wouldn't pay for a choreographer. I agonized over this and ended up doing a somersault over a couch — one of the most imaginative things I've ever done. In retrospect I wish I'd hired one of the wonderful dance teachers I've worked with over the years. I would've been assured of a solid series of actions to perform, and would've given another professional a chance to earn a good credit. It's fun to work with someone. It's not fun to agonize. I sometimes wake up in the middle of the night wondering what happened to the footage that ended up on the cutting room floor. I hope it was burned!

— Erin

DAILIES

Covered In This Chapter:

- Definition & Purpose

- Who Watches & Who Doesn't

- To See Or Not To See

Dailies are a terrific morale booster. Film almost always looks good in daily form, sometimes deceptively so.
— Gregory Goodell

A finished film never looks as good as the dailies, or as bad as the first cut.
— Francis Ford Coppola

DAILIES

DEFINITION & PURPOSE

Dailies are those all-important bits and pieces of scenes that come directly from processing (in the case of film) to a screening room and are viewed at the end of the day by Producers, Director, Cinematographer, numerous other crew members, studio executives, and sometimes actors.

The reasons for dailies are all technical. The Director of Photography needs to check to see his lighting is working. Make-up and hair need to see that their work is reading. Each person in the room has something specific he or she is watching for, usually to the exclusion of everything else.

WHO WATCHES & WHO DOESN'T

Comments usually flow freely during these sessions, and usually they're critical — often they're self-critical as someone realizes the adjustments needed for subsequent shooting. The editor often gets his or her comments from the director in dailies, comments the director may not wish to have overheard.

We say this to point out that, although this is part of the creative process for many of the people working on the film, it is not for the actors. This isn't an opportunity for you to watch your work, suggest changes, and reshoot a scene. If you have any such thoughts, you are not invited to share them. In the old days of Hollywood, there was a time when actors were expected to be at dailies, and if you didn't show up, there was a black mark against your name. That probably changed because actors began being too vocal in these sessions. Whatever the reason, the general belief now is that actors do not understand the real purpose of dailies, and don't know the first thing about what's going on technically. Dailies are not color-corrected, for example, so if you do go to dailies, don't complain about how blue your shirt looks.

TO SEE OR NOT TO SEE

As an actor, assuming you're invited at all, to watch or not to watch dailies is a very subjective decision only you can make. Generally, there are strong opinions among actors as to whether or not it's the right thing to do.

On the negative side, you risk throwing yourself outside your work, placing yourself on the outside looking back at work you're trying to make immediate and vibrant, and this can sometimes make it impossible to maintain the spontaneity and vigor of your performance. On the positive side, you may catch yourself in a move or attitude or habit that you wish to eliminate — or confirm for yourself that a choice you made was the right one.

Our best advice on this is to find your own best way of working, perhaps striking a compromise between obsessing about dailies throughout the project on the one hand, and on the other hand, adamantly refusing to get a glimpse of yourself on screen lest you jinx your performance.

> *I was once shooting in the middle of nowhere for three months, and dailies became like home movies. We'd have snacks and enjoy ourselves. We thought we looked great, but, in fact, the movie turned out not to be good. I had completely misread the dailies. Now I like to look at dailies the first couple of days' worth. It helps me to know how hair, makeup, cinematography is working. I like to have a sense of all that, and then I stop going. It's like doing a dance routine in front of the mirror, where you check your body-lines. But after that, it becomes a disservice because the creative process needs to be a subjective one, not an objective one. I don't go in with a performance meter. I leave the critic outside and just look at the technical aspects.*
> — Linda Purl

> *I once watched myself in dailies for a two-part episode of "Starman." I found that in a particular scene I "thought big," but actually did very little, and it read very strongly and well, which gave me the confidence that I was working in the right direction. On another occasion, in "Born*

> Beautiful," I watched the dailies, and found myself being so upset that I basically threw a tantrum and cried all night. Call it vanity and ego, but they had chosen to use a blue gel for all my lighting, and it made me look drawn and unattractive. The Director and I talked many times through the night, and ultimately, many emotions came to the surface, and I was able to use them in the work. Since we were both honest and frank about our differing approaches, this event brought us closer together. We each had intelligent reasons behind the choices we'd made. Although we made peace and the production continued, it was at the same time so disruptive, that for the duration of that project, I never watched dailies again.
> — Erin

Actors are sometimes cordially uninvited to watch dailies, if Directors and Producers feel that this disrupts the actors' work, and/or they have comments to make which they prefer not be overheard by actors. When actors are starring in a project, they will sometimes choose to watch dailies, in spite of a producer's or director's policy.

> On one project the director told all of us that we were banned from dailies. I went anyway and so did fellow actor John Rhys-Davies, who in this case was far more experienced than the director was. Ultimately, I realized this was just a control issue for the director, and not only that he didn't want to be judged.
> — Linda Purl

If you feel strongly that you need to watch dailies, and know that you can do so as a professional, you should probably simply go, sit quietly and unobtrusively, and get such information as you require from what you see on the screen. If you do choose to watch dailies, remember you're there as an actor, not as a director or producer, and your production comments will, therefore, not be welcome.

You'll find Directors and Producers make choices based on technical considerations, which for them outweigh performances, and this may drive you crazy as you see your best work overshadowed by superior lighting in what you consider a lesser take. Keep these thoughts to yourself, and glean what you can from what you see. When you produce your own project, you can bear production responsibilities. If you are able to separate yourself from the emotions involved, dailies can be an excellent place to learn how and why scenes are cut, shaped, paced, and edited.

THE BUSINESS OF THE BUSINESS

Covered In This Chapter:

- Treating Yourself As A Business

- Creating Your Data Base & Your Day Planner

- IDs, I-9s and Legalities

- Business Cards

- Mailings

- Gifts

- Thank You Notes

Never lose sight of being professional. Even when you hit it big – remember where you came from.
— Abby Singer

Don't lost sight of the fact that this is a business to make money. Remember, "Show Business," not "Show Friendship."
— Ricki Maslar

THE BUSINESS OF THE BUSINESS

As we've said time and again throughout this book and in many ways: this is a collaborative business. That means it's made up of people – and people you will most likely see again and again. You may not always know when or where – but chances are you'll see people again. It's a small world. And it's a very small business.

TREATING YOURSELF AS A BUSINESS

This is a *business*. Treat yourself as though you're a business person, someone who plans to be around for a long time.

> When I was first starting to audition in L.A., I met with the head of casting at Universal Studios, Monique James. She asked me to come back in a week to audition with a scene from a play called "Blue Denim." During that week I moved to New York. Eleven years later, I showed up in her office. By then I'd become a well-known New York model, but never dreamed she'd remember me. She looked at me, said, "Just a moment," reached into her files, and looked at me again. "So are you ready now to do the scene from 'Blue Denim'?" She taught me a valuable lesson.
> – Erin

People remember. People keep notes. People treat this as a business. You must do the same.

CREATING YOUR DATA BASE & YOUR DAY PLANNER

There are many ways to be organized and we'll share some of our discoveries with you. However, remember your own style of getting organized is as personal as your handwriting. The important thing is to develop a system of your own – and use it.

In the pre-computer days we tried all sorts of things. There were index cards. There were endless color-coded file folders. There were binders. There were stickers. To some extent, we still have the binders and folders. But things have changed dramatically with the advent of the computer.

Whatever you do, you must have a comprehensive day planner or journal of some kind, be it hand-written or computer-generated. Make this a running list of contacts, phone calls, appointments, and notes. This will be your "chron" file.

> *I was recently contacted on-line by a jazz discographer who had found my name in connection with an album I co-created with Charles Lloyd in the late 70s. The discographer asked if I knew any of the details of the recording of that album, as no notes were included on the album liner. I went through my journals – these were hand-written, since the album was done pre-computer – I had the name of the recording studio, the name of the engineer, and the names of all the personnel on that recording session. All this detail has now been added to his web site as a permanent record. Apparently I was the only one who knew.*
> —Mara

- Have a notebook. There are so many excellent options these days, you have no excuse not to find a notebook you love. For example, there's the Day Planner from Franklin Covey; there's the Day Runner; the Day Timer; there's the Levenger notebook; and there are, of course, spiral binders in every size and color, with do-it-yourself tabs of every description.

- As an alternative, have an electronic day planner. These hand-helds are fabulous tools offering maximum portability and instant access to all your critical data. The Palm is the best known and now has several versions, each suited to different needs, so investigate before purchasing. Sharp has an updated version of *The Wizard*. Microsoft has an excellent hand-held device as well. Do some homework and check web sites to learn more which device might be right for you. Bear in mind you'll want a device that has compatibility with your computer so names and other info does not have to be entered twice. The Palm and other devices offer a "Hot Synch" function which updates both the device itself and the desktop in a matter of seconds. And there are also keyboards available into which the Palm fits, in case you want to type your data instead of hand entering it.

- Whichever method you use — electronic or paper — use it! Don't just lug it around and refer to it occasionally. Take notes. Scribble down people's names, addresses, idiosyncrasies you notice in someone's casting office, a birthday if you overhear it, someone's spouse's name, or the team they like to follow. Don't obsess over this, but do get into the habit of jotting down your observations.

- Work with your notes. Before you go to bed at night (or in the morning) review the things you wrote down today, and transfer them to whatever logging system you devise. You might have a permanent calendar with everyone's birthdays on it. You might have a complete list of casting directors, with notes about things that you noticed when you met. Process this information when it is fresh in your mind. And here's a hint. Review your lists again first thing in the morning. Go over your goals and activities for the day. It's a simple and very powerful technique for keeping you on course, in a business that often makes you feel rudderless and adrift in a sea of "we'll call you"s and "keep in touch"s.

- Have a filing system. Keep at least two basic categories — subject and chron. Your "chron" file can be the rough notes you took before you transferred information to your database. Your "subject" file can be listed by name of project, name of casting director, name of theatre or production company — whatever makes the most sense to you.

- Get computerized if you can. Getting names and addresses into usable computer files will take time to input. However, you'll more than make up the time when it becomes easy to generate mailing labels, letters, envelopes, updated résumés, and many other things. There are many excellent programs that connect word-processing with record-keeping intelligently. Microsoft Office is a good one. Corel's WordPerfect Office Suite is an excellent one too. Both these programs have components which allow you to input names, organizations, and so forth, and then to link them to other names, organizations, etc. So if you can't remember a person's name but you know you met them at a certain event, you can find them that way. It's ingenious, and a tremendous time-saver.

However you decide to do it, enjoy taking charge of the details of your own career. No one will ever do it better than you will — no one will ever be as interested.

IDs, I-9s and LEGALITIES

What would happen if you were notified a long-lost and extremely rich relation had just left you a million dollars? When you went to collect it, you'd have to prove who you were, right? Well, the same rule applies on the set when it comes to taking care of paper work.

As with any profession, there is now LOTS of paper work and it can't be done properly without proper documentation. And without proper documentation, you don't get paid. So this is *important*. Got it? When you come to work, bring your legal identification. You'll need a set of two items — driver's license and social security card, or passport and birth certificate.

> Getting actor's contracts signed has become one of the many jobs that the 2nd A.D. now has to do, and the pesky I-9 is such a pain because the A.D. has to physically see the actor's identification and then sign the I-9 to verify that. It is such a help when the actor brings a photocopy of his/her driver's license and social security card or of a passport or birth certificate. That copy can be attached to the I-9 and the 2nd A.D. then does not have to see the ID and sign off. Some

actors already know to do this but it would be great if it became common practice.

– B.C. Cameron

BUSINESS CARDS

To put it simply – we advocate having them. If you're computerized, you can generate and print your own. If not, you can have them created quite reasonably at photocopy stores and quick print shops. Keep the card simple. Don't make it pretentious. But rather than scribbling down phone numbers on the back of your bank deposit slips, isn't it more professional to hand someone a card? We think so.

MAILINGS

What's the first thing you want to do when you get a part in a play? Send out invitations and notices, of course.

Traditionally, the best way to find an agent in L.A., for example, is to get a showcase. So you send out invitations. Agents or their assistants are always going out to review these performances. How else can people get to know your work? If you don't yet have anything on film, this is the way to be seen. And as we've already discussed, auditioning is not necessarily the best way to show your work. So inviting professionals to your "home" turf on stage is critical.

Don't expect other people to send out these mailers. The theatre has its own agenda. Be responsible for your own business details.

> Steven Macht became a well-known actor. When he was making the transition from theatre to TV, he sent out postcards with an amusing cartoon of his face for each and every episodic appearance he did. People remembered him – they never were given the chance to forget.
> – Mara

In this electronic age, there's still something to be said for receiving something attractive via snail mail.

At the bookstores for actors — Samuel French (Los Angeles, New York, London), Drama Bookshop (New York), Act One (Chicago), Intermission (Philadelphia), etc. — you can now purchase mailing labels. In New York, for example, there is Henderson's Mailing Labels with targeted lists, such as Soaps or Agents. In Los Angeles we've even found these lists available at the local Kinko Copies store. Take advantage of these lists! They're great time savers.

E-MAILINGS

If you do decide to send announcements via e-mail, be careful with your mailing list. We've heard some nightmare stories about people who get highly annoyed when they receive "Spam" — that is, mass mailings via e-mail. We heard about one person against whom an e-mail hate-campaign was launched because he sent out too much Spam. Though that reaction seems excessive, we do sympathize to some extent. We each received hundreds of e-mail messages every week and it's an enormous task to screen them, sort them, respond to them and even to delete them.

We do advocate collecting genuine e-mails lists person-by-person through your own contacts, and/or purchasing targeted lists similar to the mailing labels mentioned earlier.

Your e-mail should be short and sweet and it should be inviting, not pretentious. Respect the person who's going to receive the e-mail. Don't be another sender of obnoxious electronic messages.

GIFTS

Unless you're rich and famous by the time you're reading this book, you don't necessarily have a budget to go out and buy gifts for your cast and crew at the end of every shoot. We're not saying you should. We do, however, want to make you aware of the ritual gift-giving which often takes place to punctuate the closure of professional relationships, and to celebrate the project which is reaching completion.

Your own work in a project may or not coincide with the final shooting day. But it is still the time to exchange tokens of the esteem you have developed for your colleagues. It is not necessarily bad form to give to some individuals, and not to others. In fact the gifts you give should probably mark some sort of actual exchange which has happened between and the people to whom you are giving.

It might be that your make-up person was particularly helpful, and you might give her a scented candle; it could be that your Second A.D. saved your car from being towed, and you find a small flashlight which he can hang on his key ring.

> *On "Evening In Byzantium," the First A.D. spent the first several days yelling at me. He was constantly furious that I wasn't where I should have been, and wasn't doing what I should have been doing. After the first two weeks of the shoot, there was a knock on my dressing room door. I opened it, and found the First A.D. kneeling in prayer. "Tell me this isn't your first job," he implored. I looked down at him and said, "It's my first job." He then realized that I wasn't stupid or stubborn. I just didn't know how to be professional yet. At the end of the project, I found a paperweight engraved with the slogan, "Don't Tread On Me." When I gave it to him, he loved it. It mended our relationship, and was the first time an actor had ever given him a gift. It was truly appreciated.*
>
> *– Erin*

> *I'm a firm believer that everyone needs recognition. And when you've worked with someone who's made a difference to your project, that person truly deserves acknowledgment. When my radio drama Milford-Haven was in production I gave annual cast and crew parties. Everyone who worked in the show received a certificate when our show had its*

first big success on the BBC. When Erin and I produced our Public Service Announcement, we mailed hand-signed certificates to each and every cast and crew member. For other projects I have sometimes given engraved paper weights to commemorate the work. In and of themselves, these are small things. But what they represent is genuine gratitude, and that truly is a valuable gift.
— Mara

THANK YOU NOTES

We advocate cultivating your relationships at every level. After a shoot is over, perhaps nothing cultivates friendship and appreciation more than a simple note.

> I always follow up with note writing! To everyone, for everything. My father was in PR. I keep the notes light and usually include a joke, I keep them short. I call these "touch notes." It's good business.
> — Joan Van Ark

Of course, you won't be able to send these notes unless you have each and every person's address from the shoot. Of course, you got all those, right? Just in case you hadn't thought of it, this chapter is for you.

THE INTERNET AND YOU

Covered In This Chapter:

- Using the Internet

- Useful Web Sites

This business moves fast. Actors who are serious about their careers need to be aware of how much is already out there on the web.

— Gary Marsh
(Founder, Breakdown Services)

THE INTERNET AND YOU

Just a few short years ago "network" meant something quite different from what it means now. A Network used to be a string of television stations each of whom had a signed agreement with a certain broadcasting company – NBC, ABC, CBS, and later, FOX. With the advent of Cable TV, we began moving toward smaller, more focused networks. Eventually we'll move beyond this paradigm all together, and the user will no longer be "fed" programming, but will decide what to view from a huge selection, effectively creating his or her own network of favorite programs.

"Networking" always meant connecting with other people, but it was generally limited to "who you know." The Internet changes all that and gives you access to "who you don't know." It also – for good or ill – gives others access to you.

The Internet is the ultimate networking tool. While our privacy may sometimes suffer, still, when it comes to marketing, researching and networking, the advantages are extraordinary.

USING THE INTERNET

If computers are still foreign objects to you, take heart. We ALL were beginners at some point. Believe us – we were there. And here's another little known secret – everyone who uses the computer is more or less self-taught. You may feel you have no aptitude for such devices, but computers have come a long way toward becoming user-friendly and we feel anyone can master the basics.

If you have no desire or ability to own your own computer at this time, public libraries all over the country will allow you to access the internet. Whether you own your own system or borrow one, we encourage you to make a habit of "surfing" periodically for sites that will help your career. You'll find all kinds of marvelous resources. And you'll have fun doing it.

USEFUL WEB SITES

The list we provide here is just a start. We keep finding new sites every week, and we're sure you will too. (If you find some good ones, let us know and we'll add them to our next revision. E-mail us a Actright@aol.com!)

Some sites listed here are better than others. Some are growing and expanding regularly. Perhaps you'll be one of the next people to create a brand new site which will become indispensable to actors! It's an exciting new frontier – jump in and explore.

Auditioning & Casting	
Breakdown Services	www.breakdownservices.com
Casting	www.thecastingsite.com
Casting	www.casting-america.com
Sides for Actors	www.showfax.com
Getting to Auditions, Meetings & Jobs	
Driving Directions (Map Quest)	www.mapquest.com
Driving Directions (Yahoo)	http://rd.yahoo.com/search/iy/maps/maps/*http://maps.yahoo.com
(L.A.) Traffic info from Caltrans	www.dot.ca.gov/hq/roadinfo/index.htm
Directories	
Academy players director	www.acadpd.org
Hollywood Creative Directory	www.hollyvision.com
Regional Sites	
Florida - The Acting Studio	www.actingstudio.com
North Carolina - Film Workshop	www.filmws.org

Resources for Actors	
Acting Books, Casting and more	www.acting.com
Actor Fest Annual Event	(link through www.backstage.com]
Actors Post – list of agencies, photographers, and schools	www.actorspost.com
Actor Site – networking	www.actorsite.com
Reel Mind – upload your reel	www.reelmind.com
Resources & Networking	www.redbirdstudio.com www.tvistudios.com
Working Actors Guide	www.workingactors.com
Movies, Television & Plays	
actors appearing on TV this week	www.tv-now.com
movie reviews	www.filmscouts.com
movie data base	www.imdb.com
playbill	www.playbill.com
episodic guide	www.xnet.com/~djk/main_page.shtml
Professional Organizations	
Academy of Television Arts & Sciences	www.emmys.org
Aacademy of Motion Picture Arts & Sciences	www.oscars.org

Publications	
Backstage	www.backstage.com
Hollywood Reporter	www.hollywoodreporter.com
Inside	www.inside.com
Reel West	www.reelwest.com
Variety	www.variety.com

Unions & Organizations	
ACTRA (Canada)	actra.com
AFTRA - American Federation of Television & Radio Actors	www.aftra.org
AFI - American Film Institute	www.afionline.org
DGA - Director's Guild of America	dga.org
SAG - Screen Actors Guild	sag.com
WIF - Women in Film	www.wif.org
WGA - Writers Guild of America	wga.org

We thought we'd share with you a short list of sites created by colleagues and/or friends. These sites are included because each of them has some or all of the following qualities. When you design your own site, think of some of these qualities.

- Each conveys a sense of who the person (or group of people) is. Style, attitude, tone, are all reflected in colors, fonts, layout, graphics and word content.
- Internal links are easy to use and interesting. By navigating the site, the user can travel among the various activities and interests of the person. We get more than just a resume (though resumes are available) — we get a sense of life choices both personal and professional.
- Current events. While past history enriches a site tremendously, users also like to feel they're up to the minute — otherwise, they could be reading a book published several years ago. These sites are frequently updated and users can tell what the person is up to now: their current performances, projects and activities.
- External links. Although some people fear "linking out" will dilute their site, we feel the opposite it true. Why? Because it makes your site a resource for your visitors. At caryn.com you can find musings on the acting business. Amanda McBroom lists her latest favorite books. Mark Wolfram created an extraordinary sub-site all about the L.A. Lakers which widens the appeal of his site.
- If you want to create sub-networks, there are various types of "Rings" you can join, linking you both to and from colleagues' sites and generating mutual traffic. Check out Marilyn Harris's use of Songwriter Rings. Here's a young actor's site we found by searching yahoo's actor rings. His site has his head shot and is followed by (on the right) his lift of credits (always updated) and (on the left) some great on-set photos: http://msnhomepages.talkcity.com/studiorow/johnnyalonso/
- Feedback. Want to make your site interactive? Be sure to design a way for your visitors to "talk" with you. The simplest way is by e-mail. Be sure to have more than just your webmaster's e-mail. Have your own listed clearly. You'll be amazed what interesting comments visitors provide. If you want to get a little more advanced, you might

try creating a bulletin board, which is a threaded conversation: i.e., a visitor's e-mail gets posted, and so does your response, and subsequent responses, leaving a trail of your conversation, which can lead to further conversations....

Actors & Other Artists

Host Sites for Various Actors	www.mrshowbiz.go.com www.safesearching.com
David Baldacci	www.davidbaldacci.com
Ed Begley	www.edbegley.com
Stephen Bishop	www.stephenbishop.com
Caryn's Actor site	www.caryn.com
Doobie Brothers	www.doobiebros.com
Whoopi Goldberg	www.whoopi.com
Erin Gray	www.eringray.com
Marilyn Harris	www.marilynharris.com
Mary Helsaple	www.helsaple.com
Louis L'Amour	www.louislamour.com
Amanda McBroom	www.amcbroom.com
Alyssa Milano	www.alyssa.com
Kathleen Noone	www.kathleennoone.com
Linda Purl	www.lindapurl.net
Mara Purl	www.marapurl.com
Joan VanArk	www.joanvanark.com
Mark Wolfram	www.markwolfram.com

There are several ways to get your web site created. Most ISPs (Internet Service Providers) offer the services of an in-house web designer for an additional fee. Or, you might find a friend or colleague who'd work with you in exchange for some kind of favor or service you could provide. Or, you may be one of those intrepid technofiles who wants to create your own.

In case you want to teach yourself to build your own site, or enhance to web-building skills you already have, we'll end this chapter with a short list of terrific sites full of advice, guidance and tips about web building.

Whatever method you chose, we encourage you to consider this as yet another part of your creative process. You're creating your life, you're creating your career, and your web site is a chance to clarify and represent all that you're creating. Have fun!

http://www.builder.com/
http://www.jars.com/
http://javascript.internet.com/
http://msdn/microsoft.com/workshop/
http://www.websitepreloader.com/
http://www.wsabstract.com/
http://www.phpbuilder.com/
http://thescripts.com/
http://www.idevnet.com/
http://www.freewebtools.com/
http://www.weberdev.com/

GLOSSARY

Covered In This Chapter:

- Key Terms You'll Need To Know

Arriving on the set and not knowing the terminology is like landing in Paris and not speaking French.
— Mara

If you're an actor who doesn't know the language of a professional set, it's like trying to work with one hand tied behind your bank.
— Jim Lewis

GLOSSARY

ABBY SINGER — Penultimate shot – the one just before the last one. Abby Singer, a well-known producer, often walked onto the set toward the end of the day's work. When he saw that the Director was about to do the second-to-last shot, he'd notify the crew so they could start wrapping things up. Once the crew caught on to this pattern, they named the second to the last shot for him, and it caught on industry-wide. (We interviewed Mr. Singer and got the story straight from him.)

ACTION — The most famous word in film vocabulary – the word which only the Director may say. Not for actors to say, but very important for actors to listen for – this is your cue to begin. But – a word to the wise. Wait for a second or two before beginning. Those few seconds could protect your performance, or could even capture a moment of "real" behavior which is more compelling than the "acting" you're about to do. And by the way, the word "Action" is generally not used is taped TV programs (like Soaps) where instead the Stage Manager will repeat the countdown coming from the control booth. What you will probably get is more of a hand signal to begin than the word "Action," which is reserved for film and filmed shows.

ALL CLEAR — Whatever technical problem was holding things up has now been solved. "All Clear" is called out to indicate that production can resume.

Glossary

ANSWER PRINT — This is the preliminary print, a kind of rough assembly of all the shots which will ultimately comprise the film.

APPLE BOX — Although apples may have been in the original boxes, they are no longer. The box is wooden and sturdy — useful for standing on, and that's just what it's for. There are many configurations. A Full Apple can have "stories": first story means flat; second story: on its side; third story; on end. There are also the half, quarter, and pancake (about half an inch). All these are for height adjustments for cast or crew, to see or be seen correctly. Also see "Half Apple."

ATMOSPHERE — When you get out the CD player and pipe some John Coltrane music through the sound stage. Just kidding. Atmosphere is another name for "Background" "Extras," people without speaking parts, who add to the scene by creating a realistic background or "atmosphere."

BABY — Those noisy and sometimes cute creatures rarely allowed on the set. True. But actually a Baby is a lighting instrument. To be precise, it's a Fresnel, which is a light with a condensing or focusing lens. Its lenticular design is a piece of glass with concentric circles, which make the instrument provide an even field of light, giving the same amount of foot-candles wherever it shines. "Baby" is one of the smaller ones — a 1000 watt globe. A "midget" is even smaller, 300 to 600 watts.

BACKGROUND — (See Atmosphere)

BACKSTEPPING — What you do when you've just insulted your Director, forgetting that your mike was still on? Not really. Technically, it's an important technique used by the actor to ensure that he or she hits his/her mark. The actor walks backward from the end position in a scene to the previous position and counts the number of steps it will take. See "Hit Your Mark" and see the "Shooting" chapter.

BANANA — No, not the fruit. When the director says "give me a banana," he doesn't mean you should run to the catering table. Instead, walk into your shot in an arc, rather than a straight line. Now that you know what to do, don't you want to know why? Because, from the perspective of the camera — and that's what this is ALL about — it may be necessary to keep a certain object in view because it's a story point.

BEST BOY — The person who carries the ring in a child marriage? Wrong again. There are actually two departments which each have a best boy, but the job itself is similar in either case. This important person is in charge of materials and details relating either to lights, or to rigging. The Best Boy Electric keeps track of lights, and is in charge of the electricians' paperwork. The Best Boy Grip keeps track of materials and items on stage, and is in charge of the paperwork for Grips or Hammers. In either case, there's also a lot of physical strength and dexterity involved in the job.

BIBLE — An inspiring text which will always tell you what's really going on. Actually, we're not joking. If your agent asks if he should send you one, always say yes. This is what the writers put together before and during the writing of their scripts. It has tremendous detail about characters, much of which may never show up overtly in scripts, but all of which informs the text, and informs the actor as well.

BLUES — Not what the lady sings, but rather the color of the pages for the first set of rewrites.

BOOM — A mechanical, extendable arm to which equipment is attached. The camera boom, also called a crane, extends from the dolly, to which the camera can be attached. Facilitates difficult shots generally incorporating height and swooping motion. Can be operated hands-on, or by remote control. The microphone boom holds a microphone just out of frame, allowing for dialogue to be spoken at a normal level in a scene.

CALL TIME — "Your call" or "call time" is the time you are expected to arrive on set.

CAMERA READY — Not the art work for a print ad, but you – dressed, made-up, including final touches and ready to work.

CHINESE ANGLES — This refers to a particular kind of lighting technique, wherein shutters (also called "Barn Doors") across the front of a lighting instrument are closed almost down to a "slit" or "Chinese angle."

CLEAN ENTRANCE — Making a "clean entrance" means the actor starts the scene outside the first frame of the shot and comes in "clean."

CLINT EASTWOOD SHOT	Clint Eastwood is famous for many things, not the least of which is his Adam's apple. Early in their careers, both he and Burt Reynolds were let go from their movie contracts, Reynolds because he "couldn't act," and Eastwood because his Adam's apple was too large. Reynolds quipped he could work on his problem, but that Eastwood would have trouble fixing his. Too bad neither of them had careers after that. So, where does this shot frame the actor? You got it, from the top of the head to just below the Adam's apple.
COWBOY SHOT	A strange term which makes perfect sense once you know it, the Cowboy Shot includes just the hips — the area of the body framed by the six-shooters and their holsters and gun belt. See also "Holding."
COVERAGE	We warned you about this when we discussed nudity. (Just kidding.) Actually coverage is an important term describing the various ways a scene is shot. By shooting a master, a close-up, and perhaps other shots, the director is giving him- or herself the maximum options when it comes to editing.
CRAFT SERVICES	Another term for caterers, although Craft Services is more comprehensive, in that they provide a variety of meals and snack foods which, depending on the set, are replenished throughout the shooting day. Be nice to these people. You need them.
CUE	Usually the line spoken immediately before yours, but it might be a hand signal, a movement, an

	action. Whatever it is, you must memorize it, and respond to it as your signal to begin.
CUT	In shooting – what the Director – not the actor! – says at the end of a shot. Our advice is not to end your work the *instant* the Director says "Cut." Hold for a second or two - you'll give the editor a break. In editing, the word refers to where the editor is going to cut from one shot to another.
CUT TO	Script designation indicating the method in which the final script is to move from one scene to the next. A cut is a clear definite move rather than a gradual one.
DAILIES	One day's worth of shooting, usually processed overnight as quickly as possible with limited corrections so the footage can be viewed the next day by the Director, D.P., and Editor. Sometimes the producers watch and also the heads of various departments such as Make-up, Hair, Wardrobe, and any member of the crew.
DIRECTOR OF PHOTOGRAPHY	The D.P. is responsible for the look of the film, and has three departments under his/her directo control: camera department, grip department, & electric department. The D.P. is responsible for the technical interpolation of the other creative departments. In some cases the D.P. also becomes the Second Unit Director.
DIRTY CLOSE-UP	Does this refer to a nude scene? No. Essentially, this describes a shot somewhere between a close-up and an over-the-shoulder. It's a close-up which

	includes a small section (an ear, a shoulder) of your scene partner.
DR. FEELGOOD	A legendary doctor who shall remain nameless, who used to be sent out to see if you were really sick. Whatever his diagnosis, his treatment generally was to boost his patients with B12 shots which temporarily solved the energy problem but took a toll on the actors later.
DRIFTING	What actors do to drive the crew crazy — and we're not joking. Some actors have a nervous habit of shifting their weight from side to side. This can mean that half their face disappears from the shot, or that they move out of focus. Don't go there.
DRYING UP	Forgetting your lines. Don't go there either.
DUB IN	Adding sound elements.
DISSOLVE	What happens to an actress when she finishes an emotional scene. Just kidding. A post-production term describing a gradual transition from one image to another.
DIVING BOARD	They say you must take the plunge when you get into this business. Metaphors aside, sometimes a camera with both its Operator and its First Assistant have a difficult time getting into the correct position to capture a shot. The diving board is a platform attached to the camera dolly for someone to stand on.

DOUBLE	Usually refers to the Stunt person who doubles the actor in action sequences. See the Stunt Work chapter.
DUTCH ANGLES	Also known as Canted Frame. This is when a camera moves in a tangent, or slant. Normally, a camera sits on what is called a pan head, which allows the operator to move the camera horizontally or vertically. When a second pan head is used in addition, it allows the camera to move tangentially. The result is that the audience sees a slanted frame.
DOLLY	A moving platform on which the camera is mounted. It allows the camera operator to position himself and his camera at varying heights and angles with relation to the actors and the set.
DOLLY SHOT	Any shot made from a moving dolly.
DUBBING	Substituting sound or dialogue in a later looping session, in place of what has been recorded during shooting.
EIGHTH OF A PAGE	Increment of page to be shot. It comes from folding a piece of paper into 8ths.
EYELINE	Not what the Make-up person puts on you, but rather what you are able to see from where you are. While you are working, it's important that nothing disturbing be in your eyeline. Refer to the Shooting chapter.
FADE IN	Coming from a black screen, an image appears. Typically used at the beginning of a film.

FADE OUT	The image on screen is gradually overtaken by black. Typically used as the final shot in a film.
FEED LINE	Another term for "Cue."
FIRST TEAM	You remember this from your days on the Varsity bench, right? It's not so different. First Team refers to the actors — as opposed to the stand-ins, who are sometimes called the Second Team.
FIRST UNIT	First Unit shooting involves the actors, and everyone who is involved with shooting what the actors do, their dialogue and their actions. It does not refer to stunt shots, nor to establishing shots of exteriors which don't involve actors. Since you're an actor, you're involved in the First Unit shooting.
FORCED CALLS	Good news and bad. You may be sleepwalking but it's a bonus to the checkbook. A forced call occurs when a player is called back to work before receiving the union prescribed rest period, and is therefore entitled to a substantial set fee, or a day's pay, whichever is less. The union put this in so the actor isn't worked to death, since it discourages the producers from doing it too often. It really comes into play on a series.
GOLDEN TIME	To a still photographer it's the moment when the sun is setting and the light is golden. To an actor or crew member, it's those hours after you've been working for what seems like forever. After 18 hrs you go into "golden time" and begin earning double scale.

Glossary

GRACE PERIOD — To avoid paying a meal penalty, there is a twelve-minute grace period to which the producers are entitled, so long as they don't start work on a new set-up. Relates to lunch, not dinner.

GROUCHO — Groucho was as well known for his physical as for his verbal comedy, and that has created a move which can save your shot. From the camera's perspective (the only one that counts) if you POP into or out of a chair, you will seem magically to appear or disappear from the shot (leave that for special effects). Instead, "Groucho" into or out of your chair by stooping slightly before sitting or standing. Your crew will be happy campers.

HALF APPLE — All you're allowed to eat and still fit into your costume? No. At some point in the history of filmmaking, it was discovered that half a wooden apple box was just the right height to stand on. Writer Carl Esser was visiting the set of one his first low-budget feature film. When the Director called for a "half apple" Carl tried to be helpful. He went to the catering table, cut an apple in half, and brought it back to the Director, who looked at him as though he were insane. It certainly was a fast way for the crew to find out how green their writer was.

HANG THE BABY & SHOOT THE MIDGET — The closing lines you deliver as the anti-hero of the sick low-budget film you're starring in. Not really. A Baby is a lighting instrument, and so is a Midget — see separate definitions. In this case the expression describes a situation where first you're going to hang a Baby, which is a 1K light; it is then going to project light onto a lighting instrument which is actually part of the set, in this case a Midget. The simple explanation? In this shot a guy is standing next to a light.

HAVING HAD	When the second A.D. calls and says, "Report to work tomorrow at 2:00pm 'Having Had,'" he means having eaten lunch.
HIT THE BLOWERS	Reminds us of a joke we heard at the Comedy Club. But in this context, it's an order to a crew member to turn on the air conditioners after Sound is no longer rolling.
HITTING YOUR MARK	The original title of our book. (True! But there's more.) One of the most important things you do on the set. You may know your lines and have your motivation figured out, but if you fail to hit your mark, your performance won't show up on film. See "Shooting" chapter.
HOLDING	Vera Miles walked up to the camera operator on her set one day and said, "What are you holding?" His only reply was "Shoulders." She said "Thank you" and proceeded to do her scene. What did all this mean? The actress wanted to know the framing of the shot, or exactly on what part of her the camera would be "holding." The camera operator's reply was an abbreviated way of saying that he was "holding" on her head and face, and then down far enough to include her shoulders, but, for example, not as far as her waist. This would let her know what gestures would be visible.
HONEY WAGON	Everyone's favorite euphemism for the trailers containing the toilets.

IN THE CAN	Where you hide when you don't know your lines? Wrong! "In the can" refers to film footage which has already been shot, and is therefore "in the can" – completed, finished.
KEY LIGHT	The dominant light used to illuminate a scene.
LOOPING	Not something you do in an airplane. Many times various segments of dialogue must be re-done after all the principal photography is completed. Perhaps a plane did fly by – in the background – or perhaps an actor's words were not as clear as they need to be. There may occasionally even be situations where a change has been made in the script which may not necessitate re-shooting, so long as it can be fixed by altering the tone of the dialogue. Whatever the production needs, the actors are asked to come to a sound stage, where they watch themselves on screen, and lip-synch their own mouths.
MARTINI SHOT	The _real_ last shot. Self-explanatory, after a 16-hour shoot.
MARKS	When rehearsing a scene, at each move you will be given a mark on the floor. This is essential for the camera operator and camera assistant to make sure you are properly framed and in focus. Sometimes chalk is used, sometimes tape, or sometimes even a sand bag. "Hit your mark" doesn't mean shooting it with your (prop) rifle. If you think we're joking, be sure to read the story in the Shooting chapter.

MASTER SHOT	A wide shot, encompassing all the actors in a given scene, so all their exchanges, in dialogue and action, are visible. This is a story-telling shot, rather than a shot which focuses on one particular character.
MATCHING	So tough to do with wallpaper. Even tougher, actually, when it comes to shooting. We wrote an entire chapter on the subject. Have a read.
"MAY DAY"	As explained in the Shooting chapter, this is a final run-through, or technical rehearsal for the Crew.
MEAL PENALTY	How you feel when you're on a diet. No, actually this is quite important. The producers work really hard to finish the shot they're working on before the required lunch period begins. If they run over this, and go past their grace period, cast & crew receive meal penalty checks.
MIDGET	A Midget is a lighting instrument. To be precise, it is a Fresnel, which is a light with a condensing or focusing lens. Its lenticular design is a piece of glass with concentric circles which make the instrument provide an even field of light, giving the same amount of foot-candles wherever it shines. A Midget is one of the smaller ones — with 300 to 600 watts. A Baby is slightly larger.
MISE-EN-SCÈNE	Generally, this term (French, but often used in English) refers to the overall look and feel of a production. It is the result of the collaboration between all the artists who design and create the set and is ultimately the manifestation of the Director's vision. Some Directors feel quite passionately that the Mise-en-Scène describes

	their whole creative process, particularly including the work they do with actors. See the Shooting chapter for further information.
MIXER	No, it's not what you add to an alcoholic beverage. This refers to the sound technician, who must mix sound levels appropriately.
MOS	Stands for "Mit Out Sound." "Mit" means "with" in German, Germany being the original home of the finest recording equipment.
MOW	Movie Of the Week. Today the term "TV Movie" is more commonly used.
OBI	No, not a sash on a Kimono but a tiny light which sits right on top of the camera lens. Designed originally for Merle Oberon, this light highlighted her dark eyes.
ON A BELL	The first thing to happen in the order of shooting: putting the set On A Bell turns on the red lights, and tells everyone to be quiet in preparation for shooting.
ORDER OF SHOOTING	(1) On A Bell (2) Rolling (spoken by First A.D.) (3) Speed (spoken by Sound mixer) (4) Slate (5) Action (spoken by Director)
ORDER OF REVISIONS	This refers to script pages which are printed on successive colors as revisions continue to be made, in the following order: BLUE, PINK, GREEN, YELLOW, TAN, SALMON, ORCHID.

OUT TAKES	Pieces of film footage not used in the final cut of a film. Often it's moments when an actor didn't remember to match movements, and the editor can't cut to him/her.
PAN	Not to be confused with kitchenware. A move the camera makes, from side to side, moving across a landscape, or a room, or from one face to another on a horizontal plane.
PICK UP	It's not always necessary to re-shoot an entire scene. If the first part worked, the Director may ask for a Pick Up from a designated line.
PLACES	When you hear this word, you stop everything you are doing instantly, and go to the exact mark where you begin the scene about to be shot.
PORK CHOP	What's for dinner? No. This is a small platform (shaped something like a pork chop) on the side of a camera dolly, making it wider so the Operator can have another standing position. See also Diving Board.
POV	Point Of View. An important term in scripts. Technically, this refers to point of view of the camera. Metaphorically, this will then refer to whose eyes we are seeing through.
REVERSES	What you experience when you are no longer on a series. (Well, that's true, but that isn't what we mean here.) First one person's close-up is shot; then the other person's: this is referred to as a "reverse."

ROCK INTO IT	Proper behavior at an Elton John concert. Well, perhaps. But as explained in the Shooting chapter, this refers to a suggestion of movement which an actor must employ as he/she steps into a shot, in order to match the Master Shot, where he/she might have been moving.
ROLLING	What the First A.D. says just before shooting begins. Tells you film has started to roll.
ROOM TONE	Believe it or not, every room has its own sound, even when most of us would describe it as silent. This basic ambience is crucial for Sound mixers to capture on tape, for use later in editing.
RUN-THROUGH	This derives from the idiom, "Let's run through it again," meaning "Let's rehearse this again." When working on a sitcom the "run-through" is usually the time the actors do a performance of the entire show for the producers, say on the third day or at the end of a tech day for the producers and network.
SET-UP	Each separate shot in a film or television program has specific angles from which it is shot, and therefore requires specific lighting. Each time the production shifts from one shot to the next, is called a Set-up, because set, lighting, sound, actors, and all elements must be set up differently for each shot.
SEVEN O'CLOCK ACTORS	May sound derogatory, but it's actually a complimentary term for actors who deliver their performance before the crew goes into overtime.

SCRIPT SUPERVISOR	The critically important crew member who takes notes about every detail of the shoot – including matching – for later use by Editor and Director.
SECOND TEAM	Team of "Stand-Ins" who literally stand in for the principal actors for purposes of proper lighting, and in some cases, for actual shots. Stand-Ins are not usually the same as Stunt Doubles.
SECOND UNIT	A completely separate crew with its own Second Unit Director, which typically shoots on location rather than at the studio, and which does not use the principal actors, but instead usually uses stunt doubles. The Second Unit Director is responsible for shooting establishing shots and any stunt work. In many cases the D.P. on the show is also the Second Unit Director. You'll find that if you are supposed to appear in an establishing shot or an action shot, it won't be you. Do you get to go to St. Tropez for those heavenly sunset scenes? No. They'll find someone who looks enough like you from a distance that the audience will think it's you. You'll do your shots down the street in Santa Monica. Shucks.
SIDES	A section of the script. Certain scenes which are either being shot or performed at an audition.
SLATE	Or "Clapper" has information on it for purposes of identification, such as production title and number, scene and take number, and the Director and Director of Photography's names and is photographed at the beginning of a scene on the first few feet of film. Occasionally it can be filmed at the end.

SLOPPING	When an actor's role isn't finished on the planned day, an actor "slops over." So when the A.D. says "You're slopping over," he/she doesn't mean you're doing a sloppy job. It means you'll continue shooting at a future date. That's right! More days and more money.
SOPHIA LOREN SHOT	Named for some of the Italian film star's obvious assets, this shot holds on the actor from the top of the head to just below the breasts.
SPEED	When the sound mixer on the set yells "speed," he or she doesn't mean amphetamines, nor that you're to deliver your lines fast. The word "speed" is short for "up to speed." Sound mixers must deal with something called a "wow" factor – this refers to the tape reels which take a moment to get going fast enough to be at full speed. Actually "speed" is the synch point, at which the film, which travels at 24 frames per second, and the sound track will synchronize. The Director must wait until he hears "Speed" before saying "Action" – which is your cue to begin.
SOTTO VOCCE	Literally "soft voice."
STUNT CASTING	Where the casting ITSELF is a stunt. All the cameos are performed by well-known people.
STUNT COORDINATOR	Responsible for designing the stunts which will fulfill the script's and the Director's requirements. Responsible for hiring the stunt men and women. Occasionally the Stunt Coordinator will be the Second Unit Director.

SWISH, FLASH ZIP PAN	Nothing to do with sexual preference, clothing, or the lack thereof. A panning motion wherein the camera is moving fast enough to cause blurring of the image. Used to indicate the passage of time in such notable TV series as "Batman."
TILT	Not the same as when your video game goes down. A move the camera makes up and/or down, moving for example up the length of a tree, or down from a moon to a landscape.
TURNAROUND	A twelve-hour period between work periods, which is required by the unions.
TV Q	It is not legal in the U.S. to maintain a policy against hiring anyone for inappropriate reasons. Therefore when asked, network executive deny the existence of the "TV Q" list. However this non-existent, imaginary, and unheard of listing determines your hirability. You have one. It may be zero, but you have one, whether you know about it or not.
V.O.	Stands for Voice Over. See the Sound chapter for a complete explanation.
W.A.G.	Wild Ass Guess. Used by anyone, at any time, under any circumstances, but it usually has to do with time estimates. Not a good idea to apply this to the lines you were supposed to memorize.
WALK-THROUGH	Usually an early rehearsal on-book (using scripts).
WILD LINES	Lines spoken out of context, which will later be edited into the scene.

WIPE	Nothing to do with the honey wagon. (What's a honey wagon?) A term used to describe a hard transition between shots, in most cases with the screen going to black momentarily, sometimes in a specifically defined way such as a line, a circle, or a square.
WRAP	End. Finito. Kaput.
WRAP PARTY	Celebration of the end of a project, where everyone involved is invited, and all manner of back-slapping occurs. It's considered good form not to miss your wrap party.

BIBLIOGRAPHY

Covered In This Chapter:

- On Acting

- On Creativity

- On Technical Advice

- On Career Advice

- Biographies (Some Of Our Favorites)

ON ACTING

"A Challenge for the Actor"
©1991 by Uta Hagen
Scribner

"Acting For the Camera"
©1997 by Tony Barr, Eric Stephan Kline, Edward Asner
Harper Collins

"Acting In Film: An Actor's Take on Movie Making"
©1990 by Michael Caine
Applause Theatre Books

"Acting In Television Commercials for Fun and Profit"
©1986 by Squire Fridell
Three Rivers Press

"Advice To The Players"
©1980 by Robert Lewis
Harper & Row

"An Actor's Handbook"
©1924 by Constantin Stanislavski
edited & translated by Elizabeth Reynolds Hapgood
Theatre Arts Books

"An Actor Prepares"
©1936 Constantin Stanislavski
edited & translated by Elizabeth Reynolds Hapgood
Theatre Arts Books

"Building A Character"
©1949 Constantin Stanislavski
edited & translated by Elizabeth Reynolds Hapgood
Theatre Arts Books

Bibliography

"Creating A Role"
©1961 Constantin Stanislavski
edited & translated by Elizabeth Reynolds Hapgood
Theatre Arts Books

"Free To Act"
©1978 Warren Robertson
G.P. Putnam

"Method or Madness"
©1958 by Robert Lewis
Samuel French, Inc.

"How To Audition"
©1977 by Gordon Hunt
Harper & Row

"On Acting"
©1986 by Laurence Olivier
Simon & Schuster

"On Singing Onstage"
©1978 by David Craig
Schirmer Books

"Sanford Meisner On Acting"
©1987 Sanford Meisner & Dennis Longwell
Vintage Publishers

"Respect For Acting"
©1973 by Uta Hagen
Macmillan Publishing Co., Inc.

"The Actor and the Camera"
©1994 by Malcolm Taylor
A & C Black

"The Golden Buddha Changing Masks: Essays on the Spiritual Dimension of Acting"
©1989 by Mark Olsen
Gateway/IDHHB Publishing

"To The Actor: On The Technique of Acting"
©1953 by Michael Chekhov
Harper & Row

also republished with additional material as:
"On the Technique of Acting"
©1991 by Michael Chekhov
Harper Collins

ON CREATIVITY

"Marry Your Muse"
©1997 by Jan Phillips
Quest Books

"The Artist's Way"
©1992 by Julia Cameron
Tarcher/ Putnam Books

ON TECHNICAL ADVICE

"Accents: A Manual for Actors"
©1998 by Robert Blumenfeld
Limelight Editions

"The Art Of The Film"
©1963 by Ernest Lindgren
Collier Books

"The Film Director"
©1971 by Richard L. Bare
Collier Books

"Independent Feature Film Production:
A Complete Guide From Concept Through Distribution"
©1982 by Gregory Goodell
St. Martin's Press

"When The Shooting Stops... The Cutting Begins: An Editor's Story"
©1979 by Ralph Rosenblum & Robert Karan
Viking Press

ON CAREER ADVICE

"How To Break Into Motion Pictures, Television, Commercials & Modeling"
©1978 by Nina Blanchard
Doubleday

"How To Sell Yourself as an Actor"
©1996 by K Callan
Sweden Press

"The Actor: A Practical Guide To A Professional Career"
©1987 by Eve Brandstein
Donald I. Fine, Inc.

"The Los Angeles Agent Book"
©1996 by K Callan
Sweden Press

"The Seven Habits of Highly Effective People"
©1989 by Stephen R. Covey
Simon & Shuster

"The Seven Spiritual Laws of Success"
©1994 by Deepak Chopra
New World Library

"The New York Agent Book"
©1995 by K Callan
Sweden Press

BIOGRAPHIES

Lauren Bacall
"By Myself"
©1978 by Lauren Bacall
Ballantine Books

Eleonora Duse
"Eleonora Duse: The Mystic In The Theatre"
©1965 by Eva Le Gallienne
Southern Illinois University Press

Charles Grodin
"It Would Be So Nice If You Were Not Here"
©1990 By Charles Grodin
Vintage Publishers

Katherine Hepburn
"Me: Stories of My Life"
©1991 by Katherin Hepburn
Alfred A. Knopf

Laurence Olivier
"Confessions Of An Actor - An Autobriography"
©1982 by Laurence Olivier
Simon & Schuster

Ali MacGraw
"Moving Pictures"
©1991 by Ali MacGraw
Bantam Books

Patrick Macnee
"Blind in One Ear"
©1989 by Patrick Macnee
Mercury House Publishers

<u>Marion Seldes</u>
"The Bright Lights: A Theatre Life"
©1978 by Marion Seldes
Houghton Mifflin Company

<u>Donald Sinden</u>
"A Touch Of The Memoires"
©1982 by Donald Sinden
Hodder and Stoughton

<u>Liv Ullmann</u>
"Changing"
©1976 by Liv Ullmann
Alfred A. Knopf

"Choices"
©1984 by Liv Ullman
Alfred A. Knopf

<u>Tennessee Williams</u>
"The Kindness of Strangers"
©1985 by Donald Spoto
Little Brown

Home

Tai Chi, the Woo Way in beta testing... - THE Raygun - collectors edition is here...

- News Page
- Life's Pursuits
- Personal Appearances
- Photographs
- Erin Gray Fan Club
- Biography
- Filmography
- Celebrity Events
- Links
- Erin's Online Store
- Web Announcements
- Projects

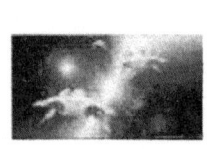   

Aloha!

Welcome to my web site! You may know me as an actress... I'm also a producer, teacher, speaker and writer, and I'm a wife and a mother. My life is about balance, creativity and healing, and these are some of the things I'd like to share with you in these pages. I greet you with "Aloha" which in Hawaii, where I spent much of my childhood, means "hello", "goodbye" and "I send you love." In India when people meet and part, they often say "Namaste" which means: "I honor the place within you where if you are in that place in you and I am in that place in me, there is only one of us." Just as these two words overlap and blend, so do the different aspects of my being, a strange but perhaps unique blend of West and East, of the outer ease and simplicity of the island paradise, and of the inner serenity and discipline of the ancient arts of Asia.

Namaste!

http://www.eringray.com/

Erin Gray
Current Activities

ACTING

As we go to print, eight independent feature films in which I co-starred either have just been released or are about to be. Production was just completed on "Clover Bend" with Robert Urich and "The Last Producer" with Burt Reynolds was recently released. Several interesting projects are in development.... I'll keep you posted through my web site.

WRITING

*Beyond Yoga (working titl*e*)* I'm developing my ideas about Chi Kung (the art of energy) — the basis of both Yoga and Tai Chi — and how to incorporate its profound healing potential into one's daily life.

PRODUCTION

My husband Richard and I are working on my Chi Kung/ Tai Chi videos. Mara and I are working with the National Coalition Against Domestic Violence to create a Training Video for cosmetologists.

TEACHING

The *Act Right* seminars are getting better established as an important aspect of professional training for actors, in Los Angeles and across the United States.

My *Tai Chi Classes* continue at U.C.L.A. and I have now taught my Tai Chi class in almost every state (Montana and North Dakota — you're on my list!) at personal appearances and conventions. Please continue to check my web site to find the class closest to you.

SPEECHES & SIGNINGS

At Sci Fi Conventions, where I sign photos for fans, I meet and greet so many fascinating people and often teach my Tai Chi class as well.

Several subjects, all dear to my heart, are the topics of my speeches (many of which I co-write with Mara.) My web site calendar lists the details.

Mara and I will be showing up all over the country at signings for our Revised Edition of *Act Right!*

BOARD MEMBERSHIPS

National Coalition Against Domestic Violence Advisory Board and Spokeswoman
Haven House (Shelter for Battered Women)

Erin Gray is an actress, producer, teacher, speaker, writer, wife and mother, not necessarily in that order. Her life is about balance, creativity, and healing.

Erin redefined our public image of the beauty with brains, when "Buck Rogers in the 25th Century" became a hit series, her sleek, sophisticated "Colonel Wilma" became a role model, and Erin Gray became a household word.

For five years on NBC TV, she was the American public's image of the ideal woman. Her "Kate" in "Silver Spoons" managed to have it all — marriage, family, and business career.

Recently Erin guest starred in a recurring role as Congresswoman Karen Archer in NBC's "Profiler" and played a recurring role in ABC's "Port Charles." In the past few years, she has co-starred in eight films, "Clover Bend" with Robert Urich, "Woman's Story" (with Kent McCord), "Social Misfits," "The Last Producer" (with Burt Reynolds), "Touched by a Killer" (with Isabelle Hoffman), "Delicate Instruments," "ManFast," "S.W.A.T." and "Serial Intentions."

Erin was one of the best known models in the country before her acting career started. Hers was the face that launched some of America's most glamorous beauty products. She was the original "I'm Worth It" woman for L'Oreal, one of the first Sports Illustrated models, the Maxi Girl for Max Factor, and the Bloomingdale's spokeswoman for ten years.

Erin has co-starred in literally scores of TV movies including "Born Beautiful," "Starman," "Laker Girls," "Coach of the Year," "Police Story," "Code of Vengeance," "Breaking Home Ties," "The Avenging Ace", "Addicted To His Love," "Official Denial," "Honor Thy Father & Mother: The Menendez Trial," and feature films "Six Pack" with Kenny Rogers," "The Myth that Wouldn't Die" (with Thierry Lhermitte) "Jason Goes To Hell (Friday the 13th Park IX)," "Dangerous Place" and "T-Force."

Erin's theatre work includes 'La Moure N.D. 58458' in which she starred at 'The Bitter Truth Theater in Los Angeles, and her work earned her a best actress nomination for the Valley Theatre League's Artistic Director Award.

Erin and Mara have been partners in PurlGray Enterprises for fourteen years and have written sitcom & TV movie scripts, book proposals, infomercials, workout videos, and over one hundred speeches. In 1998 their domestic violence PSA "Step Forward" was co-produced with Women In Film, aired in nine states, and in 1999 they won the Women's Peacepower Award. In 2000 they wrote and co-produced  "Empowerment," the first official training video for the National Coalition Against Domestic Violence. They raise funds for Haven House, the oldest shelter in the U.S.; Erin serves as board member and spokeswoman, Mara serves as advisory board member. They also conduct their seminar "Act Right," together and individually, for professional and student groups (see flyer).

Possessing a highly developed sense of public service, Erin serves as spokeswoman and advisory board member for the National Coalition Against Domestic Violence and has also served as advisory board member for Child Quest International, & and the Childhood Leukemia Foundation, and board member of the Multiple Sclerosis Association. She has given speeches for organizations including Athletes & Entertainers for Kids, National Council on Alcoholism & Drug Dependence, Women Against Family Violence – San Antonio, Texas, Mothers Against Sexual Abuse, Lifetime TV's First Annual Community Outreach Forum.

Erin teaches Tai Chi classes regularly at U.C.L.A., at public appearances nationwide and taught her introduction to Tai Chi at the renowned Spa at the Broadmoor in Colorado Springs. Erin and her husband, the noted Director of Photography Richard Hissong, are currently producing a Tai Chi video.

Erin is the recipient of eight community service awards, including Taharih, the Guardian Angel., the Leadership Award from the County of L.A., the domestic violence awareness award from the City of L.A., & the Woman of Distinction Award from T.H.A.W.

Erin has two children. Her son Kevan Schwartz has started a promising business career and her daughter Samantha is in fourth grade.

www.marapurl.com

Mara Purl's Home on the Internet

Welcome to the official web site of

Mara Purl

- Author
- Performer
- Producer
- Teacher
- Milford-Haven
- Music
- Photo Gallery
- Family & Friends
- Interviews
- Calendar

Thank you for visiting! I like to think of my web site as an eco-system with interconnecting gardens...and I like to think of life in terms of metaphors. If my life were a garden, it would be a combination of a Kyoto rock garden and a French garden of herbs and flowers. If it were a history of spirituality it would include the I Ching, Yoga, and Christianity. My life is about creativity -- mine and others I am fortunate to work with, learn from or mentor. The source of the creativity has its roots in Japan, where I grew up, and the Northeast where I went to school It has its branches by the California ocean and the Colorado mountains. Perhaps you'll find some unexpected blooms (experiences) in these pages or have some interesting seeds (ideas) to share. Let me know what you think! Peace and love, *Mara*
mara@marapurl.com

http://www.marapurl.com/

Mara's Current Activities
(a 2001 Sampling)

WRITING
2000-2001-2002-2003-2004 Etc...
The Milford-Haven Novels. Based on my BBC radio show, but with the depth, breadth and addiction to detail only fiction can satisfy... First, there's the series of twelve novels which ultimately will form one huge serial-novel. Cliffhangers? Sort of...it's more the ongoing saga of my little town full of eccentrics, but I warn you it *is* addictive once you start reading. Next, there'll be the stand-alone novels which will focus on one story-line at a time. Tony and Sally – the Vietnam vet and the waitress with the heart of gold – are first, in "Home At Last." Come find yourself in your new favorite little town, Milford-Haven.

PRODUCTION
Erin and I are working with the National Coalition Against Domestic Violence to create a Training Video for cosmetologists.

TEACHING
The *Act Right* seminars are taking off in some exciting new directions. We now teach the seminar both together and separately and with some new partners, and we're expanding across the United States, into Canada and beyond.

My brand new seminar *Ten Keys to Creativity* debuts shortly and puts tools into your hands, no matter what your field of endeavor. Hope to see you at a session soon.

At least once a year I teach *Student Radio Drama* and really show students (and their schools and parents) just how amazingly creative they are. Check my site for upcoming performances and classes near you. Topics of student dramas include domestic violence, toxic water, corporate greed, academic pressure, date rape, gang pressure, teen pregnancy, drug abuse, and many other social issues.

I'll be teaching my new curriculum *Student TV Drama* at the Colorado College in 2002. Stay tuned for an exciting production....

SPEECHES & SIGNINGS
Too many to list here but that's what the web site is for! For me, the public speaking is a joy and privilege and makes use of everything I know as both writer and actress.

MUSIC
Co-Producing my new CD "Koto Kapacity"

BOARD MEMBERSHIPS
National Coalition Against Domestic Violence Advisory Board
Los Angeles District Attorney's Crime Prevention Foundation Board
Haven House (Shelter for Battered Women) Advisory Board
Kennedy Center Imagination Celebration Steering Committee
Colorado Springs Film Commission Advisory Board
Dominique Dunne Film Festival Judging Board

Mara Purl is a producer-writer-musician-actress-sister-daughter-partner-wife-stepmother, whose name means *flow*, and who has been described as a one-woman-river-of-the-arts.

Mara created her hyphenated show **Milford-Haven**, the first environmental radio soap opera and the only American radio serial ever licensed by the BBC where it reached 4.5 million listeners throughout the U.K. The show is in development for television, and the Milford-Haven web site is www.milfordhaven.com.

Mara's popular **Milford-Haven** novels, *What The Heart Knows*, *Closer Than You Think*, *Child Secrets*, and *Cause and Conscience* are the first four in a series of twelve. She now gives talks and book signings across the country (Alaska to Florida, California to Virginia!) and she loves to hear from her readers. Audio cassettes and CDs of her original BBC radio drama are also available.

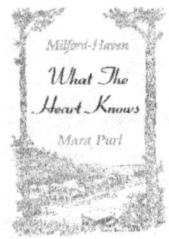   

As a model and an actress, Mara worked regularly in Tokyo, where she grew up and was well known there for starring in a TV series for NHK. In L.A. she guest-starred in several television programs and performed leading roles in many theatrical productions. Paramount screen-tested Mara to play "Saavik" in the motion picture "Star Trek III," and she played "Darla Cook" as a regular in the NBC-TV soap opera "Days Of Our Lives."

Mara plays koto (Japanese harp), performing music for the New York City Ballet. She also plays with Doobie Brothers Keith Knudsen and John McFee. She has two CDs "Koto Kist" and "Manhattan Malibu".

Mara has written for *Rolling Stone, The Financial Times (of London),* the Associated Press, the Christian Science Monitor, *Working Woman Magazine, The Mainichi Daily News,* among others, and has written two previous non-fiction books.

The recipient of grants from AT&T, the Kennedy Center Imagination Celebration, and Communities in Schools for her original curriculum **Student Radio Drama,** Mara has taught to over three hundred high school students in public and private schools in California and Colorado. She has also become a guest professor at the Colorado College and at the University of Alaska, Fairbanks, Fine Arts Camp.

Mara and Erin have been partners in PurlGray Enterprises for fourteen years and have written sitcom & TV movie scripts, book proposals, infomercials, workout videos and over one hundred speeches. Their domestic violence PSA "Step Forward" was co-produced with  Women In Film, aired in nine states and earned them the Womens' Peacepower Award for 1999. They raise funds for Haven House, the oldest shelter in the U.S.; Mara serves as advisory board member. They are members of the Advisory Board for the National Coalition Against Domestic Violence, for whom they are creating a training video.

Mara gives an exciting new seminar, **Ten Keys to Creativity** through libraries and other organizations. Mara and Erin also conduct their professional **Act Right Seminar** together and individually, nationally and internationally. Their book "Act Right" is in the process of being translated into French.

Mara has worked with the Native American Sports Council, was a board member of the Los Angeles District Attorney's Crime Prevention Foundation and on the advisory board of Communities In Schools and serves on the Colorado Springs Film Commission. She has worked actively with many environmental organizations and was a crew member of a Greenpeace voyage to save whales.

Mara comes from a theatrical family which includes director Ray Purl, actress/dancer Marshie Purl, actress/singer Linda Purl and up & coming actress/director Amelia Norfleet. Mara is married to Dr. Larry Norfleet, and has two stepchildren, Matthew and Amelia.

Student Radio Drama

Fully produced audio dramas available as teaching materials or for local broadcast

San Feliz
Plot: An investigative reporter discovers a company is producing a dangerous soft drink.

K-R-A-P
Plot: Employees at TV station K-RAP discover a lethal ingredient in a popular and addictive candy.

Cruising
Plot: An FBI agent tracks two credit-card thieves onto a cruise ship.

Westland High
Plot: A high school senior is the star athlete of his school, but hides the beatings his father gives both him and his mother.

Ashton Valley, Inc.
Plot: Employees at a small company discover not only that their missing boss has absconded with company funds, but that she's planned a clever scuttling of the firm.

Friendz
Plot: At the Center for teenage girls who are wards of the State, two girls give birth – one to a crack-addicted infant.

Changes
Plot: A young woman flirts outrageously, but is shocked when she is raped by a fellow student.

In or Out
Plot: A young woman is pressured at school by class mates who want her to join their gang.

Toxicity
Plot: Students competing for a national science prize discover chromium 6 in the local water supply and uncover a plot by a so-called philanthropist.

The Peak Mystery
Plot: An FBI investigator searches for a student missing from Peak College, to discover a complex web of fraud and conflicting stories, as each of four narrators tells the same story from his or her own point of view.

Fountain Hills Mall
Plot: A mall owner contrives a kidnaping to increase publicity for his mall and is horrified when his own daughter is taken.

Going Somewhere
Plot: A college athlete pressured to "throw" a game disappears from his dorm and friends take a road trip to find him.

Alaskan Stories: Frozen Hearts
Plot: Through three generations, a bi-cultural family deals with the legacy of a Senator who has children with both a wife and a mistress.

Alaskan Stories: Deep Freeze
Plot: Two voyages embark for the arctic – a US sub, and a Russian ice-breaker. Scientists onboard must work together when the sub is trapped beneath the polar ice cap with a pompous movie star.

Index By Issues:
Academic Pressure -- Going Somewhere; The Peak Mystery
Date Rape – Changes; Toxicity
Domestic Violence – Westland High
Drugs: Friendz
Environment – Toxicity; Deep Freeze
Family – Dysfunctional Relations: Frozen Hearts; Westland High
Gangs – In or Out, Friendz
Politics – Deep Freeze
Race Relations – Frozen Hearts
Sports Competition – Going Somewhere
Teen Pregnancy – Friendz
White Collar Crime – Cruising; Ashton Valley

Order these original tapes!

Do you know teens? Do you work with students?
Play them these tapes, created by their contemporaries and peers, and create a unique opportunity for communication and mutual understanding. Send $10.00 per tape to:
Milford-Haven Enterprises
PO Box 7304-629, North Hollywood, CA 91603

Educational Strengths & Cross-Curricular Opportunities

Research & Current Events Curriculum

Writing Story Structure & Dialogue

Acting Technique & character development

Voice & Microphone technique

Producing & Directing

Engineering & Sound Effects

Broadcasting & Marketing

Live Performance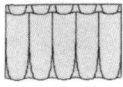

Teachers Are Saying...

Summer Diebel, Crittenton High School.
"Co-teaching Radio Drama with Mara Purl at Crittenton High School has been one of the most rewarding experiences of my teaching career. We taught a group of at-risk, teenaged girls and I truly enjoyed seeing the sense of pride these students felt with their finished product."

**Sheila Ryle, Chair of Drama
San Pedro High**
"Student Radio Drama was one of the most creative and interactive teacher/student curricular projects in which I ever had the privilege to 'play.' From start to finish, the symbiotic creativity of all artists involved was incredibly dynamic. I wish more students had access to the program."

David Manley, Chair of Drama, Fountain Valley School:
"Mara Purl's Radio Drama course is one of those all-too-rare occasions for creative collaboration in the busy high school curriculum. Her course syllabus and structure seduces students into active participation, and enables each student to make contributions. That's what I love about the program."

**Diana Sweeney,
North Hollywood High School**
"Student Radio Drama as created and coached by Mara Purl is an invaluable tool that not only addresses many of the standards set forth by the Department of Education, but also engages students in a fun, stimulating and rewarding experience. My students learned to research topical issues while honing their writing skills and their time in the studio to record the finished product is something they still rave about."

Questions?
Studentradio@aol.com

Order Tapes:
Student Radio audio cassettes are available as teaching tools or for your review.
$10.00 per tape.

Send checks to:
Milford-Haven Enterprises
PO Box 7304-629
North Hollywood, CA 91603
818- 762-2945 Voice Mail
818- 508-0299 FAX

Co-Teaching:
Working with the staff Drama or English teacher, Ms. Purl co-teaches her curriculum then brings in the production team for foley and studio recording.

Full Program:
Ms. Purl teaches a full semester, including the production team of engineer & foley artist.

**Jenette Brewer,
Fountain Ft. Carson High School**
"Student Radio Drama was ideal because it was flexible – very challenging to advanced students yet accessible to students who needed a chance to find themselves."

**Walt McDowell
Chatsworth High School:**
"The strength of Student Radio Drama was switching peer pressure to peer cooperation, forging a team to create an original drama."

**Professor Larry Oliver,
L.A. County H. S. for the Arts**
"Student Radio Drama is a an innovative approach to forging a creative team from a diverse group of individualistic students."

"We are very excited to have an innovative, original program like Student Radio Drama at our school, and hope to provide it to students annually."
– Dr. John Highland, Principal, North Hollywood High School

"Student Radio Drama is the kind of program we look to support to help at-risk youth."
– Kara Fox, District Attorney's Crime Prevention Foundation

Visit our Publisher's Web Site....

Welcome to Haven Books!

| Fiction | Non-Fiction | Audio | Authors | Authors' Kitchen | Authors' Garret | Events | Order |

Haven Books Home

Haven Books
10153 ½ Riverside Drive #629
North Hollywood, CA 91602
Ph. (818) 503-2518 Fax: (818) 508-0299
Publisher: reya@havenbooks.net
Sales & Marketing: joyce@havenboks.net
Webmaster: sky@havenbooks.net

10409

Haven Books Home

Haven Books
10153 ½ Riverside Drive #629
North Hollywood, CA 91602
Ph. (818) 503-2518 Fax: (818) 508-0299
Publisher: reya@havenbooks.net
Sales & Marketing: joyce@havenboks.net
Webmaster: sky@havenbooks.net

| Fiction | Non-Fiction | Audio | Authors | Authors' Kitchen | Authors' Garret | Events | Order |

Haven Books Non-Fiction

Erin Gray

Mara Purl

Non-Fiction   Readers' Comments   Quotes & Excerpts   More at www.tvnow.com

http://www.havenbooks.net/nonfiction.shtml

Do you know how to ACT RIGHT?
Only if you attend the comprehensive training session

ACT RIGHT

The Professional Seminar

by Erin Gray & Mara Purl

Includes information not contained in their book Act Right

YOU WILL LEARN FROM SEASONED PROFESSIONALS:
- How to audition
- How to "match"
- When to ask questions, and of whom
- How to relate to Wardrobe, Props and every other department
- How to hit your mark
- How to get hired for your <u>next</u> job

YOU WILL PARTICIPATE:
- Defining your professional goals
- Doing cold readings
- Preparing scenes for in-class audition and performance work

YOU WILL RECEIVE:
- Ten Keys to your acting career
- 21-day follow-up access to Erin & Mara for professional questions
- A discounted copy of the book Act Right

Call now to schedule this excellent seminar for your group, theatre or school!

in the U.S.:
Haven Books
10153½ Riverside Drive
North Hollywood, CA 91603
Tel: 818-503-2518
Fax: 818-508-0299
Email: ActRight@aol.com
joyce@havenbooks.net

in Canada:
Rééjean Plouffe
Tel: 819-773-1301
Fax: (819) 281-8102
Email: grpi@cyberus.ca